W9-ASF-952

THE CHURCH'S WORLDWIDE MISSION

THE CHURCH'S WORLDWIDE MISSION

edited by Harold Lindsell

an analysis of the current state of evangelical missions, and a strategy for future activity.

WORD BOOKS  WACO, TEXAS

WORD BOOKS • WACO, TEXAS

Library of Congress Catalog
Card Number: 66-22156

Proceedings of
the Congress on the Church's Worldwide Mission
April 9-16, at Wheaton College,
Wheaton, Illinois
Coordinator: Vergil Gerber
Sponsored By:
The Evangelical Foreign Missions Association
Clyde W. Taylor, Executive Secretary
and The
Interdenominational Foreign Mission Association
Edwin L. Frizen, Jr., Executive Secretary
Edited by Harold Lindsell, A.M., Ph.D., D.D.,
Associate Editor, Christianity Today

CONTENTS

PART 1

THE BIBLE EXPOSITIONS

PART 2

MAJOR STUDY PAPERS

PART 3

THE WHEATON DECLARATION

PART 4

AREA REPORTS

APPENDIX

CHAPTER 1

The Call to the Congress

(This statement was prepared for the Full Congress Committee and was released under the title, "Historical Brief," some months before the Congress convened. Thus it is anticipatory and appears in the future tense.)

The Congress on the Church's Worldwide Mission is a Christian response to the mandate of Jesus Christ to His Church to disciple all nations. Twenty centuries have gone by since those words of the Great Commission were spoken, and multiplied millions around the world cry out: "The harvest is passed, the summer is ended, and we are not saved" (Jeremiah 8:20).

Since 1917 the Interdenominational Foreign Mission Association and subsequently the Evangelical Foreign Missions Association have been contributing to the worldwide missionary leadership of the Church. These organizations are committed to historical Christianity, are evangelical in their convictions and affirm unequivocally the inspiration and authority of the Bible as the infallible revelation of the Word of God incarnate. Many of the denominational and non-denominational agencies flying the evangelical banner were born just before the turn of the twentieth century or shortly thereafter. Most of them grew slowly and matured only after passing through difficult early years of great testing. These missionary agencies found their own natural constituencies usually among their own small denominations or, as in the case of faith missions, among evangelicals in independent churches or in denominational churches whose missionary programs did not command their allegiance.

As a result of earlier historic missionary conferences, e.g. New York (1854), London (1888), New York (1900) and Edinburgh (1910) which included not only old line denominations but representatives of faith missions and other agencies not now identified with the Ecumenical Movement, the International

Missionary Council was set up in 1921. For many years, through its member councils, this agency included in its fellowship missionaries from large and small denominations and from some faith missionary groups. Since many missionaries from denominations connected with the National Council of the Churches of Christ in the United States of America (earlier known as the Federal Council of the Churches of Christ in America) were theologically conservative, it was not difficult to cooperate with conservative missionaries from other backgrounds and at no compromise to the historic faith. The Congo Protestant Council, a member council of the International Missionary Council, was in earlier days one of the happier examples of broad cooperation in the interest of missionary endeavor.

The birth of the World Council of Churches and the pressures to integrate the International Missionary Council into the framework of that organization brought to the forefront the problem of conservative theological missionary cooperation in an agency which was theologically inclusive and which numbers in its ranks Eastern and Russian Orthodoxy. At Accra, in the newly formed Republic of Ghana, in December 1957, the majority of the delegates at a conclave of the International Missionary Council voted to recommend to its thirty-five constituent councils that a merger be consummated with the World Council of Churches, despite great reservations on the part of some delegates. A large majority of the national councils approved the recommendation, and in November 1961 at the Third Assembly of the World Council of Churches in New Delhi, India, the merger was accomplished and the International Missionary Council became the Commission on World Mission and Evangelism of the World Council of Churches.

As a result of the integration, those missionary agencies related to the IFMA and the EFMA, and other unrelated denominations and missionary groups, because of their theological convictions, could not entertain any formal relationship with the new Commission on World Mission and Evangelism of the World Council of Churches. The World Council's inadequate doctrinal commitment, its inclusive policy in theological matters, the rising tide of universalism on the part of certain key spokesmen, and its movement from direct evangelism toward greater emphasis upon changing the social and economic structures instead of personal regeneration pointed up the problem.

Meanwhile the growth of those missionary agencies unrelated to the ecumenical complex has reached such proportions that the IFMA-EFMA missionary strength alone is numerically greater than those societies represented in North America by the National Council of Churches. Millions of missionary-minded supporters of IFMA-EFMA make possible the overseas ministry of more than thirteen thousand missionaries. This is six thousand more than the number of missionaries having full membership in the Division of Overseas Ministry of the National Council of the Churches of Christ. The Congress, therefore, represents the major North American missionary force today.

The necessity to call for a Congress on the Church's Worldwide Mission arises then,

*In the events of the past decade which culminated in the demise of the International Missionary Council in 1961,

*In the subsequent need for evangelicals to define their own position in the light of this change,

*In the desire for a closer fellowship of evangelicals committed to fulfill the terms of the Great Commission,

*In the realization that changing modes of thought require a reaffirmation of Biblical missionary principles and a re-examination of missionary attitudes,

*In the conviction of the continually pressing spiritual needs of a world that is shrinking in size but increasing in complexity.

Therefore it becomes the duty of evangelical leadership to make plain to the world their theory, strategy and practice of the Church's universal mission.

The Church of Jesus Christ cannot ignore today's new and radical challenge. Facing the judgment of God on their stewardship, evangelicals have a sobering responsibility and obligation. The clarion call has gone forth to those who share this heritage to join in a Congress which has for its compelling aim to bring into new focus the Biblical mandate to evangelize the world.

CHAPTER 2

Overview of the Congress

by Dr. Harold Lindsell

The Congress on the Church's Worldwide Mission convened on the campus of Wheaton College in Illinois from April 9th to 16th, 1966. Called by the Interdenominational Foreign Mission Association and the Evangelical Foreign Missions Association representing more than 13,000 missionaries overseas, the Congress registered 938 delegates from 71 countries. One hundred and fifty mission boards sent delegates, fifty of these agencies being non-IFMA-EFMA boards. Thirty-nine special interest groups, 14 non-North American missionary agencies and 55 schools were represented.

For eight days the delegates considered the mission of the Church and adopted a Declaration (printed in full in Part 3 Chapter 19) which was addressed to the constituencies of the delegates, fellow believers beyond these boundaries and to a non-believing world. The calling of the Congress was an epoch making event in itself. Twenty-five years ago such a gathering would have been an impossibility for evangelicals. Even in 1966 the call to gather at Wheaton carried with it no automatic guarantee either of immediate or future results and success. It was immediately apparent once the Congress was over that important gains had been registered and a significant document forged by the delegates. Whether or not enduring consequences will flow from the immediate gains remains to be seen; the Congress must be analyzed and an assessment made.

The accomplishments of the Congress must be viewed against the background of the total world missionary situation. Thus the agencies at the Congress do not exist independently of others which also serve Jesus Christ even though they were not at

Wheaton. No one should or would claim that they represent major denominations of the Christian movement today. They do, however, represent an important segment of Christ's Church on earth with a geographical spread of international significance. How shall such a movement involving these servants of God be evaluated and how does it fit into the missionary scheme of our day?

The Congress was called, in part, because the Church faces grave problems and needs to explore the issues, seek solutions, and express a common consensus. In one sense the crises of our age did not occasion the Congress. Everyone knows that the Church lives between the times: i.e. between the time of its beginning at Pentecost and the time of its consummation when Christ returns. During this period the Church is always in crisis, and its problems will be many, its outreach will always be threatened and its life in danger. At times it is necessary to pause for reflection, to take stock, and to get bearings. This is true because, while the Church is always in crisis, the specific challenges to its ongoing ministry vary from age to age.

One hundred years ago the Church did not have to face the menace of worldwide Communism. The population explosion had not erupted. The complex problems of urban communities had not surfaced. The Ecumenical Movement was non-existent and there was no *aggiornamento* in the Roman Catholic Church. Furthermore there had been no knowledge explosion; radio, television, atomic energy, airplanes, and space ships were unknown to men.

Second, there has been a remarkable and profoundly important manpower shift in the missionary movement in recent years. As late as 1936 the number of missionaries recruited in North America was still fewer than those sent out from Europe. Since then there has been a radical inversion. Whereas approximately one-third of the missionary force came from North America in 1911, approximately two-thirds do so today. There has been a corresponding increase in the financial support of missions from North America as well. It is now the key bastion for recruiting and supporting missionary personnel.

Third, significant theological changes have overtaken the

churches of Europe and North America. Nineteenth century German liberalism infected the continent of Europe and ultimately invaded North America. The unceasing struggle between liberalism and orthodoxy led to important changes. Smaller denominations came into existence, theologically conservative and devoted to missionary advance. Bible institutes, and later Bible colleges, dotted the North American landscape. Independent Bible churches multiplied. Mainline denominations were infiltrated with liberalism and the social gospel gained ascendancy as the good news was subordinated to good deeds.

Fourth, the Ecumenical Movement, evangelical in origin and embracing those committed to an authoritative Bible, has come of age. But in coming of age it has moved away from its earlier theological foundations. Inclusive in its theology and its fellowship it has sought for a consensus based on a limited statement of faith. The first structural form of the Ecumenical Movement was the World Council of Churches which came into being in 1948. It was not intended that this should be the final form nor was it envisioned that it should remain as a council of churches. Its leaders envisioned as its ultimate goal the reunion of the churches, the end of denominationalism, and the attainment of a universal church.

One of its first presidents was G. Bromley Oxnam, a bishop in the Methodist Church. It was he who, in an episcopal address to his church and speaking for his fellow bishops, stated that he looked for the moment when all the Protestant churches would be one and when only two great churches existed, Protestant and Roman Catholic. Then he envisioned that day when Protestant and Roman Catholic churches would come together to form the one holy catholic church.

As the World Council of Churches developed after 1948 at least two important events transpired. One had to do with the International Missionary Council formed in 1921. This agency brought together in fellowship and for united action missionary organizations and included in its local councils fundamentalist denominations and faith missionary agencies. During the period when some missions in the International Missionary Council became more liberal and even before it became a part of the

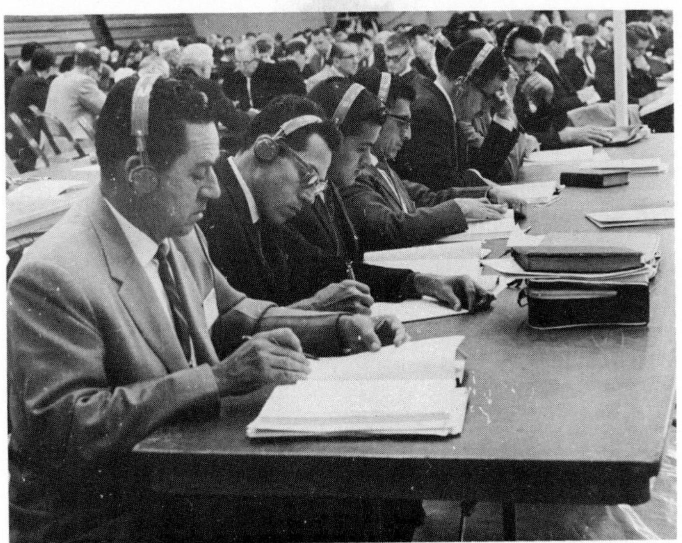

Simultaneous translation of the major addresses into French and Spanish were received by overseas delegates.

Delegates covenant together to implement declaration.

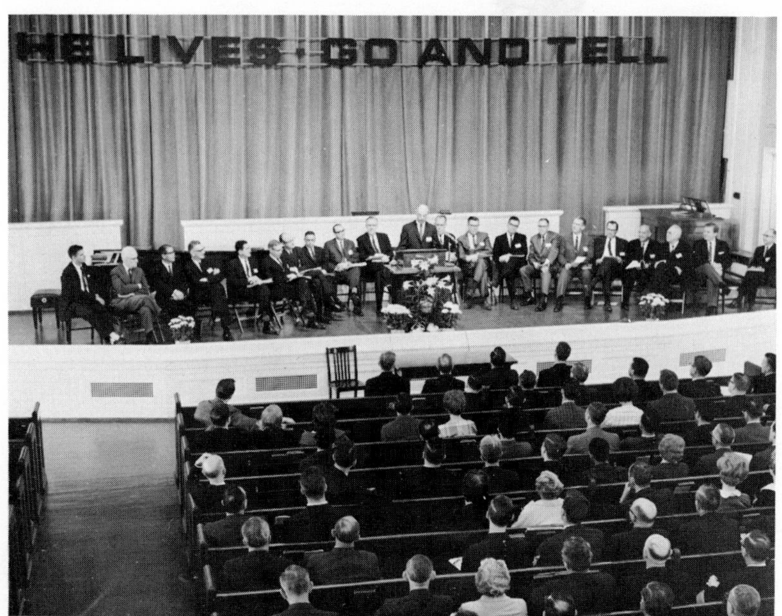

Hundreds of delegates opened with a multilingual prayer meeting on Saturday afternoon.

Full Congress Committee with members of International Advisory Committee. Left to right: Cummings, Blocher, King, Lores, Baker, Gerber, Taylor, Hatori, Mortenson, Kamau, Davis, Rockness and Frizen.

Handel's Hallelujah Chorus highlighted the Easter afternoon rally.

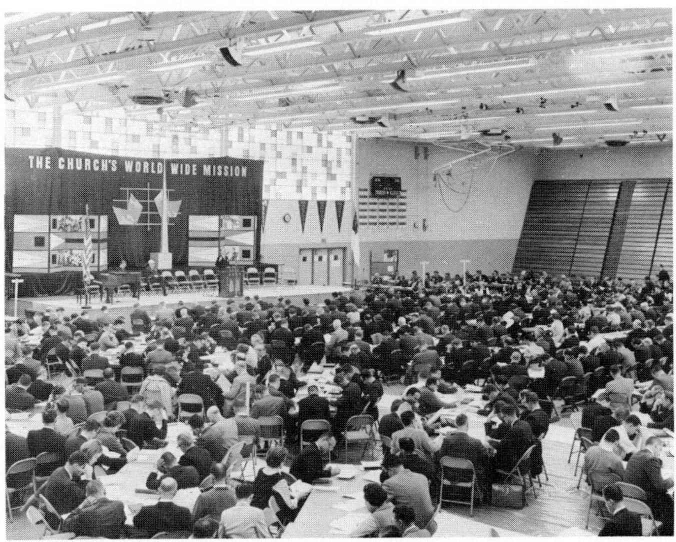

Over 900 delegates follow reading of major study paper.

Final revisions committee worked late each night considering suggestions from discussion groups.

Warmth of fellowship characterizing the Congress is expressed in the faces of EFMA Secretary Taylor, Wheaton College President Armerding, and IFMA Secretary Frizen.

World Council of Churches a number of its members withdrew. The union with the World Council, designed to produce unity, also produced further division. Those evangelicals who for conscience's sake withdrew had to look elsewhere for a larger fellowship. This threw them together and strongly influenced developments among missionary-minded evangelicals since then.

The second important event was really a twofold one. In its early stage the Russian and Eastern Orthodox bodies were brought into the World Council of Churches. These have long been regarded by evangelicals as sub-Christian if not actually apostate churches, and missionary experience shows that most of the adherents have little or no knowledge of regeneration. Moreover evangelicals experienced continued persecution and harrassment whenever they tried to do missionary work among them. It was looked upon as proselytism, in the worst sense of that abused term. The second aspect of this same thrust is the increased rapprochement with the Roman Catholic Church which church has been looked upon by many evangelicals as apostate, and indeed was so thought to be by the Reformers. John Calvin proclaimed that it no longer bore the marks of the true church. Obviously this does not mean there are no regenerate people in the Roman Catholic Church. It also does not mean that the presence of some regenerate people makes it a true church. When, in its official teachings, it holds to that which nullifies the essence of the Christian faith it cannot be a true church although some within it may be truly Christian. The Roman Catholic Church has not yet changed its basic stance. It still rejects the basic views of the Reformers and until it accepts them it cannot be called a true church.*

Fifth, evangelical missionary endeavor has also come of age in the 1960's. The significance of this statement lies in the fact that most of the EFMA and IFMA missionary organizations are less than a hundred years old. Many of them were commenced around 1900. The Baptist General Conference of America started its own missionary work when it disassociated itself (1944) from the American Baptist Convention. The Conservative Baptist Foreign Missionary Society arose after schism in the same convention (1947). The Christian and Missionary Alliance missionary effort sprang from the ministry of A. B. Simpson (1887). Of all the faith agencies tied to the IFMA and the EFMA only two, the Overseas Missionary Fellowship (China Inland Mission—1865), and the Woman's Union Missionary Society can claim to have existed more than one hundred years. Large agencies like TEAM, SIM, the AIM, and Wycliffe, began in 1890, 1893, 1895, and 1933 respectively. The Assemblies of God began in 1914, the International Church of the Foursquare Gospel in 1928.

Furthermore the agencies connected with EFMA and IFMA have experienced their greatest growth in the past thirty-five years. So enormous has that growth been that in the Church's effort to evangelize the world, evangelicals have assumed a leading role, but this in no sense implies that the evangelical task force is adequate for the job at hand. Along with growth and development has come a sense of maturity and acknowledgement of the need for concerted action if the Great Commission is to be completed. Twenty-five years ago there could have been no Wheaton Congress. The passing years have brought together diverse agencies, agreed on essentials, but widely disparate on other matters. For example, the Pentecostal churches, markedly used of God in missionary endeavor, have often been suspect because of their Arminian theology and stress on glossolalia. Understanding and appreciation have come between them and other evangelicals in agreement with Pentecostals on the essence of the Christian faith but having reservations about tongues and Arminian theology. The Spirit of God has shown them their common unity based upon a commitment to an authoritative Bible, a conviction of the lostness of men, and of their need for personal regeneration.

Lastly, a decisive shift in the direction of American Protestanism has forced evangelicals to look at themselves to find out where they are and where they are going. This shift includes the emergence of radical theology of various schools. One is that of Bultmannism which has risen alongside the decay of Barthianism. Bultmannism has demythologized Jesus and seeks to destroy the Bible as a credible source of authority. Secondly, a new modernism has risen connected with names like Bonhoeffer, Tillich, J. A. T. Robinson and James Pike to mention but a few. Even more recently the Death-of-God school of atheism has challenged the Church and has done so from within its structures rather than outside of them. Thus Elton Trueblood of Earlham College has said: "Never in my life have I known a time when the attacks on the Gospel were as vicious as they are now. I see about me a far more militant atheism than I have ever known, and I see it pressed with evangelistic fervor."

Christianity is a minority religion and threatens to become more so as we approach the end of the twentieth century. Whatever the accomplishments of the past, the revolutionary nature of our day and the challenge this age presents, has forced evangelicals to call a summit conference to learn that they do not labor alone each in his own little sphere; that God has called out people from every race and tongue and nation who love Him devotedly; that a strategy for world evangelization must be worked out; that evangelicals need, as never before, the presence and power of the Holy Spirit as they engage in the missionary task; and that the evangelization of the world is the true biblical objective for this generation.

Moreover in Protestantism there has been a decided shift to the left in eschatology. Frequently good works are emphasized more than the good news and men seek simply to change the structures of society. This has been due in no small measure to the new universalism of this hour. The stress on a God of love has denigrated eternal punishment, the wrath of God, and the lostness of men who are not in Christ until they have been converted, and who will be eternally separated from God if they are not regenerated before physical death overtakes them. American Protestantism is rapidly losing its sense of urgency in evangelism; no longer are men pressed for individual decisions since they are regarded as being in Christ whether they know it or not; no longer is there sturdy adherence to the eschatology of Jesus and of the New Testament.

There is another facet of evangelical eschatology that must not be overlooked. Great numbers understand the Scriptures to teach that in the closing days of the age just prior to the Second Advent of Jesus Christ the professing church will be apostate. This eschatology sees the Roman Catholic Church involved in the apostasy; it will be a worldwide ecclesiastical organization under the sway of Satan, persecuting true believers. This church will be made up of apostate Romanism and Protestantism. Therefore evangelicals tend to look upon the present movement toward church union as a fulfillment of the prophetic Scriptures. Because they believe this to be true, their distrust of ecumenism is not only built upon what they see in it now, but also upon that which they are confident will come to pass. Many of those outside the evangelical fold do not understand this viewpoint and for this reason they cannot come to grips with the real problems that separate evangelicals from agencies like the World Council of Churches. So far as the agencies attending the Wheaton Congress are concerned there is little evidence to suppose their eschatology is undergoing significant revisions now or in the immediate future.

In the light of all this the Congress that convened in Wheaton met at a junction point in Christian history. There have been other great missionary conferences; some have been largely evangelical and others have not. The evangelical missionary congress of greatest size in the United States convened in New York City in 1900, but differed from the Wheaton Congress in that it was largely denominational. It was also ecumenically oriented and the proceedings were published in two volumes by the American Tract Society. The first printing ran 25,000 sets. In some sense the Wheaton Congress inherited both the evangelical stance and the ecumenical orientation of this earlier meeting.

The Wheaton Congress was characterized by harmony and unity from beginning to end. Differences of opinion were expressed freely, but the meetings generally were harmonious and serious. The arrangements were handled superbly and there was no breakdown in the mechanics. The sessions went like clockwork. Even the weatherman cooperated. While it was chilly, there was no rain during the days the conference was in session.

Five Bible expositions were presented and of them two fell within the range of great controversy. The first one by the Dean of Trinity Evangelical Theological Seminary, Dr. Kenneth Kantzer, dealt with the Scriptures. He strongly advocated propositional revelation, an inspired, authoritative and inerrant Bible which is the Word of God written. There was no dissent from this high view of the Bible.

The second Bible exposition, which by its very nature was most provocative, was delivered by President John Walvoord of Dallas Theological Seminary. Evangelicals have not given much scholarly attention to ecclesiology. While they have always agreed on the need for spiritual unity they have not led in the movement to eliminate the denominations nor have they felt that denominationalism is sinful. Many of them are affiliated with small denominations or with Bible churches of strong Baptistic leanings and for that reason they think more largely in terms of "the churches" rather than "the Church" with regard to visible organization. Independency is often a benchmark of evangelicalism and thus is inherently opposed to monolithic church structure. But the biblical and theological support for this has not been spelled out with great skill or in depth. Dr. Walvoord's paper strongly favored spiritual, but not organic, union. He faced up to the challenge of the Ecumenical Movement. Undoubtedly some of the comments from observers like Dr. Eugene Smith of the World Council of Churches indicate how greatly they fail to understand the deep currents underlying evangelical thought. At Wheaton it was clear that the overwhelming majority of the delegates have grave reservations about the Ecumenical Movement.

The authors of the major study papers worked hard to insure a scholarly product. Some of them succeeded better than others. Most of the writers are missionaries or missionary administrators and were forced to do their research while continuing their normal labors. Most of them are not publishing scholars and yet, with the support of the consultants, the final products were of good quality which bodes well for future missionary writing by evangelicals. In zeal, a number of them exceeded the limitations imposed by the time factor and left portions of their papers unread in order to stay within the Congress schedule. The papers also had to be cut considerably for publication. The discussion groups met and discussed the position papers freely. The delegates were frank in their appraisals and in at least one instance (nationals from Latin America) opposed any concessions to Roman Catholicism, a sore point for many who had resisted its hegemony and experienced restriction and persecution in their countries. The preliminary draft of the Declaration was revised considerably as a result of national and missionary influence and a harder line was taken. No one was ready to assert that no Roman Catholics are numbered in the body of Christ, but many delegates wanted to be sure this aspect was not emphasized. Moreover, while it was not stated categorically, the final draft of the Declaration implied that the Roman Catholic Church is not a true church.

Syncretism was considered in its religious and cultural contexts. The uniqueness and the finality of the Christian faith were affirmed, clearly reflecting the conviction of the delegates that the non-Christian religions are not saving vehicles nor are their adherents within the household of faith. A warning was sounded against those cultural accretions which tend to obscure the true biblical message.

In the treatment of neo-universalism the Congress weighed apparently opposing teachings of the Bible which seem to favor both universal redemption and eternal separation of the lost. The Declaration strongly affirmed the reality of both heaven and hell and earnestly called upon evangelical theologians to present an adequate exegetical defense of their viewpoint. One trenchant statement warned against an incipient universalism of which evangelicals can be guilty when they fail to evangelize the world in the light of their principle that men are and will be lost without the knowledge of Christ.

The paper on the thorny problem of proselytism was presented by Dr. Blocher from France who has had extensive experience among Roman Catholics. Both among them and the Eastern Orthodox any effort to convert their adherents is looked upon unfavorably because they teach baptismal regeneration which means that baptized infants are already in a state of grace. The Congress came out strongly for religious liberty, the right to change one's religion and also one's church affiliation. At the same time the Congress opposed unethical practices sometimes employed to persuade people to change their church or ethnic religious affiliations. Proselytism was recognized as a biblical practice and its rightful meaning was endorsed and its proper use favored.

On church growth, the Congress proposed more research into the principles of church growth enunciated in the Scriptures, and more contemporary studies to find out why churches are not growing as they should and what corrective steps can be taken to insure an ingathering among receptive peoples. Missionary leaders were encouraged to send in substantial reinforcements in fields where populations are especially receptive even though unreceptive fields should not go untended.

The discussions on Mission and Foreign Missions clearly showed this to be an unworked field calling for extensive research and a new literature. Some of the delegates stated the distinction between mission agencies and the church on the field should not be maintained. The delegates were not unmindful that, in many instances, the term "foreign missionary" is being abandoned but in the end the majority did not endorse this line of thinking. They drew attention to the need to define the role of those called to pastoral or missionary service. The act of calling for a definition implied the uncertainty. Indeed, few agencies have worked out clearly the lines of authority and the relationships between the churches on the field and the missionary agencies. These problems are surely related to the question of the nature and function of the church. Faith missionary agencies, because they are not churches, have tended to bypass this problem and have not produced a literature in any sense comparable to that which has come out of Faith and Order Studies in the past decades. The discussion cannot end with the Declaration which simply reaffirmed that there is a distinction between missionary agencies and national churches—a distinction few evangelicals seem to deny, but which needs to be worked out and undergirded by first class scholarship.

The thorny problem of the Church emerged again in the essay on Evangelical Unity. The Declaration espoused spiritual unity and encouraged the organization of evangelical fellowships at the national, regional and international levels. Mergers were also recommended as was the avoidance of competing and overlapping work. But it remains for evangelical spokesmen to state more clearly how spiritual unity finds expression in visible organization. Precisely what the creation of regional fellowships and international ones means, how they are to be organized, what powers and authority they may have, what their attitudes and relationships to other ecumenical organizations will be, have been left open. These are important questions and will become more so in the decades ahead. They cannot be avoided and unless they are articulated adequately the situation will probably decay. Such articulation is particularly important since the Ecumenical Movement has reached out and is reaching out to extend fellowship to national churches that were born out of the ministry of IFMA-EFMA agencies. Moreover the churches on the field do not always understand what the issues are nor do they always feel free to register their real opinions. The report of the Congress in the *Christian Century,* lacking in understanding as it was, should nonetheless cause evangelicals to find out whether the national churches simply tell missionary agencies what they want to hear, and whether the agencies themselves hear what they want to hear rather than what is really said. There is need for greater intercommunication between missionaries and nationals to discover what nationals really think and in what direction they will ultimately move.

The Declaration called on missionaries to evaluate their methods and to familiarize themselves with the insights of psychology, anthropology, sociology and business management in missionary outreach. At the same time the Congress guarded against subordinating spiritual preparation and Bible knowledge. The call to use these other areas of knowledge means: (1) there is an awareness of the failure to use them sufficiently in the past, and (2) evangelicals cannot afford to lag behind others who have learned much from their researches in these areas. Implementing the Congress findings constitutes the true necessity, for recognizing the need serves no long range purpose unless it is followed up by whatever action the circumstances require. No one should underestimate how far the Congress went, nor suppose that it was in a position to do more than it did. The individual agencies at the Congress are the only ones who can carry out the recommendations and coordinated action by many agencies working together should eventuate.

The Congress faced the issues of proclamation and service in the essay on Mission and Social Concern. Evangelicals of late have emphasized proclamation (*kerygma*) at the expense of service (*diakonia*). Therefore it was heartwarming to note the clear-cut stand for social justice and human welfare. Indeed the document went so far as to say "that evangelical social action will include, wherever possible, a verbal witness to Jesus Christ." Thus the Congress said that at times there can be no proclamation or verbal witness, but social action must continue in the hope verbal witness will be possible. But likewise there was agreement that anyone who engages in service without proclamation, when verbal witness is possible, falls short of what is required of him by the Scriptures. In all probability evangelicals will not go far enough in service (*diakonia*) to please their critics, nor should they do so. They must, however, not back away from a commitment to service, and make certain that their actions support their profession in tangible ways so that the world will believe for their works' sake.

The closing position paper on a Hostile World brought into focus the evangelical philosophy of history. Behind the paper and the Declaration lies the deepest conviction that two forces are arrayed one against the other. God and a personal being called the Devil are on opposing sides. While the ultimate victory of Jesus Christ is assured, the Devil still remains the Prince of the power of the air. The whole world lies in the lap of the evil one. The struggle is not simply for the earth and for men; it is a titanic battle waged in the heavenly places and encompassing the whole universe. Men have to decide. Some go to heaven and some to hell. Evil is not only a force. Behind it lies a person of great intelligence. The people of God, in deadly combat with this malign person, battle in the confidence that God is sovereign and he will be victorious. Thus the warfare is not between flesh and blood but principalities and powers.

On the closing day the Congress listened to and voted on the Declaration section by section. One delegate registered dissent at two places. This dissent was withdrawn later so that the approval of the Declaration was unanimous. Louis L. King of the Christian and Missionary Alliance prefaced the reading and adoption of the Declaration with a statement, the summary of which is contained in the chapter on the Declaration. Included also is a chart showing the procedure leading up to the final draft of the Declaration. It guaranteed, as those who were involved can testify, that the drafters honestly attempted to present the thinking of the delegates. This is not to say that every delegate was in agreement with every particle of the Declaration but it did have the overwhelming support of most of them in every regard. Most of the amendments made from the floor at the time of adoption were incorporated into the document. The only exception was a suggestion which would have reversed the meaning of one statement contrary to the intention of the delegates. The original rendering was retained when the committee inserted the other changes after the Congress had adjourned. To have made even that single change would have broken faith with the majority of the delegates.

Throughout the Congress one could sense the presence of the Spirit of God. This was most obviously manifested when the delegates, in unison read their pledge of support of the Declaration. "In support of this declaration we do covenant together to seek the mobilization of the Church for the evangelization of the world in this generation." There was no mistaking the commitment of the delegates and their intention to fulfill the terms of the Great Commission. This reading was followed by the singing of the hymn "A Mighty Fortress". Pierce Chapel rocked as hundreds of male and female voices offered praise to God and declared their faith in him who cannot be defeated. Black, yellow, and white children of God then sat down at the undivided table of our Lord where together in true unity they ate the one bread and drank the one cup. This ecumenical drama into which all were drawn in obedience to the command of the Lord of the Church was celebrated joyfully and solemnly. It was a testimony to all who work for the unity of the Church but who cannot sit down at a common table because of differences that divide them. However great the differences that divide evangelicals, they ate and drank together in remembrance of Christ's shed blood.

So the Congress closed leaving behind it a document for men to think about. What the delegates do now that the Congress is over will be more important than what they did when meeting together. Certainly the meeting was not a final act. It was only a curtain raiser to other Congresses which must follow. It was a laudable start in the right direction. It did not solve all the problems nor answer all the questions. It did not go as far as some would have liked for the Congress to have gone. But it went far enough to give its constituency plenty of room to march forward. In not going too far it kept contact with its constituency thus demonstrating the highest order of maturity and the deepest concern to move ahead but to do so without losing the bulk of its people. If it was a modest effort, it also pointed the way to attainable goals. Those who were responsible for calling the Congress and who, more than anyone else, knew what its purposes and goals were, came away with the conviction that their highest hopes had been realized and that truly God had met the members of the Congress.

This is but a human overview, the insights and opinions of one who sat in on the meetings from beginning to end—and did so as a reporter, a former professor of missions, and one whose contacts have enabled him to observe congresses involving other people, and who, in personal experience, has some knowledge of the Christian world outside the evangelical complex. No reader needs to accept what has been said by this writer but will have the privilege of deciding for himself what the Congress thought and what it committed itself to—as each reader scans the documents of the Congress, and reads aloud the Wheaton Declaration which will long be remembered when those who constructed it have passed beyond the veil. And may every reader join in the solemn pledge "to seek the mobilization of the Church for the evangelization of the world in this generation."

* For example, when Vatican Council II commenced in 1962 every delegate was required to sign and assent to a "Declaration of Faith" which committed them to acceptance of the seven sacraments, the necessity of baptism for salvation, the teachings of the Council of Trent on original sin and justification, transubstantiation, purgatory, images, indulgences, obedience to the Roman Pope "successor of St. Peter, the prince of the apostles and the vicar of Jesus Christ", and the primacy of Rome's bishop and his infallible magister.

CHAPTER 3

THE KEYNOTE ADDRESS

God's Gift to the Church

by Dr. Louis L. King

Ephesians 1:22,23: "(God) . . . gave Him to be the head over all things to the church, which is His body, the fulness of Him that filleth all in all."

Today the eyes of God are surveying the whole earth. He sees the ostentatious gatherings of people. He sees them in the places of exchange, the halls of learning, the council chambers of industry. He sees them in their buildings of magnificence. It may be for convenience, for business, or for amusement that they are gathered together. God, however, is not centering His interest in such assemblies. Rather, He glances over them all and rests His all-pervading eyes directly on the Church. And of the Church He says in Ephesians 1:23 that it is Christ's body and that it has "the fulness of Him that filleth all in all."

I. *The Church Encompasses All the Redeemed.*

The Church which is Christ's body does not refer to a building or yet to an organization. True, in our everyday speaking, we employ the word *church* to mean a building and also an organization. In the Bible, however, this is not its meaning. In its biblical sense and usage, the Church refers to the whole mass of redeemed men and women and not to so many separate and unrelated parts. It is a society in which man is perfected. It is a kingdom in which God is glorified. It is the grouping together of the individually redeemed to form the society of God. Our Lord—and the apostles, also—used the word *church* to refer to a spiritually free, saved, called-out-of-the-world people who fulfill certain qualifications and to whom a certain work is committed.

A. *The Church Is Indwelt by God.*

God who is a Spirit cannot dwell in houses of material fabric; He does not dwell in buildings made by man's hands. He dwells in our spirits. In the collected life and spirit of the Church, God claims to reside. The Church is the vessel of His Spirit, and He fills it with His glory. "Know ye not," cries the apostle to the Corinthian fellowship of believers, "that the Spirit of God dwelleth in you" (I Corinthians 3:16).

B. *The Church Was Established Specifically as God's Habitation.*

The deliverance from our personal sins, our reinstatement in God's favor, the assurance of salvation, the earnest of the Spirit—all of these blessings were not bestowed upon us to end there. These great results of Christ's sacrifice were meant for a further end. That end is that we might be the body of Christ to which pertains the "fulness of Him that filleth all in all" (Ephesians 1:23). The house, the body, the temple—call the Church what you will—was established for God's abode, His place of residence among men. It is the "habitation of God through the Spirit" (Ephesians 2:22).

In the Bible, many glorious things are spoken of this redeemed society, the Church.

But the most glorious thing—that which exceeds all other glory—is disclosed in Ephesians 1:22,23: "And (God) gave Him to be the head over all things to the church, which is His body, the fulness of Him that filleth all in all."

II. *The Church's Head Is Christ.*

The first glorious fact mentioned in the text is that Jesus Christ is Head of His body, the Church. And He is Head in a twofold sense.

A. *The Living Head.*

First, He is the living, vital Head of the Church—the Church which is called His body. Consider for a minute our own natural bodies. The head sees for the whole body, thinks for the body, provides for the body, receives nourishment for the body. If the head is honored, the whole body is honored. In similar fashion, the exalted Christ is united to His body, the Church. He as its living, vital Head thinks for it, provides for it, sees for it, receives the nourishment for it; and from the Head the whole body receives all that is provided. The anointing upon the Head comes down upon the members. The glory of the Head—at least in a measure now, and fully later—is the glory of His body, the Church. He is the source of its light; the seat of its authority; the center of its unity; the inspiring, ruling, guiding, and sustaining power of its spiritual being and blessedness.

B. *The Governing Head.*

Christ, however, is not only the vital head of the Church; He is also its governing head. The voice of Christ is supreme in the decisions of the Church. For the believer, not what other Christians do, but what the Lord says, is vital. Christ is the sole king and the only lawgiver in Zion. Even a church council's right to legislate is ruled out in all questions of faith, practice, and worship if the Lord through His Word has spoken on these matters. The Bible as the Word of Christ, therefore, becomes the ultimate constitution and the only law book of the Church. It is also the daily guide giving practical answers to life's problems. Indeed, for every problem in the Church or in our personal lives, Jesus, the governing Head, has given an answer in the Bible. Or if there is not an outright solution, there is a principle applicable to it.

For instance, Paul visited Corinth on his second missionary journey. He stayed there eighteen months and raised up a sizable congregation. When he resigned the pastorate, he went to Ephesus. He had been in Ephesus three years when ominous news reached him about conditions in the Corinthian church. From knowledgeable sources Paul learned there were ten grave problems in the Church. The problems were (1) factional strife, (2) immorality, (3) lawsuits between Christians, (4) marriage and divorce, (5) eating meats offered to idols, (6) women's forsaking the modesty becoming their sex, (7) unworthy partaking of the Lord's supper, (8) abuse of spiritual gifts, (9) denial of the resurrection, and (10) stinginess in money matters. As soon as Paul learned of these problems, the Holy Spirit came upon him; and under that divine inspiration he wrote a specific answer to each one. Here then are specific answers given by the governing Head of the Church to ten common problems that are in the Church.

In similar fashion, if we know our Bibles well enough, it will be discovered that Christ has not left us to ourselves; but as Head of the Church, He has given a precise answer to every difficulty, the right method of meeting every opposition, the one true solace that can get into the heart and heal it with the succour which it needs.

The problems of life are not answered by the voices of the current age. It is indeed interesting and important to know what is being said and written. It is proper to keep ourselves abreast with such things. We need to know what thoughtful men inside and outside the Church are thinking. It is good to know the spirit and tenor of the age; but the solution to our problems, our proper guidance, and our message do not come from them. Instead of listening to and following the voices of the current age, we listen to the correcting and directing voice of all ages—to Jesus Christ, the Head of the Church.

In the Bible He has supplied the answers to the new morality as well as the mission of the Church. The answers concerning church unity—the nature and basis and form and extent of the Church's unity—are clearly set forth. The question of man's eternal destiny—whether some are saved or all are saved—is answered in the Book.

The questions of divine inspiration and the integrity and worth and authority of the Bible have been settled by Jesus. Since He, the King of Truth, recognized the Scriptures as nothing less than the infallible record of His heavenly Father, we do, too. Since Scripture was to Him the infallible guiding-star of His life, it is just that to us also. Since He reverently bowed to every jot and tittle of Scripture, we do too. It is not in the power of any man mighty in dialectics and rich in learning to deprive the Bible of its validity. The Bible cannot be loosened. Other books may come and go, but this Book stands forever. We have the word of Jesus

Christ, the Lord and the Head of the Church, on that. He hath said, "The Scripture cannot be broken" (John 10:35). This Holy Book is the word of Christ, the governing Head of the Church, and is relevant to the 20th Century and to every century.

We see, therefore, that the first glorious fact mentioned in the text is that God has given Christ to be the essential, living Head and also the governing Head of His body, the Church.

III. *The Church's Fulness Is Christ.*[1]

The second glorious fact mentioned in this text is that the *fulness* of Christ has been given to the Church (v. 23). Now this word *fulness* means the entire number, the entire measure, the plentitude, the perfection. For an understanding of the *fulness,* we need to go back and consider the Lord in His preincarnation as Son of God, then in His incarnation as Son of Man, and finally in His glorification as the God-man. Only as we comprehend Him in this threefold manner will we begin to know what the *fulness* is.

A. *The Preincarnate Christ.*

First and assuredly concerning Him in His preincarnate state, it can be declared that:

- God's character, His divine nature, His express image were Christ's. The whole unbounded powers and attributes of Deity—all the divine glories—were His.
- His love, joy, peace, longsuffering, and gentleness were the same as the Father's.
- He lived in God and God in Him—in a full dependence on God, and receiving blessed and glorious communications from Him.
- He was the center of things—Supreme, Eternal, Governor of all.
- His was the hand that moved all things.
- He knew all that can be known.
- He was head and source of creation.
- He held the helm of the universe in His hand.
- He caused the rays of light to flow thousands of millions of miles and to fall upon our eyes that we may see.
- He made celestial bodies of different magnitude that move

through the heavens at different velocities.

- He made the heavens, the earth, the seas—stars, clouds, trees, fields, and rivers.
- He was head and fountain of life.
- He linked all creatures and all forces into a cooperative whole.

But, further, He was eternal love—compared to an everlasting burning. He was infinite infinity, eternity itself. He was immediately present—from everlasting everywhere—extending Himself from the utmost bounds of the everlasting hills, surrounding and filling the universe. Communicating Himself in His infinite unchangeable goodness, there was no variableness—no shadow cast by His turning. Being the essence of infinite wisdom, goodness, power, lustre, authority, glory, He was superior to cherubim, angels, and man. He stood forth as the glory, joy, and treasure of all His hosts, the sun of every eye, the crown of every head, the jewel and joy of every bosom, the ineffable, fathomless, eternal object of all delight, our Author and our End.

Thus was Christ in the eternal past in His preincarnate state as Son of God.

B. *The Incarnate Christ.*

But Christ laid aside this power and magnificence and equipage for a time. When He came to redeem man, He emptied Himself of His glory. He veiled—hid—himself in flesh. He took upon Him the form of a servant. He was made in the likeness of man. He lived among men as a man. He became linked to us as a brother by a common human nature. He learned the weakness, the longing, the temptations, the diversified experiences of child life. Passing from childhood to youth, He went through all those mysterious transitions which are common to all adolescents. He became a working man, earning his own bread by the sweat of the brow. He knew fatigue, hard toil, and scanty remuneration. He knew poverty, privation, physical exhaustion, helplessness in the presence of pressing duties, fame, and defamation. He experienced the bitterness of misunderstanding and trouble at home. He was raised to the pinnacle of popularity, then dashed down and stranded on the shores of absolute isolation. He associated with sharp, keenly educated men as well as with dull, stupid, infinitely inferior men. Yes, our Lord lived a varied life. He was baby, child, boy, man; son, servant, friend, master. He truly acquainted Himself with every part of life. He experienced every conceivable form of human experience. So much so that the great apostle states, "He became like unto His brethren." "He was tempted in all points like as we are" (Hebrews 4:15). Indeed, He qualified in the whole of His earthly life in compassionateness and humanness and sympathy.

Thus He lived. Then He died and was buried.

C. *The Glorified Christ.*

Now look at Jesus where He was. See the poor, tortured, wounded body—slain for our sins. It was lying cold and still in Joseph's grave. But now lift up your eyes and see Him where He is—He is risen, ascended, and enthroned in the wonder and worship of heaven! Look at the terrific powers arrayed against Him; these were manifested in His brutal death and sealed vault. But look again and see Him alive forevermore! Look at Him despised and rejected of men. Look again—He is exalted high over all! Look and measure the distance between earth's grave and heaven's high throne. Behold, He has traversed the gulf and is now seated on the right hand of the Majesty on high.

Christ conquered sin, the devil, and all demons. He overcame the powers of death and the sealed grave in might and power and glory. He ascended on high. Up and up through the rent clouds and the ranks of shouting angels He went. He passed under the lifted-up heads of the everlasting doors. He ascended until He took His seat to reign forevermore. Now He is at the topmost height of His glory. He is risen and exalted. Into His humbled, emptied-out form was poured back the brightness of the Father's glory. Given back to Him was the infinity of heaven's authority and power. The majesty which in preincarnation was His was restored in undiminished measure. Thrones and princedoms are beneath His seat. All power has been given unto Him in heaven and in earth. He is the supreme, unequalled potentate in all the realms of heaven and all the kingdoms of earth. He is indeed "God of God, Light of Light, very God of very God," the Lord God Almighty. He possesses the entire measure, the entire number, the plentitude, the perfection of Deity, He is fully God. But more wonderfully precious to us is the knowledge that He is not there solitarily as God. When He ascended to heaven, "He carried up to His Father's house not only the Deity He had brought with Him when He came to earth to obey and to submit and to suffer among us; but He carried back more than He brought, for he carried back a human heart, a human life, a human character, which was and is a new wonder in heaven. He carried back His humility, His meekness, His humanity, His approachableness and His sympathy" (Alexander Whyte). And he sits there on the throne, fully man. He is our Elder Brother, one like unto us. He possesses the entire measure, the entire number, the plentitude, the perfection of mankind. And this entire measure of Deity and this entire measure of man have been joined, linked together, in the one Person, Jesus Christ the Lord. He is, therefore, fully acquainted with and wholly sympathetic toward man and, at the same time, completely able to help the very weakest. This is the Christ which has been given to the Church. The fulness of Him that filleth all in all has been given as a gift to the body of Christ.

IV. *The Church's Wealth.*

How rich the Church is! God has given to it a gift: "Him He gave . . . to the Church . . . gave, the fulness of Him that filleth all in all."[1] Christ in His fullness. Christ powerful and glorious, is ours. Son of God, Son of Man, the God-man—Christ the conqueror dwells in and works through the Church. He penetrates the Church with His gifts and life-powers.

Oh, let us recognize the Church's pedigree and wealth in Christ. He has been given to the Church. All of His fulness belongs to the Church, and Christ's resources are limitless. Let us therefore rid ourselves of all talk about a weak or poor Church. We must tear such words out of our speech. There is no poor Church. There can be no weak Church. The Church is not like a commercial institution. It is not concerned with monetary investments, endowments and revenue. If this were so, we could speak of a Church's being poor and weak. The Church, however, is the body of Christ; and He is its head. Like the physical body receiving nourishment and direction, its very life, from its head, so the Church obtains from the fulness of Christ His strength and blessing. If it is a Church, it has Christ's presence, power, and resources. God has given it all that pertains to His fullness. Christ's Person and Godhead, His offices and all His interest and His resources—all of these in fulness have been given to the Church. Nothing, absolutely nothing, is withheld. All that He is as the Son of God; all that He is as Son of Man; all that He is as Mediator between God and man; all of His service, His time, His care, His thought, and His very life—all of these in fulness have been dedicated and given to the Church. With this sure knowledge, never let the words *weak* and *poor* be used again with reference to the Church.

---

1. Reverend Professor G. G. Findlay, in *The Epistle to the Ephesians (The Expositor's Bible,* W. Robertson Nicoll ed., Grand Rapids: Wm. B. Eerdmans), p. 92: "'Him He gave . . . to the Church . . . (gave) the fulness of Him that fills all in all.' In the risen and enthroned Christ God bestowed on men a gift in which the Divine plentitude that fills Creation is embraced. For this last clause, it is clear to us, does not qualify 'the Church which is His body,' and expositors have needlessly taxed their ingenuity with the incongrous apposition of 'body' and 'fulness'; it belongs to the grand Object of the foregoing description, to 'the Christ' whom God raised from the dead and invested with His own prerogatives. The two separate designations, 'Head over all things' and 'Fulness of the All-filler,' are parallel, and alike point back to *Him* who stands with a weight of gathered emphasis—heaped up from verse 19 onwards—at the front of this last sentence (v. 22b). There has been nothing to prepare the reader to ascribe the august title of the *pleroma,* the Divine fulness, to the Church—enough for her, surely, if she is His body and He God's gift to her—but there has been everything to prepare us to crown the Lord Jesus with this glory."

PART 1

THE BIBLE EXPOSITIONS

Introduction

Five Bible expositions on themes basic to the witness of the Church and at the heart of the Christian faith were presented to the Congress by distinguished scholars, missionary leaders and nationals. The expositions dealing with the Bible, the Church, and the consummation at the end of the age were especially strategic in the light of contemporary problems and discussions. While the expositions were not discussed by the delegates as were the position papers, nor were any specific declarations derived from them, they undergirded the Congress and made clear the theological foundations on which it rested.

In one sense, at least, the preamble to the Declaration reflected the Bible expositions when it came out forthrightly for an inerrant Scripture, bespoke the need for the fulness and working power of the Holy Spirit and looked to the Second Advent of Jesus Christ which will be preceded by the fulfillment of the Great Commission. The central message of the Gospel was reaffirmed. Perhaps more than in any other Bible exposition, ecumenicity was discussed in the paper on Mission and the Church's Nature. Neither the Ecumenical Movement nor the World Council of Churches were mentioned directly in the final draft of the Wheaton Declaration, however. The absence of such references sprang from the conviction that the Congress had not met simply to oppose such movements. Rather it wished to speak affirmatively about its own outlook and objectives. That a number of the Bible expositions directing criticism to ecumenism met with the approval of most of the delegates was obvious. Observers, representing ecumenical agencies, were present during the meetings and were received with friendly respect.

The Bible expositions, like the study papers, express the viewpoints of those who wrote them. It may be said, in general, that they also reflect the viewpoints of many of the agencies involved in the Congress. Their inclusion in this volume serves to round out the thrust of the meetings. Each exposition stands on its own feet and is to be studied against the backdrop of the Word of God. Each is to be understood within the larger context and no one paper should be divorced from the totality of the Congress.

These expositions have been edited and deletions made to conserve space. Any editing defects are not the fault of the writers, although care has been taken to maintain continuity and intelligibility.

CHAPTER 4

Mission—And the Church's Authority

by DR. KENNETH S. KANTZER

The mission to world evangelization and Biblical or Evangelical Christianity are two sides of the same coin. A distinguished missionary once said: "Some people do not believe in missions. They have no right to believe in missions. They do not believe in Christ."[1] Nor, I would add, do they acknowledge the Lordship of Jesus Christ over their lives.

As Evangelicals, we confess Jesus Christ as our Saviour from sin and its awful consequences. We also confess this same Jesus Christ as the Sovereign Lord over all our life and thought.

"Christianity," so we hear, "*is* Christ." This is true. The grand theme of the Bible and of the Evangelical church across the centuries is the person and work of Jesus Christ. In Jesus Christ, lost men have found God. In the deepest sense possible Christianity is the good news that the great God of the universe out of a heart of infinite love for wayward man came down into this world to become one of us in order that He might redeem us from our sin and bring us as forgiven sinners back into fellowship with Himself. Christianity *is* Jesus Christ—who He is, what He has done for us men, and how man responds to Him.

Christianity, so it is also said, is the religion of a book. This, too, is true. Where do we learn about the Saviour Jesus Christ? In the Bible. Where may we discover the benefits brought to us by Christ? In the Bible. Where do we become personally acquainted with Jesus Christ and grow in His love? In the Bible. Where do we find fellowship with our Saviour, and come to experience His comfort and exhortation? His encouragement and strength? In the Bible. Where can we become apprised of his glorious plan and program of the ages—the plan of the God who works in history to meet man and to achieve His goals? In the Bible.

"I want to know the way to heaven," wrote John Wesley. "God has written it down in a book. O give me that Book! At any price, give me the book of God!"

Christianity *is* Christ but it is the Christ of the Book. Only as Christianity is the religion *of a book* is it really the Christianity *of Christ.*

The Evangelical is, therefore, and must ever remain the man of a book. The true Evangelical believes the book and seeks to live by it.

The basis for this Evangelical conviction that Holy Scripture is God's true and authoritative word to man is Jesus Christ, Himself. In the pages of Scripture the Evangelical has met Christ personally, and the Spirit of God has opened his eyes to see that Jesus Christ is really what He claimed to be–Lord and Saviour. From his experience with Christ, the Christian believer is led to accept the Scriptures as God's Word because our Lord regarded them so and commanded all His disciples to regard them so.

No teaching of Jesus Christ on any subject is clearer than His teaching on the Bible's complete authority. In His Sermon on the Mount He declares heaven and earth would sooner pass away than the dotting of an "i" or the crossing of a "t" from the law (Matthew 5:17-19). In a similar passage in Luke 16:17 He adds that it is impossible for one particle of the law to be set aside as void; and He rebukes His disciples for not believing all that the prophets had spoken (Luke 24:25). In controversy with the Jews (John 10:34,35) He argues that Scripture cannot be broken, dissolved or discarded. On one occasion He introduces an isolated passage from the Old Testament with the formula: "God (the creator) says." In the thought and teaching of our Lord, the law of Moses is explicitly labeled the word of God (Mark 7:6 ff.).

This testimony of Jesus Christ validates directly the Old Testament, but indirectly it includes the New Testament as well. Our Lord constituted His disciples as His witnesses who should follow Him. He promised to guide them into all truth (John 14:16-17). He assured them of confirming signs of their apostolic authority in predictive prophecy and miracles. After His death and resurrection His apostles claimed to represent their Lord and to have the right to speak with authority in the Church of Christ (Galatians 1-2). Their claims were confirmed by diverse miracles and gifts of the Holy Spirit (Hebrews 2:4).[2]

The world of scholarship, by and large, whether it is Christian or non-Christian, liberal or conservative in its view of Biblical authority, freely admits that the Jesus Christ of history believed and taught the divine inspiration and impregnable truth of Holy Scripture.

H. J. Cadbury, Harvard professor and one of the more extreme New Testament critics of the last generation, once declared that he was far more sure as a mere historical fact that Jesus held to the common Jewish view of an infallible Bible than that Jesus believed in His own messiahship. Adolf Harnack, greatest church historian of modern times, insists that Christ was one with His apostles, the Jews, and the entire early Church in complete commitment to the infallible authority of the Bible. John Knox, author of what is perhaps the most highly regarded recent life of Christ, states that there can be no question that this view of the Bible was taught by our Lord himself. The liberal critic, F. C. Grant, concludes that in the New Testament, "It is everywhere taken for granted that Scripture is trustworthy, infallible, and inerrant." Rudolph Bultmann, a radical anti-supernaturalist, but acknowledged by many to be the greatest New Testament scholar of modern times, asserts that Jesus accepted completely the common view of His day regarding the full inspiration and authority of Scripture.[3] The basic question about the inspiration and authority of Scripture is, "What do you think of Christ?" If we accept Him as Lord, it is consistent to submit to His teaching on the complete authority of Scripture. To accept Christ's lordship and at the same time to reject the inspiration and authority of the Bible is inconsistent. This simple logic explains why evangelical Christians, out of obedience to Jesus Christ as their Lord, insist that the Bible must be believed and obeyed as the very Word of God.[4]

This does not mean, of course, that Evangelicals espouse every foolish view of the Bible with which men may occasionally charge them. Evangelical Christians, for example, are not bibliolators. They do not deny the human authorship and characteristics of the Biblical writings. They do not insist that every word of the Bible must be taken literally. Our Lord never commanded His followers to believe such absurdities.

There are other things that the doctrine of the divine inspiration of the Bible does *not* mean. It doesn't suggest that all the Bible was verbally dictated by God to the apostles and prophets. It does not mean that the Bible was written in exact, precise language. It doesn't assert that the Bible employs up-to-date scientific terminology. It doesn't suggest that the New Testament must always quote the best text of the Old Testament. Nor does it maintain that all recorded statements contained in the Bible are true. It doesn't imply that everything taught as binding upon Israel is best in an absolute sense and ought to be obeyed by all men of all times. There is such a thing as progressive revelation without involving false teaching. I may properly teach a child to eat potatoes with a spoon and not with his fingers. Later I may properly instruct that same child to eat his potatoes with a fork and not with a spoon.

When properly understood, the Evangelical view of the Bible is simply that God by His Spirit so guided the writers of Scripture that their words—properly interpreted in the light of their grammatical and linguistic analysis and in light of the historical and cultural context they were written in—teach the truth, never teach what is false, and that this truth comes to man with divine authority.

Properly understood, the Bible is believable. Our Lord commanded us as His disciples to believe it. For those of us who seriously call upon Him as Lord, there is no alternative but to accept His Word. We are under orders.

This is the great strength of the Evangelical position. It acknowledges Jesus Christ as Lord and then it takes His lordship seriously.

To the Liberal

To our friends who insist upon a more liberal view of the Bible we express our understanding and appreciation of their problem. We sympathize with their valiant endeavors to make the gospel "relevant" to the Twentieth Century. We are aware of the yawning chasm of twenty centuries which separate us from the Biblical documents and the historical earthly life of Christ. We, too, stand in awe of the stupendous increase in human knowledge by which the sum total of all human achievement may be doubled in a ten-year span. But when it comes to the ultimate question of being and of goodness, of life and of death, what does modern man know more than the ancients? Either God in Christ has moved into our human sphere to act in our behalf or man stands alone. Either God speaks to us His word of truth in our Lord and His chosen prophets and apostles or the heavens are silent. A God who never intervenes to act for us or who never speaks to illuminate our minds and warm our hearts is no better than a dead God. It did not take Altizer and company, blasphemously propounding that God is dead, to remind us that without Christ, we are without God and without God we are without hope in this world.

As Evangelicals we believe in the living God who made heaven and earth and who long ago sent His only begotten Son down into this world to live and die and rise again for our redemption and who now today speaks to us by His Spirit the truths of His written word, the Holy Scripture.

But just here is to be found the Achilles heel of most Neo-orthodox and Liberal theologians. They, too, purport to believe in Jesus Christ. They, too, acknowledge that Jesus Christ has broken the silence of God and that in Him the living God acts and speaks. They, too, profess Jesus Christ as their divine Lord (sometimes, it must be admitted, without too careful a definition of what they mean by divine or Lord). To all such liberals, we earnestly and humbly present this challenge:

The evidence is overwhelming that the only Jesus Christ who ever existed not only claimed to be Lord but insisted that His disciples submit to His lordship by believing and obeying Scripture. In the light of this, do you really prefer to set your own mind and your own feelings as the final arbiter of spiritual and moral truth? Do you really wish on a religious question to stand in flat disagreement with Jesus Christ? Do you really arrogate to yourself responsibility for urging young people in our churches and schools to "draw their own conclusions" or to adopt your conclusions *when in doing so they must set aside the clear teaching of Jesus Christ, the Lord?*

If Liberals will honestly face such questions as these, they will be driven back irresistibly to the real issue which thinking men must not avoid, "What do you think of Christ? Is He our divine Lord, or is he not? Is He the final authority over our life and thought, or is He not?" If He is not, that settles the matter of the divine inspiration of Holy Scripture once and for all. If the Bible is wrong at this main point, it is certainly wasted effort to discuss its infallibility. With anyone who takes this position, the question to be discussed is not "Is the Bible inerrantly inspired?" but "Who is Jesus Christ?"

On the other hand, if Jesus Christ is really divine Lord and Saviour, that too settles the matter; and we should hear no more about accepting Christ but not the Bible. If Jesus Christ is Lord and Saviour, I am shut up to the position that He exercises His Lordship over me by enjoining the Bible on me (1) as my place of communion with Him, and (2) as the means for learning His will. He has sent His Spirit to help me understand the truth in the Bible, and to enable me to apply it and obey it. The inerrant inspiration and indefectible authority of the Bible is a corollary of the Lordship of Jesus Christ. All Liberals founder ultimately on the impregnable rock of the lordship of Jesus Christ and His teaching as to the complete, final and binding authority of Holy Scripture over the life and thought of His true disciples.

To the Roman Catholic

To turn to our Roman Catholic friends who frequently ask which came first the Bible or the Church and, thereby, imply that the Church is prior to and over the Bible, we reply in turn: Who came first, Jesus Christ or His Church? Which came first, Jesus Christ's commission to His disciples or the New Testament Church?

Our Lord gave to His apostles authority over the Church to teach His truth and to bear witness to their Lord. He promised to them the Holy Spirit who would enable them to perform their task. The apostles claimed this authority and the faithful Church of Christ has acknowledged that it is built on the foundation of the prophets and apostles, Christ Himself being the chief corner-stone (Ephesians 2:20).

The Christian who would be faithful to Jesus Christ must, therefore, be obedient to the teaching of His apostles as this is recorded for us in Holy Scripture.

When anyone alleges, moreover, that Scripture is difficult to understand and therefore needs an infallible interpreter, the Evangelical confesses his gratitude for every ray of light and guidance which others may shed upon the pages of Scripture to enable him to interpret more accurately and to apply more faithfully the truths of the Bible to every phase of his life and thought. But the Evangelical also notes that Christ never promised infallibility to His Church, only that its faith would never cease. He certainly never promised infallibility to those who would call themselves Bishops of Rome or who have been instituted by a segment of the nominal Church into such an office. Our Lord did promise infallibility to His prophets and apostles in their writing of Holy Scripture and warned his followers at their own peril against setting aside the jots or tittles of Biblical teaching.

As Evangelicals, moreover, we claim the best Helper of all to interpret rightly the written Scripture. God gives us the Holy Spirit who meets with us in the pages of the Bible and brings us into personal fellowship with our living Christ and leads us, who are all too fallible, bit by bit to interpret the truth of God and to apply it to life.

The Evangelical Christian, therefore, in obedience to His Lord, must ask all who would seek to add to Scripture or to subtract from Scripture: Where has our Lord commanded us to turn for truth? Where are His disciples to secure their religious guidance? What is it that they are to study so that they may know the truth and receive instruction and guidance for their souls?

To all of these questions the answer of our Lord is not an infallible Church or human leaders who may rise up in the Church. Our Lord directs His disciples to Scripture, the written Scripture of His prophets of the Old Testament and, by promise of His apostles in the New Testament. And the Evangelical who would be faithful to His Lord dares turn nowhere else.

To the Non-Christian

To our friends of the non-Christian world, we who are Evangelical Protestants humbly confess that we are not the way, the truth, or the life. By our very name, derived not from a mere protest but from a *protestimonium,* we profess to be mere witnesses to our Lord and Saviour, Jesus Christ and to His infallible word in the Holy Scripture. As witnesses, we have experienced for ourselves the wonders of God's infinite grace extended in Jesus Christ to us as lost and helpless men. We have found God in the pages of Holy Scripture as there we have come to know personally Jesus Christ and in Him recognize God acting in grace in our behalf. We have found healing of soul, comfort, guidance; yes—and rebuke and correction as needed, in our Bible which we believe to be the written Word of God.

With hearts overflowing with divine love and infinite grace, we must speak forth that which we have seen and heard and experienced for ourselves. This great gift, which has given meaning and significance to all of life, we seek to share with any who will hear and turn with us to the Saviour.

Not in pride or arrogance, not in intolerance or disrespect, but rather in humility and gratitude the Evangelical freely acknowledges that God gets all the credit, that apart from divine grace, he is no better, indeed perhaps worse than any other, but in Christ, the Evangelical insists that he has found divine forgiveness and fellowship and that His divine Christ gives him in Holy Scripture instruction and guidance for life. Just as he holds that two and two equals four, rather than three or five, so the Evangelical Christian is convinced that Jesus Christ is his Lord and that Christ's lordship is exercised through the teaching of the Bible. The non-Christian may argue that the Evangelical is wrong, but he cannot reasonably argue that the Evangelical who seeks to share his conviction is thereby sinful or unloving.

To ourselves as Evangelicals

To our own selves, finally we who are Evangelicals sadly confess that our great difficulty with the Bible is not its infallible truth and authority, but obedience to its teaching. Orthodoxy must never fall short of ortho-practice. No true Evangelical should ever rest satisfied merely with correct views about the Bible. The harshest words of Christ in all the Bible are directed not against the disbelief in the truth of Scripture but against negligence, willful misinterpretation, and disobedience to Holy Scripture.

If we believe that the Bible is true, carries divine authority and is the source of our knowledge about Christ and His will, then we must study it. And as we do, our Lord has promised His present, indwelling Holy Spirit to guide us to Biblical truth and lead His Church into joyful and obedient fellowship with Him as the Lord of Scripture.

As Evangelicals, therefore, we stand *under* the judgment of Holy Scripture. The Bible is not a Protestant Book. It is not really an Evangelical Book (or if it is, it is only to the degree that these positions are found in accord with its teaching).

The Bible is God's Book for His Church: We listen to it. We learn from it. We obey it. We are judged by it.

We must submit our own pet schemes and programs to the judgment of the Word of God. Every thought must be brought into captivity to our Lord Christ and His Word. There is no true orthodoxy or true orthopraxy that is not first of all Biblical.

My fellow Evangelicals, unless we are willing to bring the thoughts and actions of this great missionary conference under the sovereign judgment of our Lord as He has revealed it in His written Word, all our best efforts will be but sounding brass and tinkling cymbal: We must learn to think according to His Word. We must be humble to seek correction according to His Word. We must understand our task according to His Word. We must seek to relate it to our fellowmen according to His Word. We must be teachable to receive new truths according to His Word. We must be faithful always and in all things according to His Word. We must give ourselves wholly, unreservedly, radically to the sovereignty of His Word.

Here we as Evangelicals take our stand. We can do no other—so help us God.

"O Spirit of the living God, wilt Thou in grace bring forth at this conference new and living truths from the pages of Thy Holy Word, the written Scripture of our Lord Jesus Christ. Amen."

FOOTNOTES

1. Cited by J. S. Stewart, *Thine is the Kingdom* (New York: Charles Scribner's Sons, 1957, c. 1956), pp. 14 and 15.
2. For an elaboration of this evidence as to our Lord's teaching, see J. W. Wenham's *Our Lord's View of the Old Testament* (London: Tyndale Press, 1953). Jesus' teaching about the authority of the Bible includes, at least indirectly, the New Testament as well as the Old. Not only does He clearly lay down the principle as to what attitude His disciples must take toward those books which God's Spirit guided His prophets to write, but He also made very clear that He was calling out apostles to bear witness to Him. These apostles were promised, and later received, the same prophetic authority as the writers of the Old Testament (See for example John 14-16, I Corinthians 2 and Hebrews 2:4).
3. Frederick C. Grant, *Introduction to New Testament Thought* (Nashville: Abingdon-Cokesbury, 1950), p. 75. See also John Knox, *Jesus: Lord and Christ* (New York: Harper Brothers, 1958); Adolph von Harnack, *Outlines of the History of Dogma* (Boston: Beacon Press, 1957); and Rudolph Bultmann, *Jesus and the Word* (New York: Charles Scribner's Sons, 1958).
4. For a further discussion of this and related topics see author's article, "Christ and Scripture," *HIS* (January, 1966, pp. 16-20).

CHAPTER 5

Mission—And the Church's Message

by Dr. Arthur F. Glasser

> "Behave wisely towards those outside your own number;
> Use the present opportunity to the full.
> Let your conversation be always gracious, and never insipid;
> Study how best to talk with each person you meet."
>
> Colossians 4:6 NEB

I. *Introduction.*

A. *Contemporary Confusion.*

"Evangelism is something other than evangelistic preaching."

A strange mood of reaction against evangelistic preaching has descended on the Church. It is made to appear as something unChristian, unethical, sub-Biblical. Preaching for decision is downgraded to the level of propaganda and sheep-stealing. Strong and insistent are those who challenge the Church's right to stand before the human race and say: "We have a message from God for you."

And yet, at the same time, evangelism is lauded to the skies. But 'evangelism' is made to be something other than preaching. Blauw, Scherer, and others quote without negative comment, Martin-Achard's sweeping affirmation:

> "The evangelization of the world is not a matter of words or of activity, but of presence: the presence of the people of God in the midst of humanity, the presence of God among His people."[1]

Should you press these men as to the basic elements of the Gospel they would doubtless cite our Lord's death, His burial, and subsequent resurrection. But these are glossed over as somewhat unimportant. The argument goes something like this: "Why concentrate on words? You best win people by displaying love to them. Our chief task is to treat them as brothers whether they act that way toward us or not. Christianity is only learned through relationships of love, trust and understanding."

Walter M. Horton in his book, *Our Christian Faith,* attempts to define a strategy for world evangelism. He says:

> "It is a great mistake, from the point of view of strategy, to allow the straight preaching of the gospel to bulk too large in any well-rounded program of missions. . . . In terms of methods, evangelism often comes last, following modestly in the train of education and medicine. Deeds have to come ahead of words. The healing of sick bodies, the liberation of minds from the curse of illiteracy, the setting up of a new economic standard of living through scientific agriculture, or new social mores giving women and children a fair chance for the first time, all convey the love of Christ far more effectively than words."

And then Horton takes a look at Church history and comes up with the startling conclusion that "last of all" long after "heroic deeds of invincible good-will" had been performed by the early Christians throughout the Roman world, the time came "for formal instruction,—the words that explained the meaning of the deeds." "And that is how Christianity won its way all over the globe in the 19th century."[2] In the few years since Horton said this (1947) the drift toward nonverbal communication has steadily increased, until in our day evangelistic preaching is widely suspect.

B. *Apostolic Conviction.*

"Evangelism means nothing less than evangelistic preaching."

When one steps into the world of the New Testament, he soon discovers that the apostles had very clear convictions about evangelism and evangelistic preaching. According to the apostles, people became Christians because of a work that God performed upon their hearts by His Holy Spirit. In order that He might do this gracious work, these people needed to be exposed to information about Christ. The sort of information that would kindle thoughts of repentance toward God. So far as the apostles were concerned, what all men everywhere needed was this soul-transforming experience of the new birth. Only by this could they become Christians. Unless individual souls are renewed in their minds by the Spirit of God, so as to repudiate themselves and actively receive Christ as the Lord and Master of their lives, they are not redeemed people.

With these concepts all of us here are in deepest agreement. The apostles saw their task as proclaiming the Word of God to men. True, in their lives they demonstrated the love and concern that would constrain men to listen to their preaching. But they knew that only the Word of God could pierce human hearts and transform thoughts and intents. They spoke the truth in love, but their love was no substitute for the truth. They proclaimed the Gospel in a context of concern, but their concern was no substitute for the Gospel.

And yet, two words of caution are needed: First, the apostles did not *transmit* the Gospel, tossing out to people a verbal formula with a "take it or leave it" attitude. Their task rather was to *communicate* the Gospel, presenting it in an attractive, winsome form so that it might reach people in thought-forms familiar and meaningful to them.

Second, the apostles did *not* make the Gospel relevant to men. They agreed it *was* relevant because the Gospel was something in which God had taken the initiative, to make men fit for His presence and His fellowship. Their Gospel was not a set of ideas to be discussed, it was a story to be told. What the Gospel needs, they concurred, was not a philosopher, but a witness, not a lawyer but a narrator (Paul Rees).

C. *The Christian in Mission.*

"God needs men He can control."

The foundation of Mission is in the sovereign grace of God. God desires to call forth a people from the ruined human race, to become a people made like unto His Son. To accomplish this He has given to men of all nations and cultures a capacity for Himself. The heathen are not portrayed in Scripture as longing for a Saviour who was crucified. But they are portrayed as inescapably caught up in a religious quest. Man everywhere is a bearer of culture whose central, integrating factor is religion; it may even be the secular religion of the Marxist world.

The Christian involved in Mission, proclaiming the Gospel to men, must keep this religious dimension ever in view. He must be polite and appreciative of their reaching outward after *Theos* but he must end with the announcement of judgment, the call to repentance, and faith in Christ. Misunderstandings will gradually decrease as he pours new content into their old words. At no point within pagan thought will he ever find anything that will resemble an unripe fruit that can be simply taken over and utilized as a basis for his Christian witness.

The witness to Christ must involve his whole person in the task. He must sharpen the issue until it is solely an encounter between God and his hearers. His *agapé* love must show throughout. God must speak through him to the hearts of his hearers. As he preaches he prays.

D. *Paul at Athens.*

Here we find the Apostle Paul, the noblest Christian of his day preaching the Gospel in Athens, the noblest city of the ancient world. It is a record of encounter, of response, and of tragedy. But this account, as no other in the New Testament, uncovers the complex totality of all that is involved in proclaiming the Gospel of Jesus Christ in today's world. Let us read the text (Acts 17, N.E.B.):

> "Now while Paul was waiting for them at Athens he was exasperated to see how the city was full of idols. So he argued in the synagogue with the Jews and gentile worshippers, and also in the city square every day with casual passers-by. And some of the Epicurean and Stoic philosophers joined issue with him. Some said, 'What can this charlatan be trying to say?'; others, 'He would appear to be a propagandist for foreign deities'—this because he was preaching about Jesus and Resurrection. So they took him and brought him before the Court of Areopagus and said, 'May we know what this new doctrine is that you propound? You are introducing ideas that sound strange to us, and we should like to know what they mean.' (Now the

Athenians in general and the foreigners there had no time for anything but talking or hearing about the latest novelty) (vv. 16-21)

"Then Paul stood up before the Court of Areopagus and said: 'Men of Athens, I see that in everything that concerns religion you are uncommonly scrupulous. For as I was going round looking at the object of your worship, I noticed among other things an altar bearing the inscription 'To the Unknown God.' What you worship but do not know—this is what I now proclaim. (vv. 22-23)

"The God who created the world and everything in it, and who is Lord of heaven and earth, does not live in shrines made by men. It is not because he lacks anything that he accepts service at men's hands, for He is Himself the universal giver of life and breath and all else. He created every race of men of one stock, to inhabit the whole earth's surface. He fixed the epochs of their history and the limits of their territory. They were to seek God, and, it might be, touch and find him; though indeed He is not far from each one of us, for in Him we live and move, in Him we exist; as some of your own poets have said, 'We are also his offspring.' As God's off-spring, then we ought not to suppose that the deity is like an image in gold or silver or stone, shaped by human craftsmanship and design. As for the times of ignorance, God has overlooked them; but now He commands mankind, all men everywhere, to repent, because He has fixed the day on which He will have the world judged, and justly judged, by a man of His choosing, of this He has given assurance to all by raising Him from the dead. (vv. 24-31)

"When they heard about the raising of the dead, some scoffed; and others said, 'We will hear you on this subject some other time.' And so Paul left the assembly. However, some men joined him and became believers, including Dionysius, a member of the Court of Areopagus; also a woman named Damaris, and others besides." (vv. 32-34)

II. *The Athens of the First Century.*
—in microcosm, the world of today.

Four hundred years had elapsed since Athens experienced its

golden age and yet it was still "the cultural and religious capital of the world"[8]. On every side, on the streets and hilltops, Paul could see evidence of its past creativity. And yet, it was an Athens in decline and decay. Philosophy had degenerated into sophistry. Political power had passed into the hands of the rougher Romans. Oratory was now only rhetoric, poetry just verse-making.

True, the philosophers still taught the folly of idolatry. Their pupils still mocked the superstitions of the less cultured strata of society who thronged the temples. But in their ethical debates, philosopher and pupil alike were unable to come up with anything to replace the idolatry they scorned. Not unlike the poverty of contemporary philosophy with its myopic preoccupation with semantics.

The text mentions Epicureans and Stoics. The former were virtually atheists, the disciples of Epicurus (341-320 B.C.). They sort of acknowledged God in words, but denied His providence and superintendence over the world. Whatever higher sense Epicurus might have attached to this type of pleasure, his followers in Paul's day were given to gross sensualism.

In contrast, the Stoics were the pantheists of the Greco-Roman world, the disciples of Zeno (340-265 B.C.). To them everything was God. God was the soul of the world, the world was God. Self-sufficiency was to be pursued as the highest goal. Virtue brought its own reward, vice its own punishment. Pleasure was not a "good" and pain was not an "evil."

In Athens Paul also contacted the local Jewish synagogue, stark and severe in its monotheism. Its adherents scorned alike the religious life and philosophical debates of the Athenians. They gathered around the Name of the God of Abraham, Isaac, and Jacob—the Lord and Creator of all things. True, they must have been somewhat vocal in their witness as evidenced by the Gentile "god-fearers" ("devout persons") who were drawn to their worship. The record says that Paul's conference with this synagogue involved him in an "argument" ("dispute"). Were they so deeply intrenched in their religious life that he couldn't stir them up and lead them on to something better? The record is too incomplete for us to know for sure.

As Paul's eyes ranged from temples to altars to schools to synagogue he was confronted with the totality of the religious quest of man, and the beginnings of God's response to that quest. We see these same elements today in the world of our generation. Religion, philosophy, Jewish monotheism.

III. *The Elements of the Religious Quest.*

—in essence: Athens of the First Century.

The first Adam was a monotheist. He knew the one and true God. When he sinned he led the human race into moral bankruptcy. He began the pattern of closing the mind to further knowledge of God. His descendants followed this example. "Instead of appreciating the glory of the Creator by contemplating the universe which He created, they gave to created things that glory which belonged to God alone." [3] Mankind's subsequent ignorance of God became a deliberate ignorance, devoid of innocence. They suppressed the truth accessible to them and perversely, even eagerly, embraced the lie in preference. Romans 1:18-32 records the religious devolution of man.

Secular scholars do not uniformly accept the Sunday Supplement view that man's religious life has evolved from primitive animism, through polytheism, and up to monotheism. There are those who confirm the biblical teaching of mankind's religious degeneration. Dr. Wilhelm Schmidt in his impressive books: "*The Origin and Growth of Religion*" (1931) and "*The High-Gods of North America*" (1932) testifies as follows:

> "There are a sufficient number of tribes among whom the really monotheistic character of their Supreme Being is clear even to a cursory examination." [4]

Dr. Langdon, late Professor of Assyriology at Oxford, also confirmed this thesis. "Both in Sumerian and Semitic religions, monotheism preceded polytheism. I have set down with care the evidence and reasons for this conclusion, so contrary to accepted and current views, perceiving fully the adverse criticism with which it will be received." [5]

Restless, unhappy, disoriented man must worship something. "Since he refused in his pride to worship his Maker, he turns the light of divine revelation into the darkness of man-made religion, and enslaves himself to unworthy deities of his own devising, made in his own image or that of creatures inferior to himself." [6]

When Paul later stood in the Areopagus (the hill of Ares) and proclaimed Jesus Christ, what did he see? The Acropolis with its temples, idols, altars, and priests. The Agora (marketplace) with its schools, philosophers and students. The Avenue(?) with its synagogue, its rabbis, and their scrolls of the Old Testament. All these elements fitted together.

The TEMPLES with their altars and the incense moving slowly, uncertainly upward into the Beyond. Man groping, reaching out of himself, upward. Driven by a longing: Wagner called it *Sehnsucht*, Koestler spoke of the "oceanic sense," Milton wrote of "enormous bliss," Wordsworth interpreted it as "intimations of immortality." This longing has produced all the religions in this world. We, too, have experienced the Numinous. We have hungered to contact Reality. In a sense, we can appreciate why Athens had its temples, its gods, its altars, its upreaching incense.

At the foot of the Acropolis, Paul saw the marketplace, the SCHOOLS with their philosophers and disciples. He could imagine the endless debates—arguing about existence, about patterns of life, about the Law of Nature. Those who remember their Agamemnon or their Oedipus, and the choruses of the Greek plays will recall that the Greek mind—those Greeks to whom Paul spoke—was always oppressed with a consciousness of the enormity of personal guilt. In his day the Epicureans and Stoics tried to rationalize away, even justify, personal failure and give intellectual coherence to life. Their answers to the question: "What governs?" were either "Seek what pleases you, only don't hurt others" (Playboyism) or "conquer by resignation, acceptance, and service for others" (Humanism). But these solutions are not real solutions. The debate in the Agora droned on and on.

Paul now riveted his eyes on that stubborn Jewish SYNAGOGUE with which he had had such an intense debate. What did it signify? Earlier I intimated that all races, cultures, and peoples were hungrily involved in reaching out to contact the Numinous. Not quite all. There was an exception: a people who stood apart. In their history they had had a sequence of experiences unrelated to what happened to their neighbors. At places in their pilgrimage, at Ur, Haran, Bethel, Egypt, Sinai, Palestine, successive invasions from "Deep Heaven" overwhelmed them. They had come to realize that the Haunter, the Numinous Power, the awe-ful Presence of the Universe was none other than the Governor, the ethical Governor of the universe. Not many gods but one God. He is "the righteous Lord who loveth righteousness," they said. We need no longer drift through life, guess about life's great questions, and dread the future.

And yet, how incomplete are the message of the Law of Moses, the Prophets of Israel and their sacred writings. God is! Yes, but His "otherness" makes us tremble. He takes the initiative to reveal Himself to mankind. Yes, but, O, that we knew where we might find Him. What of our guilt before Him? Even the worshipper in the Jewish synagogue knows unsatisfied yearnings.[7]

IV. *Paul's Reaction to the Religious Quest.*

—righteous exasperation is no sin.

What mattered to Paul was that the statuary represented deities of one sort and another. He did not think of them as gods but as demons (I Corinthians 10:20). Their worship was not spiritual but idolatrous (I Thessalonians 1:9). And the babble of the philosophers only confirmed to him the damning proof of the thesis he later expounded with telling force: "The world through wisdom knows not God" (I Corinthians 1:21). His spirit was "provoked within him." God was being dishonored.

The city "full of idols" was robbing God of His glory. In his mind and heart Paul literally exploded. He must reason, argue, debate with all and sundry. The Athenians must turn from these vanities and worship the one true God. He must speak forth. God's very glory was at stake.

At this point we do well to inquire into one another's motivation for involvement in Mission. How well do we match this Apostolic norm? Do we merely serve out of duty because Christ commanded that the Gospel be preached to all nations? Have we gone forth into Mission because our circumstances in life left us no alternative? Paul was moved by a deepest concern for the glory of God. An enemy has usurped God's rightful place in their hearts and lives. He must give them an opportunity to hear the message of "Jesus and the Resurrection."

V. *Paul's Message: The True Nature of God.*
—Christ is God's final response to the religious quest.

A. The *Setting*: The Court of Areopagus.

Areopagus means "hill of Ares," the Greek god of war. Since his opposite in the Roman Pantheon was Mars, an alternate name was "Mars' Hill." Actually, this was the most venerable institution, most exclusive court, in Athens. It traced its origin to legendary times, claming to have been founded 1000 years before by Athena, the city's patron goddess. It still retained great prestige, with special jurisdiction in matters of morals and religion. It was quite natural that a "setter forth of strange gods" (Acts 17:18) should be subjected to its adjudication. Paul must have been very grateful to God for the privilege of standing before these men, and have them say to him, "State your faith!"

B. *The Audience*: *Critical and contemptuous.*

In the market place Paul had encountered the Stoics and Epicureans. At first they only gave casual attention to what Paul had to say. Something about two strange gods. Jesus and Anastasis ("resurrection"). But the more they listened the more impressed they became. The Epicureans drew near to taste the flow of his words, to criticize his style, to weigh his choice of images, to detect whether there was harmony to his attempted balancing of sentences. The Stoics gathered for a more serious reason. What new theory of life would he propose? How had he come to terms with life, its hardships and its uncertainties? All agreed that this Jew be brought before the Court of Areopagus to hear him out. Paul was on the spot and he knew it. From every quarter cold, critical eyes fastened themselves on him.

C. *The Silence*: *Things Paul left unsaid.*

Paul saw no point in quoting the Jewish prophets, for they were unknown to his Gentile hearers. Paul saw no point in descending to the level of his philosophically-oriented hearers, and arguing from first principles as one of them might have done. Paul saw no point in blasting the worship of idols, exposing to ridicule its foolishness, and scolding the Athenians for their stupidity. Paul wanted to win men, not fight them.

D. *The Approach: Christ and the Religious Quest.*

Paul spoke with great dignity and courtesy. He commended

the Athenians for their deep interest in religious matters. With prudence and tact he told them that they were "more divinity-fearing" than other Greeks. Had he come to proclaim "strange gods?" Not at all! He then described an altar he had seen within their city. It's inscription caught his eye. It gripped him, burdened him. He felt its agony. So Paul said, "The god who is still a stranger to those men, whom they openly confess they do not know, I have come to Athens to proclaim." Paul did not combat religious systems or philosophical systems. Instead, he addressed men. He reached out after the hungry-hearted, the groping—those who like blind men confessed their blindness as they fumbled to find the latch of the door. Were he among us today he would say, "Don't preach to Buddhists, to Muslims, to Hindus. Just preach to men. Reach out to men in the tragedy of their need. And you will win them to Christ."

E. *The Argument: Christ and the Religious Quest.*

Paul's argument moves swiftly:

1. God is not made by man; He is man's Maker. He is the transcendent Creator and Lord of the universe.

2. God doesn't inhabit the material shrines erected by men. In fact, it is He who bestows life on His creatures and provides for their needs.

3. Mankind is a unity by creation.

4. God's gracious providence has provided "habitable zones on earth" for man's dwelling and "seasons of the year" for his well-being. These are intended to lead men to "feel after Him, and find Him."

5. But the days of groping and ignorance are past. Now in Christ the fulness of the Godhead has been revealed. Valid knowledge of God is now available.

6. I can well believe that at this point Paul spoke of the Lord Jesus, of His coming into the world, of His life among men, and of His staggering claims. In Him God has "put on a face" and has revealed Himself as more infinite and more glorious than man's most sublime dreams. This God dwarfs all else and leaves no room for any gods of men. Sensual worship—temples, altars, sacrifices—all becomes ludicrous in the presence of the Lord of heaven and earth.

7. And mankind is irresistibly traveling toward the judgment seat of God. There Christ sits as judge; Not as an unknown God, but a risen Christ with whom all men have to do. Repent and believe! This is His summons to His creatures.

F. *The Response: A sharp disappointment.*

Paul never really finished his address. The Athenians listened carefully until he mentioned the resurrection. The "Court" then dismissed him as unworthy of further serious consideration. The bodily resurrection is still a stumbling-block, even in our day. And it is still integral to historic, biblical Christianity. Some mocked, others temporized with indecision, but a few believed. Paul left Athens a disappointed man. We do not know that he ever cared to return.

VI. *Conclusion*

What lessons can be learned from this study?

A. *Method:*

Paul did not fail at Athens. The Athenians failed. Actually, Paul's method at Athens cannot be improved upon. He truly meant what he said about becoming all things to all men. At Athens he showed amazing versatility and became an intellectual to the intellectuals that he might win them to Christ. We must do likewise.

B. *Knowledge:*

Paul showed himself fully conversant with the religions and philosophies of his day because he skirted so easily the many traps into which a less-informed person would have fallen. We should place no premium on ignorance. The missionary today must make himself fully conversant with the religious literature and culture of the people to whom he is sent.

C. *Emphasis:*

One element in the primitive preaching is constant throughout the Acts—"with great power gave the apostles their witness to the resurrection of the Lord Jesus." Does this characterize our preaching?

D. *Caution:*

We should guard against reading too much into (Acts 17:30). "The times of ignorance God overlooked, but now He commands all men everywhere to repent." One can argue that this means

God deals with men according to the light they have, and does not hold them responsible for the light not yet revealed to them. From this one can make unwarranted conclusions regarding the eternal state of non-Christians. Gerstner tells us: "The meaning of the statement is that God did not enter into judgment with men at this time of ignorance, that is, He did not visit His (full) wrath on them. He did not declare (so clearly) His disapprobation; for *that* He has appointed a Day of Judgment."[8]

FOOTNOTES

1. Johannes Blauw, *The Missionary Nature of the Church* (New York: McGraw-Hill, 1962), p. 43.
   James A. Scherer, *Missionary, Go Home!* (Englewood Cliffs, N.J.: Prentice Hall, 1964), p. 129.
2. Walter M. Horton, *Our Christian Faith* (Boston: Pilgrim Press, 1947), p. 88.
3. F. F. Bruce, *The Epistle of Paul to the Romans* (London: Tyndale Press, 1963), p. 82.
4. A. Rendle Short, *Modern Discovery and the Bible* (Chicago: Inter-Varsity Press, 1958), pp. 16-19.
5. Ibid., pp. 16-19.
6. James Packer, "Christianity and Non-Christian Religions," *Christianity Today,* Vol. IV, No. 6 (December 21, 1961), p. 213.
7. C. S. Lewis, *The Problem of Pain* (Geoffrey Bles ed., Saunders, S. J. R., Christian Challenge Series, 1940), pp. 1-13 contains an interesting expansion of the thrust of this section on the religious quest of man.
8. John H. Gerstner, *Acts (The Biblical Expositor,* C. F. H. Henry, ed., Philadelphia: A. J. Holman Co., 1960, Vol. III), p. 216.

CHAPTER 6

Mission—And the Church's Endowment

by THE REVEREND PHILIP TENG

When the Lord Jesus was on this earth with His disciples, they needed no endowment. He himself was their constant help. He was always in their midst to guide, to protect, to encourage, and to deal with every problem. All they had to do was to be with Him and hide themselves in Him in a very real sense. They could cast every burden on Him. He was their All-Sufficiency.

But what happened when their Master left them and went back to His Father? What endowment did He bestow upon them to take His place?

His disciples were greatly dismayed when He said that He was going to leave them, so He encouraged them and prayed for them, as recorded in John 14:17. In speaking of His endowment to them, He said something which was too much for them to take in: "Verily, verily, I say unto you, He that believeth on me, the works that I do shall he do also; and greater works than these shall he do; because I go unto my Father" (John 14:12). They could not understand these amazing words, but later they learned to know they were true.

What is this endowment, of which the Lord spoke so much? We have a definite answer recorded in John 16:7. "If I go not away, the Comforter will not come unto you; but if I depart, I will send Him unto you."

"Another Comforter." The word "another" indicates the Holy Spirit was going to be to the disciples all the Lord Jesus had been to them previously. Through this "Another Comforter" they would be enabled to do greater works than Jesus Himself had done!

We can never overestimate the importance of the Holy Spirit.

He was the center of the Lord's last discourse (John 14:16), and it was none other than the Holy Spirit concerning whom Jesus gave His "last commandment" to His disciples just before His ascension: "Tarry ye in the city of Jerusalem until ye be endued with power from on high" (Luke 24:49). There are four Great Commandments in the New Testament: the First Commandment, "Thou shalt love the Lord thy God; the Second Commandment, "Thou shalt love thy neighbor as thyself; the New Commandment, "That ye love one another, as I have loved you, that ye also love one another"; the Great Commission; and the Last Commandment, just mentioned above. All four of these are to be obeyed. Any one missing would break the Divine Chain. Jesus thought so much of the Holy Spirit that He called Him "the Promise of the Father" (Luke 24:49).

The Book of the Acts of the Apostles is really "The Book of the Acts of Jesus through the Apostles by the Holy Spirit." Since the Holy Spirit is the most conspicuous we are justified in calling it "The Book of the Acts of the Holy Spirit." We see Him explicitly at work when 3000 and then 5000 people were convicted and converted; when Peter and the other disciples witnessed boldly in the face of persecution; when the early Christians overcame selfishness and gave more than liberally to the Lord's work (Acts 4:32-34, cf. 5:3); when the first martyrdom took place; when the Gospel of Salvation reached the first gentile family in the city of Caesarea (11:12); and so on through Acts (8:29; 9:31; 11:24; 13:2,9; 15:28; 16:6-10; 20:28).

Behind all these important and, in the case of some of them, epoch-making events and movements of the early Church, we find the Holy Spirit to be the real promoting and sustaining power. Moreover, no one can fail to observe that most of the events on this list have to do with missions. Are we not justified in saying that the chief concern of the Holy Spirit in the early churches was the promotion and capacitation of missions?

As a matter of fact, the supernatural sign of speaking with tongues which accompanied the coming of the Holy Spirit at Pentecost was itself a clear and divinely appointed indication that the purpose and the work of the Holy Spirit is to bring the Gospel to all races where different "tongues" are spoken.

We shall study the work of the Holy Spirit in missions under several headings, based on the records of the Book of Acts, with illustrations from the history of missions.

I. *The Holy Spirit and the Capacitation of Missions.*

The Lord committed to His followers the task of evangelizing the world. But clearly and emphatically He told them: "Ye shall receive power after that the Holy Spirit is come upon you, and ye shall be witnesses unto me, both in Jerusalem, and Judaea, and Samaria, and unto the uttermost part of the earth" (Acts 1:8).

Power is, in every sphere of work, the one all-important requisite, for we "wrestle not against flesh and blood." We need a supernatural power against a supernatural enemy, and only the Holy Spirit can supply this power. It is interesting to note that of all the "armour of God" which Paul speaks of in Ephesians 6, the "sword of the Spirit" is the only offensive and active piece, without which we can never win a battle. Missionary apparatus without the power of the Holy Spirit is dead. The Lord thought so much of this "Power from on High" that He even forbade His disciples to begin their work before they were equipped with this Divine Supply. How can we afford to think differently from the Lord?

A. *Outpourings of the Holy Spirit on Missionary Work.*

This is an historical sketch, based on the record of the Book of Acts, showing an important and special phase of the ministry of the Holy Spirit in regard to missionary work.

There is an important distinction between the in-filling of the Holy Spirit and out-pouring of the Holy Spirit. The former has mainly to do with depth of spiritual quality and character, and with power to service, whereas the latter is a sovereign act of God, to indicate the ushering in of a new era, or the beginning of a new movement or expansion. The latter happened only four times in the Book of Acts—2:3, cf. 2:18; 8:15-18; 10:44-45; 19:6. Each of these was accompanied by supernatural signs. It is most revealing to find out that all these four times were related to missions: the first time was the coming of the Holy Spirit at Pentecost, and the Lord referred to it as the empowering for world missions (Acts 1:8); the second time was when the Gospel reached the first non-Jewish city of Samaria; the third took place when Peter preached to Cornelius in the city of Caesarea; finally, the fourth time came about when Paul broke into new ground, showing clearly the distinction between the Gospel of Jesus and the teaching of John the Baptist (Acts 19:1-6). These are facts which show how concerned and how related the Holy Spirit is to missions.

B. *Capacitation for Producing Results.*

When Peter was filled with the Holy Spirit, he preached and 3000 souls were converted. It was the quality of such a large number of new converts that showed the power of the Holy Spirit—"And they continued steadfastly in the Apostles' doctrine and fellowship, and in breaking of bread, and in prayers" (2:42).

Barnabas was filled with the Spirit, and "much people was added unto the Lord" (11:24). Not unto the church, but "unto the Lord." That must mean true conversions. There were both Jews and Gentiles among them. As a result, a prosperous and spiritually-minded church was established.

Paul was filled with the Holy Spirit, and he, with a few helpers, started churches that had fellowship with him in spreading the Gospel "from the first day until now"; that showed "work of faith, and labour of love, and patience of hope" (I Thessalonians 1:3); that were "enriched by Him in all utterance, and in all knowledge, even as the testimony of Christ was confirmed in them."

Through the centuries there have been amazing instances of the rapidity of results, under the power of the Holy Spirit. In the ninety-six years following 1811, there were over a million converts in West Polynesia. In Burma, during the first 80 years of evangelistic work, an average of one new convert was baptised every three hours around the clock, and one in ten of such converts became an active worker for the Lord. In the Fiji Islands, at the end of the fifty years between 1835 and 1885, 1200 churches could be counted. In Formosa, Mackey had 1200 converts at the Lord's table after twelve years' work. Instances like these could be multiplied again and again.

C. *Capacitation for Expansion.*

The Spirit-filled church at Jerusalem expanded along three main routes: by the converted "devout Jews" at Pentecost who went home with the Gospel; by the Christians scattered after the martyrdom of Stephen and the persecution that followed; and by other scattered Christians who took the northern route to Phenice, Cyprus, and Antioch, and in turn from the Spirit-filled church at Antioch to Asia Minor and Europe.

Church history abounds with illustrations of this truth. At significant turns in the history of the Church we see special manifestations of the power of the Holy Spirit. For instance at the beginning of the Wesleyan Revival we see a visitation of the power of the Holy Spirit which is sometimes called the Methodist Pentecost. We find these words in John Wesley's Journal:

> "Jan. 1, 1739. Mr. Hall, Kinchin, Ingham, Whitefield, Butchins, and my brother Charles, were present at our love-feast in Fetter Lane, with about sixty brethren. About three in the morning, as we were continuing instant in prayer, the power of God came mightily upon us . . . as soon as we were recovered a little from that awe and amazement at the presence of His Majesty, we broke out with one voice, 'We Praise Thee, O God, we acknowledge Thee to be the Lord.'"

George Whitefield recalled the occasion and remarked, "It was a Pentecostal time indeed!" One month later he preached to 20,000 colliers at Kingswood, Bristol, with marvellous results. The great movement expanded to all England, to all Great Britain, to America and to many other countries. Many scholars agree with Prof. A. M. Renick of Edinburgh in saying that even William Carey, the London Missionary Society, and the strong Evangelical wing in the Church of England are all fruits of this mighty revival.

D. *Capacitation for Victory over the Power of Darkness.*

On his first mission field, Paul met with a formidable enemy—Elymas the sorcerer who had great influence with the deputy of the country against the faith. Paul made him blind temporarily and thereby broke the power of darkness over the island of Cyprus. He pointed out in his rebuke that Elymas was a vessel of Satan to hinder the cause of the Gospel, and he was enabled by the Holy Spirit to bring about victory over him.

The power of darkness reigns through superstition and sin which results in moral corruption. But the transformation of individual lives and communities, wherever the Gospel is preached, is an undeniable proof of the power of the Holy Spirit. J. H. Bavinck has pointed out in *The Science of Missions*, that conviction of sin cannot be brought about by a philosophical approach alone, based on natural theology, using reason as a common premise for arguing against the falsity of heathen ways of life and faith. "The Holy Spirit alone," he says, "can call to repentance, and we are only means in His hand." He goes on to say, "If elenctics (or the conviction of sin) were an human activity, the situation would be nearly hopeless." That is only too true.

E. *The Holy Spirit and Prayer Power.*

The working of the Holy Spirit is so interwoven with prayer that sometimes they are taken as one thing. They are mutually causative. In the Book of Acts, nothing is so closely linked together with the power of the Holy Spirit as prayer.

The disciples were praying when the Holy Spirit came upon them at Pentecost; the Spirit-filled church at Jerusalem was a praying one (2:42, 3:1); Stephen was filled with the Holy Spirit, and he prayed for his enemies; Paul had been praying before he came to be filled with the Holy Spirit; The Holy Spirit fell on the house of Cornelius, and they prayed and praised God in tongues; the leaders of the Antioch church fasted and prayed, and the Holy Spirit spoke to them; etc.

Church historians concede that William Carey was the true herald of modern missions. The movement which he started was born of a special monthly prayer meeting for world-wide outpouring of power from on high, which Dr. Arthur T. Pierson called a "stated monthly season of such united, organized pleading with God for a lost world." When missionaries began to labor on the island of Tahiti, the power of darkness prevailed so that the efforts of the first fourteen years seemed to be wholly in vain. There was not a single convert. The directors of the London Missionary Society seriously proposed abandoning this fruitless field. But a few people felt this was the very hour when God was about to rebuke unbelief and reward faith. A special season of united prayer was called for. Many confessed unbelief and prayed fervently. A miracle happened just at this crucial hour. Unknown to each other, two vessels started from two opposite ports, one from Tahiti bound for London, the other from the Thames bound for Tahiti, and they crossed each other's tracks at mid-ocean. The latter carried letters of encouragement to the missionaries. The former bore letters from the missionaries in Tahiti, announcing such a mighty work of God that idolatry was entirely overthrown. What a wonderful and amazing coincidence between prayer and the power of the Holy Spirit!

F. *Capacitation in the Face of Persecution and Martyrdom.*

Under great pressure from both political and religious leaders of Jerusalem, Peter, being filled with the Holy Spirit, witnessed boldly and powerfully (4:1-12). So with the whole congregation (4:31). Immediately after receiving the fulness of the Holy Spirit, Paul "straightway preached Christ in the synagogues, that He is the Son of God" at the risk of his own life (9:20). When Barnabas and Paul were persecuted by the chief men of the city of Antioch in Pisidia, they were "filled with joy and with the Holy Spirit" (13:52).

This is most relevant today in many parts of the world. How much we need this power on our mission fields!

G. *Capacitation for Working Miracles as Confirmation of the Word.*

Before His ascension, Jesus spoke of miracles as confirmation of the Word (Mark 16:20). "And by the hands of the apostles were many signs and wonders wrought among the people" (Acts 5:12).

Innumerable miracles, either in the narrower or in the broader sense of the word, could be cited in the history of missions. Instances of divine power ruling over situations when no human efforts could be of any avail, the opening of closed doors when every factor seemed to strengthen the bolts and bars, deliverance of the messengers of the Gospel where no escape was humanly possible, conversion of the most hardened heathen where all efforts looked ridiculous, provision for the soldiers of the cross when they were completely cut off from all supply, etc., have constantly inspired and renewed trust in the divine miracle-working power.

H. *The Holy Spirit and the Supply of Recruits for Missions.*

The Holy Spirit (Acts 13:4) called Barnabas and Paul for missionary service, and they went. He calls and recruits volunteers for mission fields. Please note four things in this verse: (1) It is the Holy Spirit who does the calling. (2) He calls workers for a definite service. (3) He calls the best—Barnabas and Paul. (4) They obeyed.

It is the Holy Spirit Who does the calling. None of us should be discouraged about missionary work, since the Holy Spirit is the promoter and recruiter. He moved in the latter part of the nineteenth century, and the student world of America and England was roused to join in missionary action. Under the instrumentality of men like D. L. Moody, the Student Volunteer Movement was formed, and in twenty-five years' time over 9000 volunteered for the mission field.

He calls workers for a definite service. The Antioch church had every reason to keep Barnabas and Paul at home. Yet the Holy Spirit sent them away. Gifted Christian workers have disobeyed the Holy Spirit, persuaded their ability was meant for the churches at home. No workers who have failed in the homeland can be expected to be successful on the mission field. Facts prove beyond doubt that missionaries who have done great things on the mission fields can be as greatly used of God at home. Yes, the mission fields demand and deserve our best men and women.

They obeyed. A good measure of the weakness of missionary work today is attributable to the unwillingess of gifted workers to obey the call of the Holy Spirit to go to the mission field. They prefer to stay at home. The Christian public at home should encourage their best men and women, whom they think they cannot spare, to go to the mission field.

III. *The Holy Spirit and Sacrificial Giving for Missions.*

Following Pentecost, we read of sacrificial giving in the Apostolic Church (Acts 2:44). Ananias and Sapphira "sold a possession, and kept back part of the price" (5:1,2). Peter referred to is as "lying to the Holy Spirit" (5:3). Two things are clear in this verse: first, the Holy Spirit moved Christians to give sacrificially; second, many followed the prompting of the Holy Spirit, but some tried to cheat with clever designs.

The Macedonian churches showed "abundance of joy" in "great

trial of affliction," as well as "riches of liberality" in "deep poverty" (II Corinthians 8:2). The "Macedonian giving" is not only giving of money, but is basically giving of oneself—they "first gave their own selves to the Lord" (II Corinthians 8:5). The giving of money and the giving of lives have constituted the great "Missionary Giving," all prompted by the Holy Spirit.

Pietism gave birth to a missionary thrust of which the Moravian Mission was a part. The Holy Spirit moved so clearly at Herrnhut that out of a small congregation of six hundred grew a mission which sent out 2170 missionaries in 120 years' time to many of the most difficult places in the world. In 1930, after 200 years of work, the ratio of missionaries to the total membership was, according to Dr. Robert Glover, one to ninety-two, which is probably an unsurpassed record.

IV. *The Holy Spirit and Guidance in Mission Policy.*

The Book of Acts affords at least four principles of missionary work having to do with the leading of the Holy Spirit.

A. *Occupation of Key Cities.*

Philip was led to Samaria; Peter to Caesarea; Paul started work in many key cities in Asia Minor. Today, the metropolitan areas are the strategic centers for evangelism, since this is indeed a "Metropolitan Age."

B. *Capture of Key Persons and Classes for Christ.*

When Paul went to the Isle of Cyprus, he dealt with the deputy of the country, won him for the Lord, and thereby created a favorable influence on the island. At Athens, Paul engaged the intelligentsia of the city in disputation and roused their interest in the Christian faith, which resulted in the conversion of some intellectuals, among whom was a man of position by the name of Dionysius (Acts 17:18, 34).

Philip was led by the Holy Spirit to speak to the Ethiopian eunuch, who was a leader in his country, and it was the first step towards the Christianization of that land.

This does not mean the Gospel is meant only for a certain class of people. It does teach us there is real wisdom in labouring patiently among intellectual people on the mission fields. We should never neglect them. Many missionaries or missionary societies skip over the educated class and leaders, because work among them requires a greater price to be paid.

C. *Movement to New Areas.*

Paul moved on to new areas once he had established a local church. If missionaries follow this principle, the strength of the great missionary army will not be taken up by working in churches already established, but will break out to new areas in every direction. This will start a mighty expansion in this generation.

V. *The Holy Spirit and the Establishing and Sustaining of Indigenous Churches.*

In his farewell exhortation to the elders of the Ephesian church Paul said, "The Holy Spirit hath made you overseers, to feed the church of God" (Acts 20:28). Evidently the Holy Spirit wills that the churches on the mission fields be self-governing, self-propagating and self-supporting. If you do not go with the Holy Spirit you will never raise up strong churches. "When they had ordained them elders in every church, and had prayed with fasting, they commended them to the Lord on whom they believed" (Acts 14:23). Having ordained leaders in his mission churches, Paul commended them to the Lord. So one of the most important jobs is to train national leaders.

National churches must be trained to be missionary minded. Paul could speak of the churches which he started as having "fellowship with him in the Gospel from the first day until now," and as "sounding out the Word of the Lord not only in Macedonia and Achaia, but also in every place . . ." (I Thessalonians 1:8).

VI. *The Holy Spirit and Love Service in Missions.*

"And there stood up one of them named Agabus, and signified by the Spirit that there should be great dearth throughout all the world" (Acts 11:28).

Evidently the purpose of the Holy Spirit in announcing the coming famine through Agabus was that Christians should manifest their love to one another by action at such a time. The Christians at Antioch understood the significance of this prophecy, and "sent relief" to the brethren in Judea. It was a beautiful expression of brotherhood in the love of Christ.

It is true that the primary task of the Church is to evangelize the world, but the Holy Spirit reveals to us here that love services have their place in missions. Do schools, hospitals and other welfare services come under this category? Certainly they do serve a two-fold purpose: means of evangelism, and channels of love.

VII. *The Holy Spirit and Mass Evangelism in Mission.*

As soon as the curtain is drawn on the Pentecostal spectacle, we have a scene of mass evangelism presented to us—Peter, with the Apostolic Team, full of the Holy Spirit, preaching to thousands of amazed people with wonderful results. A short time later at the Gate called Beautiful, Peter again testified to Gospel truths before a crowd of 5000, counting only the men. Even the hostile "rulers" were overwhelmed by this huge crowd (Acts 4:21).

Crowds at evangelistic meetings are nothing new. But as an organized means of evangelism, mass campaigns have sound scriptural basis if they have the Holy Spirit as their main power source. United campaigns are greatly and desperately needed on the mission fields.

VIII. *The Holy Spirit and Unity as Power for Missions.*

The Spirit-filled church at Jerusalem showed a wonderful spirit of unity (Acts 2:41-47). Paul speaks of "unity of the Spirit" (Ephesians 4:3). Our Lord said in His prayer for His disciples, "And now I am no more in the world, but these are in the world. I come to thee. Holy Father, keep through Thine own name those whom Thou hast given me, that they may be one as we are . . . that the world may believe that Thou has sent me" (John 17:11, 21).

The unity of believers produces a power which convinces the world of the reality of the Gospel. The Lord laid repeated emphasis on the oneness of believers in this great prayer. The words "that they may be one" are used four times in this chapter, and every time they take on new meaning. In view of these words of our Lord, we can never speak too much of the importance of the unity of believers.

We evangelical churches must start a decisive movement for unity on Biblical terms. There must be combined action on the mission fields if we really want more effective evangelism. We should set up committees to study the best ways for unity, with as many evangelical groups as possible taking part. We must not only speak negatively of an unbiblical unification, but we must also act positively for a biblical one.

IX. *The Great Expectation—Outpouring of the Holy Spirit Before Christ Comes Back.*

I believe there is Scriptural basis for expecting a great outpouring of the Holy Spirit upon the Church just before Christ comes back.

Peter spoke of Joel's prophecy of the outpouring of the Spirit before "the Great Day of the Lord" as having been fulfilled at Pentecost. The fulfillment of this prophecy is evidently divided into two stages. The first was fulfilled at Pentecost, and the second will be fulfilled just before the Great Day of the Lord actually comes.

May we say that the Holy Spirit began His outpouring at Pentecost and continues His outpouring in revivals and in missionary work, and that there will be a finale, just before the Lord comes back—the beginning, the continuation, and the culmination of the outpouring of the Holy Spirit as the total fulfillment of the prophecy of Joel.

There is a close parallelism between this and the fulfillment of some prophecies in the Book of Revelation. All students of this book know of the immediate, the intermediate, and the final aspects of fulfillment of many of the predictions in that book.

It is a great encouragement for us to look forward to a great time of spiritual refreshing in the foreseeable future. We should cry to God to hasten it, and we should be prepared for it.

In conclusion, let us remind ourselves of Paul's words to the Galatians: "Are ye so foolish? having begun in the Holy Spirit, are ye now made perfect by the flesh?" (Galatians 3:3). Since it was by the power of the Holy Spirit that missions were started, are we to finish it by human efforts? Even as the Galatian Christians fell prey to legalism, so the Church of this age has fallen prey to "technique-ism" which has been allowed to take the place of the Holy Spirit, who is the real source of power for missions.

There should be a renewed call to a revival of utter dependence on the Holy Spirit, and a diligent seeking after the fulness of the Holy Spirit in our individual lives, and in the lives of missionary societies. Then a true missionary revival will be realized.

CHAPTER 7

Mission—And the Church's Nature

by Dr. John F. Walvoord

The great dynamic truths revealed in the Word of God concerning the Church as the body of Christ may be considered through the Scriptural revelation concerning the relationship of the individual to this new entity. Such a study reveals that a Christian rightly related to Christ has: (1) a new position in Christ, (2) a new union with Christ and all other true believers, and, (3) a new association which changes his total relationship to God, his fellow Christians, his family, and his relationship to the world.

I. *The New Position Of The Believer In Christ.*

On the night before His crucifixion our Lord pronounced the important prophecy, "At that day ye shall know that I am in my Father, and ye in me, and I in you" (John 14:20). During the years of His public ministry our Lord had been connected most intimately with His disciples. Now a new relationship was going to be realized. As Christ had already informed them, He was going to leave them and they could not follow Him immediately (John 13:33). His coming death, resurrection, and ascension would bring a new day in which there would be a new relationship.

The intimacy and blessing of this relationship would embody two important Scriptural truths. First, the indwelling of Christ as their constant companion is embodied in the phrase, "I in you." There was to be also a new relationship dynamically expressed in the three words "ye in me." The disciples were to be intimately related to Christ in a new position.

From this new relationship would emerge all the details of their glorious salvation. Because they were in Christ they would be justified, positionally sanctified and become channels through which the power and grace of God could flow in deliverance from sin and in manifestation of resurrection power. In Christ they would have access to God. They would have the right to eternal inheritance and the promise of ultimate glorification.

The Pauline revelation is summarized in I Corinthians 12:12, 13: "For as the body is one, and hath many members, and all the members of that one body, being many, are one body: so also is Christ. For by one Spirit are we all baptized into one body, whether we be Jews or Gentiles, whether we be bond or free; and have been all made to drink into one Spirit." The baptism of the Spirit brought them into relationship to the body of Christ and because of this they are vitally related to Christ, the head of the body, and are in Christ.

This truth finds its way into the important discussion of Romans 6 where the fact that the believer is in Christ by baptism of the Spirit is seen to relate the believer to the death of Christ and to His glorious resurrection. As Paul wrote the Romans, "Know ye not, that so many of us as were baptized into Jesus Christ were baptized into his death?" (Romans 6:3). The Scriptures are plain that being in Christ means that God sees the believer as one who died in Christ and who rose in Christ and this leads to the corresponding demand of a holy life in keeping with the new position.

Similarly in Colossians 2:12 Paul writes, "Buried with him in baptism, wherein also ye are risen with him through the faith of the operation of God, who hath raised him from the dead." The new relationship of being in Christ must necessarily be at the heart of any true Biblical concept of the Church. Such a relationship necessarily supersedes all earthly relationships. It is this mystic unity which is sometimes ignored in contending for ecumenicity. The unity of believers in Christ is not lightly achieved, but depends upon a Biblical faith which has Christ as its center, and its theology is defined in specific terms by the Scriptures.

II. *The New Union Of The Body Of Christ.*

The concept of the Church as composed of all true believers united in a living union in the body of Christ is one of the central figures of the New Testament. Using the human body as an apt illustration of the living union of believers related to Christ as the head of the body, the Scriptures have much to say concerning the formation and increase of the body as the basic program of God in the present age. It is most inappropriate for a member of the body of Christ to be joined in wicked union to a harlot. Rather, the individual believer is himself a temple of God set apart for holy use, and dedicated to the glory of God (I Corinthians 6:19, 20).

The unity of the believers is again affirmed in Ephesians 2:14 where the middle wall of partition separating Jew and Gentile is broken down. It is expanded in Ephesians 4:4-6: "There is one body, and one Spirit, even as ye are called in one hope of your calling; one Lord, one faith, one baptism, one God and Father of all, who is above all, and through all, and in you all." That none of this is organizational unity, but rather a spiritual unity affected by the power and grace of God is clear.

The analogy of the human body as it corresponds to the body of Christ is detailed in Ephesians 4:16 where the body is declared to be fitly joined together, united by that which each joint supplies, and as a living entity increasing and building itself up in love.

Other references to the body of Christ are found in such passages as Colossians 1:24 and in 2:19. In the latter passage it is indicated that believers should be rightly related to Christ the head, "from which all the body by joints and hands having nourishment ministered, and knit together, increaseth with the increase of God." The body of Christ is also presented as that of which Christ is the head, emphasizing that the direction must come from Him (I Corinthians 11:3).

The supreme position of Christ—over His body the Church—is declared again in Ephesians 1:20-23. Mentioned also is the headship of Christ in Ephesians 5:23 and Colossians 1:18. It should be clear from these many references in the New Testament that the true line of authority is not through an organization, but through a personal relationship to Jesus Christ who is the head of the Church. Such guidance and direction is ministered by the Holy Spirit and enforced by spiritual rather than carnal means.

The resultant program of God is vitally related to this concept of the Church as the body of Christ. It is this entity as the body of Christ that is nurtured by Christ according to Ephesians 5:29, Philippians 4:13, Colossians 2:19. The program of God by which the earthly body of Christ is prepared for its heavenly destiny as the bride of Christ is revealed in Ephesians 5:25-27 with many other Scriptures related less directly. It is to this Church, the body of Christ, to which Christ has given varied gifts even as various members of the human body have sovereignly bestowed upon them, functions peculiar to their positions in the body. Hence, the Scriptures outline the gifts of God to His body the Church in several major passages (Romans 12:3-8; I Corinthians 12:27, 28; Ephesians 4:7-16).

All of these truths concerning the body of Christ are summarized in the central passage in I Corinthians 12:12, 13 where it is stated that we are all baptized in one body. It is through this body that there shall be increase in members of the body, and growth in grace of the individual believer. Through this body God channels His supernatural grace which enables the believer to do all things. Certainly ecumenical organization is not a substitute for this unity nor is it a proper expression of it. A true unity can only be accomplished by the power and grace of God, the ministration of the Spirit, and the bestowal of proper spiritual gifts. The unity of the Spirit is accomplished by the power of God rather than by human ingenuity.

III. *The New Association Of Members Of The Body of Christ.*

The believer who is joined to Christ and to his fellow believers has a corresponding new relationship to everything about him. First is his new relationship to God, which is the basis for fellowship, for divine blessing, for forgiveness of sin, for justification by faith, for sanctification and ultimately fulfills the total purpose of God in the glorification of the individual.

The believer, of course, is vitally related to every other true believer. It is accomplished by the power and grace of God, not by human organizations. The relationship is real and will continue throughout all eternity. To recognize this does not require any superimposed organization to effect the unity or fellowship which is involved. The Christian recognizes that other believers are proper custodians of the grace of God even as he is, and are destined to be glorified saints in the presence of God in eternity.

The new relationship in the body of Christ extends to every other relationship of life. It is designed to transform the home, the relationship of father and mother to each other and to their children, the relationship of master and servant, and the relationship of the Christian to the world. In a word, every relationship of the Christian's life now becomes colored by the fact that he is a member of the body of Christ.

IV. *The Church And The Ecumenical Movement.*

The last quarter of a century has witnessed many significant developments. The most significant innovation from the standpoint of Christianity has been the Ecumenical Movement. Church leaders, prompted by a desire to be relevant in a world antagonistic to the Church in its program, seek the organizational unification of divided Christendom so as to have a more effective impact on the non-Christian world.

The ideal of organizational unity has appealed to many as the only useful strategy in a world engulfed by nationalism, communism, and materialism, and divided by such issues as race prejudice, disparity of distribution of wealth and opportunity, social inequities, and deteriorating morality. The pressures of population explosion, impending world famine, and the threat of atomic war accentuate a situation already grave. In such a world for the Church to be divided into many organizational units seems to the ecumenist to make the task of effective proclamation of the gospel impossible.

The Ecumenical Movement, however, is faced by many serious problems, and grave questions can be raised which strike at the ideological heart of ecumenism. Is organizational unity the real answer to the quest of the most effective means of promoting Christianity? Is such a super-church possible with any dynamic common faith? Are there not inherent difficulties which would render such a universal church organization impotent by internal divisions and a cumbersome organizational structure?

Unifying Protestant, Roman Catholic, and Greek Orthodox Churches can only be achieved if the problems of a common theology, common order, and an acceptable morality are solved.

It has become increasingly apparent, that such union can be achieved only by a process of theological emasculation.

With the practical elimination of theology as a barrier to ecumenism, the question of morality is coming to the fore. No system of morality can be divorced from its theology. The new morality of liberalism which is shocking even to some liberals is, strange to say, no barrier to ecumenism, but only another area in which ecumenism tolerates differences to the point of capitulation. Although ecumenism has tried to establish an image of being a supreme illustration of Christian love and understanding, it has tended to ignore the absolute holiness and justice of God. How can such a system of belief without specifics in either theology or morality manifest the dynamic to touch a world effectively with its message and program.

Ecumenicity suffers from the inherent disabilities of an eclectic movement. Its deep-seated theological differences are not healed by adopting a creed interpreted so loosely that almost anyone nominally Christian can be enthusiastically received. In ecumenicity today such issues as the infallibility of Scripture, the virgin birth, the deity and eternity of Jesus Christ, the personality of the Holy Spirit, substitutionary atonement, the bodily resurrection of Christ, and the personal and physical return of Jesus Christ in His second coming are areas of substantial disagreement. Little uniformity of theological conviction can be observed in theological fundamentals.

The goal of ecumenicity at any price tends also to suppress and oppose those with evangelical convictions. Where ecumenism has been in control, whether at home or abroad, there has been no favorable climate for evangelical dissenters who find it impossible to affiliate organizationally with the Ecumenical Movement.

Even adherents of ecumenicity are beginning to ask whether a religious monopoly does not have serious dangers and disadvantages. Individuals and smaller groups are in danger of being steamrollered into conformity. All the problems of centralized control of any large organization composed of people with differing opinions loom large in the ecumenical approach to Christianity.

Organizationally, ecumenicity has little or no Biblical basis.

While it is obvious that Christians of various communions should fellowship where a basis of fellowship exists and various bodies of Christendom should not be competitive, it is also true that organizational unity is nowhere upheld in the Scriptures as a *sine qua non* of effective Christian testimony. The appeal to John 17:21-22 for Biblical support of ecumenism illustrates the confusion in thought between the Church as an organism and the church as an organization. Christ did pray, "That they all may be one; as thou, Father, art in me, and I in thee, that they also may be one in us," (John 17:21), but this has no reference to Church organization. This refers to the intrinsic unity of life which binds all true believers in the one body of Christ. This prayer is already answered, and no organizational structure can add one tie to improve it. It is no more necessary for all Christians to be in the same Church organization than it is to be geographically in one local church.

The early Church had no superstructure, but manifested considerable independency in its local congregations. No hierarchy seems to have existed. The domination of the local church by higher authority arose not in a period of the Church's purity, but in the period of the Church's corruption. There is no Scriptural teaching whatever that demands that all churches everywhere should submit to some central organization.

It is in this context that the true Scriptural doctrine of the Church as the body of Christ comes into its own. What ecumenicity attempts to attain organizationally, a truly spiritual Church can achieve without organizational unity being necessary.

One of the most important criticisms of ecumenism is that it has failed to define the Church. What ecumenism has attempted to inculcate is a horizontal or organizational control of the Church as opposed to the Biblical or perpendicular approach. Organizational control recognizes human leaders or church officials as decisive. The perpendicular approach relates each individual to Christ as the Head of the Church who directs the members of His body. In a word, it is the ideology of organization versus organism.

The idea of one Church is also linked to universalism theologically. If organizational unity is the determining principle, the importance of individual conversion becomes subverted to external considerations. The tendency to make church membership important, works hand in glove with the neglect of supernatural conversion.

Ecumenism tends to ignore if not deny that men out of Christ are really lost and destined for eternal punishment. The alternatives of universalism—that all eventually will be saved—or conditional immortality—that only the "fit" will be raised from the dead—are substituted for the Biblical doctrine.

We conclude that the unity of the body of Christ is a unity of the Spirit. The true goal of Biblical ecumenicity can be achieved when Christians recognize their common bond, their common purpose to serve the Lord and are united on the basis of a Biblical theology. The challenge is, while avoiding needless multiplication of divisions, to concentrate on the main task of the Church—the preaching of the gospel to the millions who have not heard. The unbelief and ignorance which characterizes the lost world should be our primary concern. In the world mission of the Church there is room for those who may differ theologically to the extent that a separate denomination is required, but who agree sufficiently on fundamentals with other fellowships to work with them side by side without friction. The Church, as the body of Christ, is one of the great facts of Scripture. Its unity is from God, not man, by grace, not by organization. The realization experientially of that unity of life which characterizes the body of Christ should be the goal of all Christians who desire to proclaim the gospel to every creature.

CHAPTER 8

Mission—And the Church's Consummation

by Eric S. Fife

Scripture reading: Mark 13:1-13, 32-37 NEB
Text: "But before the end the Gospel must be proclaimed to all nations." (Mark 13:10).
Note: All references are taken from the New English Bible unless stated otherwise.

Consummation and mission. What exciting words these should be to such a unique gathering of missionaries as we have here! Without consummation, the mission would be pointless. Without mission, the consummation would be impossible.

As the missionary theologian, R. A. Cole, has commented, "Consummation is not a call to contemplation but to action."[1] Consummation is the crowning act of God; mission is the continual responsibility of man. New Testament eschatology speaks in the language of the battlefield, not the ivory tower. It has the whiff of gunpowder, not the smell of archives.

The Certainty of the Consummation.

Today it is fashionable to be silent concerning the Church's consummation. "It is no longer possible for anyone seriously to hold the New Testament view of the world . . . we can no longer look for the return of the Son of Man on the clouds of heaven or hope that the faithful will meet Him in the air,"[2] says Rudolf Bultmann. Neither is it surprising that in the one-third of the world that is communist, it would be forbidden to preach on the consummation of the Church, because to look for any supernatural consummation of history or for any redemption of society other than that which is materialistic obviously cuts the very nerve of Marxist dogma. What is more difficult to understand is the strange silence that seems to pervade the evangelical world on the subject of the Church's consummation. Rarely indeed do we hear it preached on in a missionary conference. This is in strange contrast to the New Testament that mentions it no fewer than three hundred times, or once every thirteen verses, and frequently in a context that lends urgency to the evangelistic mission of the Church.

Part of the silence in the evangelical world on the subject of the consummation of the Church is indubitably because of the controversy that has raged so fiercely around certain details and sequence of events. Dr. John Walvoord gave a timely word when he said, "Before the first coming of the Lord, there was confusion even among the prophets concerning the distinction between the first and second comings (I Peter 1:10-11). At the present time there is a similar confusion between the translation of the Church and the second coming to establish the millennial kingdom. An attitude of Christian tolerance is called for toward those who differ on this doctrine, but may we all 'love his appearing.' "[3] It would be tragic if our disagreement concerning the sequence of certain events silenced us concerning the essential truth of the Person. Satan uses Marxist communism to enforce silence on this truth in many parts of the world; it will be a tragedy if he exploits evangelical disagreements to cause such a silence in the Christian world. It is well that the planners of this congress call our attention to the Church's consummation and link it with her mission.

WHAT IS THE CONSUMMATION?

Historically, when the Church has been suffering, its attention has frequently been absorbed by the return of Jesus Christ. The Church in the West today is too affluent and comfortable to be overly concerned with the consummation of history. It is precisely this circumstance, however, that demands a more forthright preaching of this truth. One of the surest antidotes to preoccupation with the comforts of this world is the reminder of the imminence of the next. The Church in the affluent society needs to be continually reminded of the truth that "You do not know when the moment comes . . . Keep awake." Christians expecting the Lord's return tomorrow will not likely buy color T.V. today.

Let there go from this congress a clarion call to the Church of Jesus Christ to live, proclaim, sacrifice, as those who are expecting the return of the Lord. Much of the financial struggles of our missions would be ended if we gave new emphasis to the truth of the Lord's return.

The Distracting Power of World Events.

Jesus Christ discouraged what Alexander Maclaren calls the "fidgety curiosity" concerning details. At the same time, He stressed recurring problems that could distract Christians from their main mission. In the succeeding verses, He mentions a number of such developments:

Verses 5 and 6—Messianic movements. "Jesus began: 'Take care that no one misleads you. Many will come claiming my name, and saying, "I am he"; and many will be misled by them.'" One of the distractions is the existence of false messiahs who will arise offering total salvation to mankind; "many will be misled by them." Through the centuries, there has been no shortage of such self-appointed messiahs. Some have been political, some religious, and many have been a mixture of both. One of the earliest manifestations of this was Caesar worship in the Roman Empire. In a report to Emperor Trajan, the younger Pliny, commenting on the Christians, explained how harmless they were and referred to Emperor Trajan's ". . . instructions which banned all political societies. This made me decide it was all the more necessary to extract the truth by torture from two slave women whom they called 'deaconesses.'"[4] The early Christians had been forewarned by Jesus Christ: "Take care that no one misleads you." One of these messianic movements, Islam, claims one-fifth of the world as subjects. These messiahs have come into their own in our generation. Africa has seen scores of religious messiahs that have risen and flourished in the years since independence. Kwame Nkrumah claimed himself to be a messiah for the people of Ghana and proclaimed as his creed, "Seek ye first the political kingdom and all other things will be added unto you." Recently observers have seen his decapitated statue lying in the dust, a symbol of the downfall of his regime.

False cults arise and flourish throughout the world and not

least in the United States of America. Such developments do not surprise us; they merely emphasize the accuracy of the Lord's prediction. The voice of our Lord is insistent: Do not be misled. Concentrate on the main task at hand. The greatest challenge lies in the false prophet, Karl Marx. But let it not distract us from our task, which is to so fulfill the mission of the Church that the consummation may take place.

Verse 8—Wars, earthquakes and famines. An obstacle to the mission of the Church is the wars of nation upon nation, kingdom upon kingdom. We are called to witness in times of great instability, revolutions, cold wars, hot wars; but these do not catch us unwarned. A recent estimate by the Food and Agricultural Organization of the U.N. set the number of malnourished at nearly 1½ billion; that is, half of the world population.[5] Earthquakes may not be more plentiful now than in the past but improved communications have made us much more aware of them.

Verses 9 and 10—Persecution of the Church. "You will be handed over to the courts. You will be flogged in synagogues. You will be summoned to appear before governors and kings on my account to testify in their presence." We dare not be indifferent to the fact that in many parts of the world, the Church is a suffering minority. More Christians have died for their faith in this century than in any other century of the Christian Church. For many hundreds of years the Church has been looked on favorably in most parts of the world, but we have come to the end of the Constantinian Age of church tolerance and favor. It is estimated that 10,000 Congolese Christians gave their lives for their witness to Christ in recent unrest. Persecution must not be allowed to distract us from the main task in hand. Some of the great advances of the Church have occurred in the face of intense opposition and suffering.

Jesus Christ recognized how distracting could be the power of world events. The correct attitude of the disciple in the face of world turmoil is hard to establish. Can he be indifferent to the plight of his fellowman? Certainly not. Much time at this congress has been given to the consideration of great issues of our day—social matters, the ecumenical movement, etc. In the scriptures, again and again, the men of God were men who had keen perception of the events of their day; but their distinction was that they nevertheless did not allow these events to distract them from the main purpose in hand. "The Gospel must be proclaimed to all nations" in this day of accelerating pace of world events.

The Work of God in World Witness.

After the reminder of adverse circumstances, our Lord in verses 10 and 11, tells the disciples of the superhuman power in preparing the way for the Church's consummation: "But before the end the Gospel must be proclaimed to all nations. So when you are arrested and taken away, do not worry beforehand about what you will say, but when the time comes say whatever is given you to say; for it will not be you that speak, *but the Holy Spirit.*" "You will be summoned to appear before governors and kings on my account to *testify in their presence.*" We see a literal fulfillment of this in the ministry of the apostle Paul who was a persecuting authority figure but who became a witnessing apostle before kings and governors.

Although Jesus Christ says that the mission of the Church must be accomplished in the face of persecution; yet the outcome is never in doubt: ". . . the Gospel must be proclaimed . . . for it will not be you that speak, but the Holy Spirit." Just as the spread of the Gospel is not to be frustrated by the power of secular authorities, neither is it to be subjected to the limitation of human disciples.

Down through the centuries, the resources of the Holy Spirit have proved to be more than sufficient for the persecuted Church to maintain and extend her witness to the risen Christ. Outnumbered and despised, "He has chosen things low and contemptible, mere nothings, to overthrow the existing order" (I Corinthians 1:28).

In light of what God is doing through His Church, we need not have an inferiority complex. It is not out of place to remind ourselves that these verses (Mark 13:10 and 11) stress the fact that though human preparation and method have their place, power to complete the mission of the Church and make possible the consummation is available only in the Holy Spirit. As Lesslie Newbigin has pointed out, "It is not something under human control . . . indeed, it is something that is apt to happen precisely at the point when the Church has no human resources, at the point when the disciple is called before kings and governors and does not know what to say."[6] As we look forward to the consummation, it must indeed be with tremendous boldness and confidence; yet a confidence that rests not in our own techniques and ability but in the omnipotent power of God, through the Holy Spirit.

The Consummation and Human Responsibility.

The full implication of the tenth verse of Mark 13 depends a good deal upon the hermeneutical principles we use. Is "nation" (*ethnos*) to be construed as every tribal group, with its own language, or every nation with a common political frontier that may incorporate many languages—such as India, nations in Africa, and many others? We may not be sure but our Lord is endeavoring to impress His disciples that there must be a total witness to the total world. It is evident today that despite the worldwide work of God to which I have referred, there are huge groupings of the world that yet clamor for the attention of the Church of Jesus Christ.

There is the Muslim world, numbering one-fifth of the world population, with very little witness to the saving power of Jesus Christ. The academic world exploding before our very eyes has until recently been left almost without serious attempt to reach it on the part of the Church of Jesus Christ. As we meet today, 15 million students are in the world, almost 6 million of them here in the United States. In addition to the students, there is the great world of the faculty that for all too long we have written off as being unreachable.

One-third of the world is living under a communist government. Many of these are not committed communists but they are subject to the restrictions of an atheistic ideology. Politically, they may be our enemies but, spiritually, let us recognize that they are our responsibility.

Much more could be said of other worlds—the industrial world, the professional world, the urban world, the Buddhist world, the Hindu world, the Confucianist world. But we have seen that even though in every political nation the Church has been planted, the challenge confronting the Church today, in the light of exploding population and invisible boundaries of prejudice, is not less than the challenge that confronted the disciples to whom Jesus uttered this command.

God has linked His consummation of the Church to our obedience. ". . . *before* the end the Gospel *must* be proclaimed." Though some do not share this interpretation, I cannot escape this implication, from this text and from others in the Scripture. "Since the whole universe is to break up in this way, think what sort of people you ought to be, what devout and dedicated lives you should live! Look eagerly for the coming of the Day of God and *work to hasten it on;*" (II Peter 3:12).

The Lord used the uncertainty of His time-table as a spur for alacrity on the part of the disciples. "But about that day or that hour no one knows, not even the angels in heaven, not even the Son; only the Father. Be alert, be wakeful. You do not know when the moment comes. It is like a man away from home: he has left his house and put his servants in charge, *each with his own work to do,* and he has ordered the door-keeper to stay awake" (Mark 13:32-34). Each with his work to do. Stewardship, accountability, are clearly taught here. "Each with his work to do" is a solemn thought, for it speaks to us of accountability. I cannot tell any man what God's will for his life is, but I can scripturally tell him that "each has his work to do" and that same day he must account for the way he has performed it.

I would leave with you three practical implications to take to heart:

1) *A new call for purity.* We are living today in a moral morass. Compulsory study of certain types of English literature in high school and college, the prevailing commonness of intercourse before marriage, exposure to television, all combine to put pressure on our youth and also on our older people. He is coming in glory and in purity and we are people whose standards are

based not upon the atmosphere of this world, but upon the next, and let this be obvious by our standard of conduct.

2) *A new call for unworldliness.* ". . . in the last days there will come men who scoff at religion and live self-indulgent lives, and they will say: 'Where now is the promise of his coming? . . . everything continues exactly as it has always been since the world began'" (II Peter 3:3-4). Self-indulgence is the characteristic of our age. Scoffing at the second coming is taken for granted in sophisticated circles. Let us stress that the consummation of the Church calls us to a new frugality. "We must teach Christians not to build nests in the trees of this world for they are all marked for the axe." It was in the context of self-indulgence that Peter urged the importance of the teaching of the Church's consummation. Early marriage, obtaining a mortgage on the house, making monthly payments on a car—it is not long before a young Christian today finds himself inextricably enmeshed by the "cares of this life." These things are not wrong, but perhaps the time has come when we should issue a call to some of our young people to be "eunuchs for the kingdom of heaven's sake," or at least to postpone marriage until thirty or thirty-five that they might give themselves without reservation to the work of the ministry while they are still in the full vigor of youthful energy.

3) *A new call for urgency in the mission to which Christ has called us.* This must surely be the clearest, strongest note of all as we contemplate the mission of the Church in the light of its consummation. "I solemnly charge you, Timothy, in the presence of God and of Christ Jesus who will judge the living and the dead, by his appearing and his kingdom, to preach the Word of God. Never lose your sense of urgency, in season or out of season" (II Timothy 4:1-2 Phillips).

William Barclay tells the fable of three apprentice devils who, before taking up service on this earth, had an interview with Satan and were asked what were their plans to deceive mankind. The first replied that he would tell men "There is no God." Satan told him that he would deceive very few because many men know deep down that there is a God. The second said he would tell men there was no hell and Satan replied that he would deceive nobody for everyone knows that sin brings on its own hell. The third said that he would tell them that there is a God and there is a hell, but there is no hurry. Satan replied that he would deceive men by the thousands. One wonders if this is not the lie that has deceived the Church of Jesus Christ today.

As representatives of the evangelical missionary army of the world, we have a history that is soaked in blood but written in glory. Yet it is as nothing compared with our future. Let us rejoice in it, magnify it, preach it, live it. Such an attitude cannot fail to breathe into our mission a new sense of urgency and glory.

FOOTNOTES

1. R. A. Cole, *Gospel of Mark* (London: Tyndale Press, 1963), p. 205.
2. George E. Ladd, *Jesus Christ and History* (Chicago: Inter-Varsity Press, 1963), p. 51.
3. George E. Ladd, *The Blessed Hope* (Grand Rapids: Wm. B. Eerdmans, 1956), p. 160.
4. *Letters of Young Pliny* (Baltimore: Penguin Classics, 1963), p. 294.
5. B. R. Sen (Director General F. A. O. of the United Nations, Rome), *Food, Population and Development.*
6. *Christianity and World Revolution* (Edwin Rian, ed., New York: Harper and Row, 1963), p. 161.

PART 2

MAJOR STUDY PAPERS

Introduction

Ten major study papers were prepared for the Congress. The topics were selected by the Full Congress Committee. The Wheaton Declaration came from the consideration of these topics by the delegates to the Congress.

In each instance one person was assigned to prepare a position paper and he was advised and assisted in the preparation by consultants also selected by the Full Congress Committee. The final responsibility for each paper remained in the hands of the individual to whom the paper was assigned. He availed himself of the counsel of his colleagues but was not bound by their suggestions. The purpose of the papers was to provide the delegates with information for use in their discussion groups. They were also intended to include background material from which the Declaration of the Congress was to be drawn.

Following the reading of each study paper (for which forty-five minutes was allotted) the delegates met for an hour and twenty minutes in twenty-five small discussion groups of not more than thirty persons. A presiding officer and a recording secretary were present at all of these sessions. The participants reviewed the study paper itself and the tentative Declaration. Their opinions, suggestions for changes, and actual changes were recorded. In turn the recording secretaries met in five groups of five. One leader from each of these groups constituted a final committee of five which then met with the author of the paper and his consultants. Together they formulated the Declaration document they transmitted to the final drafting committee which then met and forged out the draft that was presented to the delegates on the closing day of the Congress.

The final drafting committee was a widely representative body and composed, on an average, no fewer than fifteen members. Individuals, young and old, were drawn into the meetings to clarify issues about which there were differences of opinion as to the intentions of the delegates. The final draft of the Declaration was a consensus of the Congress, a faithful effort to reflect what the delegates wanted. As a consensus it was only representative. Many minority opinions were sent on to the final drafting committee and even suggestions made by an individual were considered. In some instances a single recommendation was carried up to the final drafting committee and included in the final Declaration because it was thought to be part of the consensus which had been overlooked but which when drawn into the stream of the discussion was worthy of inclusion.

Space limitations make impossible the publication of the study papers in full. A number of the authors exceeded the limitations imposed by those who assigned the papers. Therefore the papers have been edited and cut. Every effort has been made to insure that the resultant product is an accurate rendering of the author's intentions. Often quotations have been eliminated or severely cut without altering the impact of the paper. If the reader senses any interruption of the flow of the author's thoughts or feels that the organization of the paper has suffered, it should be charged to the editing process rather than to the author of the paper.

It must be reiterated that the papers provided the basis for the discussions that led to the Declaration. They do not necessarily represent the views of the delegates. Individuals made suggestions to the editor that this or that in one or more of the study papers be deleted from them before they were published. Unless there were obvious errors this was not done. Each reader, therefore, can decide for himself whether he is in agreement with the viewpoints expressed in the study papers even as the delegates did. The Congress, as such, was responsible only for voting the Wheaton Declaration. The study papers were neither endorsed nor rejected in part or in the whole by the delegates.

CHAPTER 

Mission—And Syncretism

by THE REVEREND JACK F. SHEPHERD

consultants:
The Reverend Junichi Funaki, Dr. Delbert Kuehl,
Dr. Harold Lindsell, Dr. Francis R. Steele

The Church's worldwide mission is to proclaim Jesus Christ as Saviour and Lord so as "to bring about obedience to the faith for the sake of his Name among all the nations" (Romans 1:5). Syncretism in a variety of forms challenges and compromises the uniqueness and finality of the message of the Saviour—the Lord Jesus Christ.

I. *Definition.*

Webster defines syncretism as "the reconciliation or union of conflicting beliefs, especially religious beliefs." The Oxford definition is, syncretism is "an attempted union or reconciliation of diverse or opposite tenets or practices;" it appends the pithy quotation, "usually derogatory."

The word and the practice have acquired disparaging associations both in origin and use. Plutarch on *Fraternal Love!* reports that the Cretans themselves lived in a constant state of internal discord, but whenever they were faced by a common enemy, they sought to show a "united front." Plutarch labels this expediency *Synkretismos.*

Hendrik Kraemer has a more precise definition which is helpful. Syncretism is "a systematic attempt to combine, blend and reconcile inharmonious, even often conflicting elements in a new so-called synthesis."[1]

W. A. Visser't Hooft in his small book *No Other Name* distinguishes real syncretism from those efforts at communication which may appear to be syncretistic but are not. He says syncretism should be reserved for the type of religious attitude which has four basic characteristics: 1) The insistence that there is no unique revelation in history; 2) The notion that there are many ways to reach the divine reality; 3) The view that all formulations of religious truth or experience are by their very nature inadequate expressions of truth; 4) The concept that it is necessary to harmonize all religious ideas and experiences so as to create one universal religion.

The kind of syncretism so far described strikes at the exclusive claim of the Christian faith as unique and final. Any admixture or amalgamation of beliefs which seeks to change the essential Christian message is wrong and Christians have reacted with apprehension and indignation to attempts to formulate "another Gospel."

We must say, however, that there is a kind of unintentional syncretism which distorts or obscures the essential Christian message. If this idea is valid, we may say that there are three kinds of syncretism:

1. Assimilative syncretism incorporates elements of non-Christian religions assuming there is no qualitative difference between the Christian and other faiths.
2. Syncretism by accommodation reduces or rephrases the Gospel message. It develops as a result of un-biblical, naturalistic thought of one's interpretation of the Christian faith.
3. There is also syncretism through accretions in which secondary beliefs and practices overlay and obscure the basic message.

II. *Syncretism in History.*

Visser't Hooft speaks of "four waves of syncretism."[3] The first of these was in the history of Israel. The "second wave" was the Greek and Roman syncretism which permeated the world of the New Testament into which the new Christian faith was not drawn. The "third wave" preceded contemporary manifestations of syncretism. This was the optimistic humanism of the Renaissance and Enlightenment. Now in the contemporary situation, we are confronted with two syncretistic movements. These correspond to the first two kinds of syncretism referred to above.

III. Why Fear Syncretism?

We must run the risk of being misunderstood. There is a wholesome and legitimate fear of syncretism as an ominous threat to the Gospel. Two important considerations relate directly to this matter: The first is the clearly biblical disallowance of syncretism. The other is the danger of syncretistic distortion of the Christian message.

A. *The Biblical Disallowance of Syncretism.*

1. The exegetical basis for the case *against* syncretism is implicit in the Bible studies on "Authority" and "Message." In both Old and New Testaments, there is a rejection of "the illegitimate blending of religions."

a. In Old Testament affirmation the one God is Creator and Lord and there is no other God (Deuteronomy 4:39; Deuteronomy 32:17-21; Isaiah 37:20; Isaiah 36:18, 19).

b. Israel is separated in thought and activity from false gods and idolatrous practices (Exodus 19:5,6; Deuteronomy 5:2,3; Nehemiah 9:13,14; Ezekiel 36:22,23).

c. The Biblical idea of revelation limits the knowledge of the true God to and through the nation of Israel (Psalms 67; Psalms 47; Isaiah 2:2,3; Isaiah 19:23,25; Zechariah 8:23).

d. Christ's claim of uniquely disclosing the only God is incontestably clear (John 1:1-14; John 14:1-9; Matthew 11:27; Mark 1:15; Luke 24:42-44; Matthew 28:18-20).

e. The expansion of the church as reported in Acts shows an uncompromising affirmation of the one Saviour (Acts 2:34-39; 4:12; 13:38; 16:31; 28:31).

f. Especially in the epistles, Jesus Christ is explicitly set forth as Lord and Saviour in exclusive terms (Romans 10:13-15; I Corinthians 15:1-4; Ephesians 2:1-12; I Peter 2:7-10).

g. The apocalyptic eschatological passages of the Old and New Testaments point to the ultimate and final headship of Christ over all things (Daniel 7:22; Matthew 24:30; Ephesians 1:10; Philippians 2:10; Revelation 1:5; 5:12, 13; 19: 11-16).

2. "Hearing the word" is necessary for salvation:

a. Our claim is that the witness of Scripture to Jesus Christ, not just He Himself as a person, is unique and final. Some seek to exalt Christ as unique, final and absolute without saying the same thing for the witness of Scripture to Him. We believe that "the faith" as message is also unique and exclusive.

b. Those who do not hear the Word and believe, come into judgment and separation from life in God. If it is true that final salvation for the individual relates to the acceptance or rejection of the Gospel, how can one keep from a kind of trembling apprehension in "handling the Word of God" lest it be done "deceitfully"?

B. *The Danger of Syncretistic Distortion of the Message.*

1. The Gospel can be garbled by human factors in transmission. We believe that "the Holy Spirit effects regeneration through the use of the truth as a means". Therefore, we must avoid any admixture which would cause the message to be ineffective, unauthentic or unattractive.

2. Crucial to any discussion of syncretism and the Gospel is the "essential core" of Christian faith. Speer sets out Warfield's "Core Confession" as a central proposition in his great book *The Finality of Jesus Christ.*[4] The three kinds of syncretism may be defined in terms of their effect on the "core" of Christian truth. Assimilative syncretism seeks to incorporate incompatible elements into it. The syncretism of accommodation is in danger of eliminating or deleting some aspects of it. Syncretism through accretions may attach things to the essential message so that it is submerged.

IV. *Assimilative Syncretism.*

The most significant and influential example of assimilative syncretism is that which is associated with the name of William Ernest Hocking. He and those who share his ideals advocate a universal faith for this one world. Arnold Toynbee, the historian, is a champion of this same thing. He strongly urges Christianity to give up its westernism and its traditional belief in uniqueness. Radhikrishnan, the Indian scholar and statesman, proposes a unifying of faiths on the basis of the common "inner essence of all religions."[5]

This kind of syncretistic tendency, as well as that which we call accommodation, is present in the World Council of Churches. It seems fair to regard many of the articles in Gerald Anderson's *The Theology of the Christian Mission* as generally representative of the WCC point of view. Little wonder that Kraemer laments that he has not been listened to by the responsible people.[6]

At the great 1910 Edinburgh Conference there was a very full and discerning statement on the non-Christian religions. In Speer's judgment, this was framed without compromise. At Jerusalem in 1928, there was not complete unanimity on the Christian faith as unique and exclusive. Nonetheless the official statement on the Christian message was strong and positive.

At Madras or Tambaram in India, Hendrik Kraemer presented the fullest and most nearly adequate treatment of the relation of Christian faith to the non-Christian religions in *The Christian in the Non-Christian World.* Since Kraemer, it is generally considered that there are four ways of relating Christian faith to the non-Christian religions: "Radical displacement" now only of fundamentalist sects; "Relativistic syncretism" as "assimilative syncretism" is still strongly influential; "Discontinuity" is Kraemer's view and is a bit more generous and thoughtful than "radical displacement," but we consider his view basically sound; we apply this idea of discontinuity not only to the personal revelation of God in Christ but to the inscripturated revelation of it. "Fulfillment" is the fourth view and is frequently held as a counter proposal to "discontinuity."[7]

It is not reduction of Christian faith or unwarranted elevation of other religions to say that the biblical faith fulfills every legitimate aspiration, answers every anguished question, and ennobles everything of value in any of man's religions. No one has taken this more seriously or worked at it more passionately than Kenneth Cragg. His colorful words summarize what seems to be the possibility of a proper missionary outlook. This can be a

Christian approach to other religions which hold the uniqueness of biblical faith and at the same time judge men to be lost who do not believe it.

> One discovers that all other religious faiths are diversely and variously concerned with just those areas and issues of life and death, of time and mystery, with which the Christian faith is dealing. Parallels are plentiful in the interrogative aspects of religions. They are present also, fruitfully, in the indicative aspects. And if these grammatical similes may be extended, points of meeting also offer themselves in the imperatives of religion. The uniqueness of what the Christian finds in Christ does not mean or argue the exclusiveness of everything Christian.[8]

V. *Syncretism by Accommodation.*

In syncretism by accommodation, the same result is achieved as in assimilative syncretism, but the method is different. Is not syncretism just the right term to apply to the thought of John A. T. Robinson in *Honest to God?* The views of Robinson as well as those of Bishop Pike and the "God-is-dead theologians" should be distinguished and opposed to what Kraemer calls "new so-called synthesis."

Surely is there not a point at which doctrines cease to be Christian in a Biblical and historical sense? Why do they not acknowledge this and step out of the church?

The syncretism of Robinson *et al* can certainly be associated with the Ecumenical Movement. To be sure some who are loyally ecumenical have sharply challenged such views as dangerous and heretical. But there are many in ecumenical fellowship who accept such radical teaching and do not seem to find it incompatible with the doctrinal agreements and stated purposes of the World Council of Churches. Not only is there a syncretism of opposing theological views in the wide range called "Christian," but especially in Robinson's exposition of Tillich there is a striking similarity between his teaching and that of Eastern pantheism. Some have even spoken of this in commendation.[9]

Notice first, that Bishop Robinson insists that the intention of his book is a missionary one. This concern, he says, "determines almost every line of what I wrote."[10] There is much to indicate that he has a sincere desire to make the Gospel, as he understands it, relevant. However, *Honest to God* and similar things may well be a demonstration of the fact that you can go so far in the attempt to be relevant that you cease to say anything and the message is lost in the communication process.

The other tendency is to agree on a minimum of doctrine in order to attain ecclesiastical union. It is sinful to disregard or damage, true Christian unity, but where union is sought at the expense of truth, even greater wrong is done. Dr. Eugene Blake's appeal for "an ecumenical consensus,"[11] sounds good, but it may well come under the kind of criticism that Dr. John MacQuarrie recently made.

> The Ecumenical Movement has undoubtedly dispelled many suspicions and opened up possibilities for co-operation and friendship. But there have also been failures, and these have occurred where there have been attempts to impose a drab uniformity, to be reached by taking the average of the beliefs and practices of the different Christian bodies. I call this the "lowest common denominator" type of mentality, and it is lamentable. It destroys the authentic traditions and puts in their place an insipid syncretism, a soulless Esperanto. Such schemes of union are usually the work not of theologians but of pragmatically-minded ecclesiastical bureaucrats, who think of churches as if they were corporations and dream of super-denominations of twenty million members, or whatever.[12]

VI. *Syncretism Through Accretions.*

Evangelicals will not be taken in by either eclectic or ecumenical syncretism. We insist that nothing shall be assimilated into the Gospel to corrupt it. But, let us ask ourselves if we have not added to and combined with the basic saving proclamation our own accretions, which in a sense get mixed up with the essential core of truth and even confuse and conceal the message. Such a blending or combination, though it is not deliberate and may be well-intentioned, is actually syncretism.

We may regard the missionary communication of the Gospel

as having two stages. The first is the formulation stage where the message which is to be conveyed takes shape. Then there is the transmission of the message to the prospective receptors. The primary danger of syncretism appears to be at the level of transmission. It is this dimension of the communication process which we have considered up to now. We must, however, carefully examine the formulation end of the process to make sure that we have not compromised our message, before we declare it, by an accumulation of non-essential accretions.

This idea of formulation of the message is directly related to the concept of an essential core of the biblical faith. It must be insisted that in translation and transmission of the Gospel there is going to be a measure of adaptation to the receiving situation so that the message is heard in a way that is relevant. This clearly involves a process in which, ideally, the essential core of the biblical faith is introduced and begins to find expression in ways appropriate to, and meaningful in, the new culture. This new shape and mold in the adaptation of the Gospel is not syncretism.

A stimulating and searching question is, "What must a man hear and believe in order to be saved?"

In the evangelistic encounter with the non-Christian, we, as foreigners, should attempt to sort out and transmit only the essential saving message. To get down to the essential core of the Gospel, we can begin by peeling away the layers of inevitable accretion that have in our own experience become attached to the central message.

The first layer to peel off is the complex of the normative way of life of North American church people which has no direct biblical sanction. Then one comes to the behavior standards which have special significance, but they are not essential to the basic message, so let this layer be peeled away.

The next layer is composed of ecclesiastical and denominational traditions. Let them be set aside. But now, we cut through into the quick of the theological system or pattern of interpretation to which we are committed. But let this, too, be taken away in order to come to the heart of the matter.

We come now to the infallible Scriptures, the written revelation

…tion of the Holy Spirit. …not every portion deals …ne redemptive message, …in any sense to be set …ated to the core of the

…t man must believe for …t include the utter lost- …o not one," and that the … Christ, God's incarnate …n's sin and justification

…necessity in a study of …y standpoint, we assert …ctices affect the central …y have syncretism. This …ssimilation, accommoda-

…tion of our message to …re or to present them as … might call it evangelical

…essage will achieve two important things: First, it will alert us to points of vulnerability where vigilance against syncretism is needed. Also, it will allow for a legitimate and creative expression in worship and witness of the life of the receiving church. We will not expect the new formulation of Christian life and faith to duplicate ours as the reshaping takes place. The core must remain the same and be faithfully conveyed in missionary witness.

Beyond this layer, however, it is to be expected, and with some excitement, that a Christianity with a somewhat different shape than ours will emerge. This will appear in new kinds of religious behavior, the expression of ethical values in changing social forms, and possibly even varying theological patterns. The real threat of syncretism arises only if there is absorption into the central core. But the surest safeguard against such corruption and compromise is to have the essential biblical faith adapted to and expressed in culturally relevant ways.

VII. *Conclusion.*

It seems proper to make some proposals for missions in view of the problem of syncretism.

A. Proposals for Missionary Thought:

1. The most urgent task is to elaborate what is the essential core of the biblical faith.
2. An important aspect of this idea is the necessity for a kind of definition of the limits of the claim of uniqueness for the biblical faith.
3. Consideration needs to be given to the view of those who have maintained that no claim of uniqueness is made for Christianity as an empirical, historical religion; it shares, in that sense, with all religions' tendencies to humanness and sin.
4. In considering the *informational* content of faith as message, we must reflect on the implications that "the saving word of God" has had more or less informational content in every age.
5. Attention must be given to the concept of the quality of "addressability" in man. We must ask how this relates to the place of reason in the experience of saving faith and in the communication of the Gospel message.

B. Proposals for Missionary Action:

1. Missionary education must have greater depth and breadth. The missionary must be exposed to thorough theological and cultural study. Anthropology and linguistics are of inestimable value in the crucial issues of distinguishing relative from absolute aspects of Christianity, thereby producing a bulwark against syncretism.
2. In the training programs of national ministers, there should be careful study of the relation of the Christian faith to indigenous religions and of the church society. Here also the social sciences can be brought to the service of theology.
3. We must have missionaries who become experts in the understanding of various religious traditions. They should be

involved not only in academic programs but in research and study centers on the fields.

4. There must be the kind of personal and administrative relationships between missionaries and nationals that will allow and encourage nationals to make the decisions in relating Christian faith to their own culture. Missionary participation in this process can bring a deeper understanding of the real nature of the faith.
5. A demanding and much needed kind of missionary action is the manifestation of a spirit of service and love which not only contends for the Gospel as unique and final but confirms it. This can only be done in the deep awareness that the saving Gospel is not our discovery or development, but God's revelation to be humbly shared with other sinners.

FOOTNOTES

1. H. Kraemer, *Religion and the Christian Faith* (Philadelphia: The Westminster Press, 1956), p. 392.
2. W. A. Visser't Hooft, *No Other Name* (Bloomsbury St., London: SCM Press Ltd., 1963), p. 11.
3. Ibid., pp. 12-34.
4. Robert E. Speer, *The Finality of Jesus Christ* (New York: Fleming H. Revell, 1933), p. 272.
5. Cf. Lesslie Newbigin, *A Faith for This One World* (New York and Evanston: Harper and Row, 1961), pp. 30-55.
6. *The Theology of the Christian Mission* (G. Anderson, ed., New York, London, Toronto: McGraw-Hill, 1961), p. 182.
7. Ibid., pp. 206-209.
8. Cf. Max Warren, *Challenge and Response* (London: S. P. C. K., 1950), p. 51.
9. E.g., Geoffrey Parrinder, *The Christian Debate, Light from the East* (London: Gallanez, 1964), p. 15.
10. Viz., Ecumenical Press Service (May 17, 1963).
11. Eugene C. Blake, "Theology Viewed as Facing Crisis," *The New York Times* (February 20, 1966).
12. John MacQuarrie, "Christianity and Other Faiths," *Union Seminary Quarterly,* Vol. XX, No. 1 (November, 1946), p. 46.

CHAPTER 10

Mission—And Neo—Universalism

by Dr. Arthur M. Climenhaga

consultants:
Dr. Horace L. Felton, The Reverend Ian Hay,
Dr. Carl F. H. Henry, Dr. Louis L. King

Ancient heresies have a way of cropping up in new garb. The cosmological universalism of an Origen not only comes to flower in a nineteenth century universalism but bursts out anew in a modern approach to an old subject. In view of the fresh garb and modified approach to an older speculation, we speak of this movement as neo-universalism or "the new universalism."

Among the anti-Nicene fathers Origen stands out as the first major thinker to espouse a system of universalism. On the basis of an allegorical interpretation of Scripture, he developed the theory that all men (and even fallen angels) ultimately would be redeemed. Thus the term "cosmological universalism." The church of the succeeding centuries rose up in opposition to this universalistic thesis both in creedal and council definitions and proscriptive acts.

In the nineteenth century once again belief in ultimate salvation for all entered the life of the Christian church. The principle of universalism was advocated on the basis of the eternal decrees of God. God in His sovereign grace was seen eternally predestinating all men to ultimate salvation. Gradually, and in some cases more swiftly, the Universalist ministers of the day not only denied other tenets of the Christian faith, such as the deity of Christ, the Trinity, and the authority of Scripture, but they openly espoused looser forms of conduct than the generally accepted norms of the day.

Once again the main stream of the Christian church (especially the Protestant denominations) rose in strong opposition to universalistic assumptions. In all of this it is noteworthy that the main stream of the "Church" stood firmly against the movement as heretical. The early Church of Origen's day and the Protestant church of the nineteenth century stood for eternal salvation or eternal damnation on the basis of the teachings of Christ in the four Gospels, and the amplifications of Paul and other New Testament writers.

What then of the day in which we live? Once again a universalistic interpretation has been introduced into the theological thinking of the Church. This time one senses a spirit of tolerance on the part of the main stream of the Church towards universalistic assumptions. Universalism is rapidly advancing in the theological expression of certain accepted leaders in Protestant churches—a striking reversal of earlier trends! In modern Roman Catholic theology there may be a parallel development which the Second Vatican Council apparently has stimulated by an extension of the notion of implicit faith and baptism by desire.[1]

Following the Second World War, and particularly in 1949, forthright expression of "new universalistic" thinking was evidenced by Dr. J. A. T. Robinson in his exchange of views with Professor T. F. Torrance in the Scottish Journal of Theology.[2] Subsequent writings by Dr. Robinson (now the Bishop of Woolwich[3]) and Dr. Nels F. S. Ferré[4] and other theologians all pointed in a greater or lesser degree to the concept of the ultimate salvation of all.[5]

The current climate of theological thinking in certain sections of the Ecumenical Movement is clearly seen in the provocative work by Dr. D. T. Niles, *Upon The Earth.* This work represents, says Bishop Newbigin, "A unique effort of cooperative thought by many Christians of many nations and churches."[6]

Dr. Niles asks the question, "Will everyone be saved?" After a fairly lengthy discussion, Dr. Niles says,

> The New Testament does not allow us to say either Yes or No to the question: 'Will all men be saved?' and by preventing us from doing this it forces on us the question: 'Will you fulfill your share of the task to which God has called you in

the church—the task of making Jesus known and lived, confessed and obeyed, by all men in every area of life?'

With the "new universalism" breaking onto the current ecclesiastical scene and theology, we are constrained in the context of our deliberations in this Congress to ask: 1. What in essence is the "new universalism"? 2. How, in the light of concepts of Church Mission, is it manifested? 3. Where, in the light of neo-universalism, is our Mission?

I. *The Essence of Neo-Universalism.*

Several classes of Scripture are produced which allegedly imply a universalistic scheme—the ultimate reconcilation of all men.

First, there are passages which purportedly predict the actual salvation of all men, passages such as: Jesus' statement that if He be lifted up, He would draw *all* men to Himself (John 12:32). Pauline statements as found in Ephesians 1:10: Paul's prediction that *all* things will be brought into unity in and under Christ. "As through one man's transgression judgment came upon all (Romans 5:18), so through Christ shall the many be made righteous again." "at the name of Jesus *every* knee shall bow" (Philippians 2:9-11). Paul speaking of the final triumph of the kingdom of Christ, the subjection of all things to Him, including death the last enemy, and thus God finally being all in all (I Corinthians 15:22-28). Peter's reference to the restoration of all things (Acts 3:21).

Second, there are passages which allegedly consist of announcements of God's will to save all men, such as: "God will have all men to be saved and come to the knowledge of the truth" (I Timothy 2:4). "God is not willing that any should perish but that all should come to repentance" (II Peter 3:9).

Third, there are passages which allegedly declare that God stands now in such a relation to all men that they must be saved. "God was in Christ, reconciling the world unto Himself" (II Corinthians 5:19). "The grace of God which bringeth salvation hath appeared to all men" (Titus 2:11). "By the grace of God he tasted death for every man" (Hebrews 2:9). "He is the propitiation for our sins: and not for ours only, but also for the sins of the whole world" (I John 2:2).

Fourth, in the same vein as the above, an attempt is made to equate Jesus' statement in Luke 12:58 and 59 and especially the words, "I tell thee, thou shalt not depart thence, till thou hast paid the very last mite," as an expression of purgatorial and expiatory suffering. Or again in such Scriptures as Matthew 16:19 or 18:18f and John 20:23 the interpretation is that Jesus is speaking in the terms of binding and loosing and remitting of the authority and intercession of the Church reaching beyond this life and beyond this world—although not necessarily beyond the last judgment.

From Paul's writing the new universalism proponents cite the difficult passage in I Corinthians 15:29 and the potency of intercessory baptism of the dead as an evidence of Pauline hope for redemptive processes beyond the grave. For them there is a feeling that the new universalism shadowed in outline in I Corinthians is fully worked out in Romans. The argument is that as man's fall is universal, so divine deliverance is set forth as including all.

Here, then, is an attempt to develop a concept of universalism on the basis of Biblical proof texts. However, Scriptures used to buttress claims of universal redemption when taken in the total context of the scriptural passage, or when juxtaposed with contextual Scriptures which clearly imply that some do perish, can be shown to have a different meaning entirely.

For example, in Acts 3:21 Peter talks about the restoration of all things but then two verses later we hear him saying, "And it shall come to pass, that every soul, which will not hear the prophet shall be destroyed from among the people" (v. 23). Or again, note Paul, who in Ephesians 1:10 speaks of the heading up of all things in Christ declaring in Ephesians 2:3 that some are the children of wrath. He states in Ephesians 5:5 that such have no inheritance in the kingdom of Christ and of God. Perhaps most telling of all is the misuse of the statement of Jesus that if He be lifted up, He would draw all men to Himself (John 12:32). When we remember the clarity of the teaching of the Lord Jesus Christ in the four Gospels on the subject of hell, the fire that is not quenched, the issues of judgment, then the insufficiency of the new universalism view of even this Scripture becomes more evident. "To *draw* all men" is entirely different from "to *save* all men." The Spirit of God can draw even where the heart of man remains in utter rebellion. The liberal use of quotations from Scripture by some of the universalism advocates does not mean that the proponent of the new universalism quotes his Bible as the word of an authoritative, infallible Scripture. The neo-universalist takes proof texts (often out of context and with highly questionable exegesis) and assumes an infallibility at variance with his usual Biblical modes of interpretation. This is done from a subjective position in which "I accept *this* from the Bible as being authoritative *to me* in *this* situation." In this the element of human reason and judgment versus divine revelation is most apparent.

On the other hand, evangelicals today stand in the historical stream of Christianity maintaining that God has given man a supernatural revelation in the Bible. Such revelation is unique and exclusive in its written form and in the person of Jesus Christ.

Where God speaks in an infinite variety of ways, but never decisively, man is thrown back on himself to determine how to reach ultimate truth. He seeks through his reason or intuition to find the answer. One senses the new universalist taking this position.[8] Equating divine love with human love, he patterns God after man. Hell there may be but it "will be adequate to cause the sinner to know that the strange country is not good for him and to come to himself enough to want to go back to his father and home."[9]

The presumptions of the neo-universalist, and particularly his usage of Biblical proof-texting, can only stand as the belief in the authority of Scripture is rendered ineffective. Thus we declare the neo-universalist has no right to lay hold of proof texts because he does not subscribe to the authority and infallibility of Scripture.[10]

In considering the essence of the new universalism, we may well question why such a theological development has occurred in the context of quotations of Scripture to buttress a viewpoint. One suspects that at the point doubt enters concerning the infallibility and authority of any area of the Bible, a propensity to move into further areas of human reasoning becomes apparent. For instance, the downward trend in statistical results of Christian evangelistic enterprises and an exploding world population with a resultant sense of hopelessness in the task may consciously or unconsciously have had a significant influence in the development of new universalism thinking. A leading evangelical theologian, Dr. Bernard Ramm, claims this to be true.

Dr. Ramm's analysis about the rise of neo-universalism undoubtedly is true of too many who at one time may have been orthodox in belief. And yet as we think of such, do we not stand amazed at the lack of comprehension of the Biblical statement, "Evil seducers shall wax worse and worse, deceiving many and being deceived," and the Biblical command, "Occupy till I come?" To be so discouraged that you cast away theological moorings is to be utterly lacking in eschatological comprehension. We see again the subjective rather than objective characteristic of such thinking. "I feel disturbed, therefore, I must change my stance"—rather than, "He that sitteth in the heavens shall laugh and shall declare a decree."

The challenge of the hour then is to recognize the validity of any and all evangelistic enterprises relevant to the hour and based on the authority of the Biblical message. The essence of that message we shall see in the third major point of this discussion.

II. *The Manifestation of Neo-Universalism.*

In the view of the *what* of the new universalism, we come to the *how* of its manifestation, especially as it applies to our consideration of its impact on missions and evangelism for, in a practical way, the concept has burst into the arena of missions, evangelism, and other church enterprises.

Here in this Congress we are using the term "mission" in a traditional vein. However, one suspects that the increasing use of the term in certain theological circles to some extent may be an outgrowth of the invasion of universalistic concepts into current programs. An example of this can be found in the statement, "From Missions to Mission."

To some this has become a pet type of cliché, more or less innocuous, just a new term, no more, no less. Or again, the word may be used as an attempt to emphasize the sense of total church involvement in witness to a total world. Here "mission" demands the elimination of the seeming dichotomy in the concepts of *foreign* and *home* missions or of *missions* on one hand and *service situations* on the other. One professor of missions puts it like this:

> The frontiers of the mission are no longer at geographical far ends of the earth, but are wherever there are men and groups unreconciled to God and fellow men in Jesus Christ. This does not lessen responsibility for points and peoples overseas, but it does mean the disappearance of a sharp distinction between mission and evangelism.[11]

If one properly understands the idea of reconciliation, there can be little quarrel with this statement. However, lest it seem to be a case of semantics to stress *mission* as lessening the impact of *missions,* and therefore much ado about nothing, we should look more sharply to see if another concept may not be back of the terms "mission," "church mission," "mission of the church."

The problem of word relativity is to be seen most sharply in theological terminology. Whereas formerly the simplicity of a fundamental versus liberal expression was one of sharp definition (e.g. Jesus, Christ, the redeeming Son of God over against Jesus the man, a great leader), now one must probe behind the term or title used, the word spoken, to ascertain what is really meant. When a preacher or scholar speaks of the incarnation fact or of the deity of Christ, just what does he mean? Is he speaking as does Nels Ferré of the Incarnation and mean by it the juncture of the Logos—the Christ—with the human Jesus at some given point within the life of Jesus?[12] Can he even state he believes in the Incarnation without the necessity of the virgin birth, even with the suggestion that Jesus could be the illegitimate son of a German mercenary?[13] One is convinced that within the demythologizing concept of a Bultmann, the use of myths by a Robinson, or the philosophical relativism of a Ferré, this too often is true.

We suggest, then, that the same process could well be true in the movement of the term "missions" to "church mission," or "mission of the church." We must repeat we certainly are understanding of any movement to combine home missions, foreign missions, relief and welfare work, and service ministries into one agency where this is functional and administrative and is effected with a theological motivation of worldwide concern to fulfill the Great Commission. However, questions are raised when an ecumenical leader declares:

> At the same time we are forced to contemplate the prospect of a giant and increasing jumble of programs and relationships if these two streams of "mission" and "interchurch-aid-and-service" continue to run in separate channels. In Europe there has been a tendency to conceive "mission" in a rather narrowly evangelistic sense. In organizational terms, therefore, the Division of Interchurch Aid, Refugees and World Service has a mandate covering virtually all the action programs of the word church except evangelism. On this continent, by contrast, the comprehensive understanding of mission has persisted and expanded.
>
> . . . Unless we are to confine mission to verbal evangelism—which means largely ineffectual evangelism—there is no way of maintaining a clear distinction between mission and services on either practical or theological grounds.[14]

We ask what is really meant here. Is this a movement pressing for the joining of the two areas of missions and service purely on a functional basis, a basis which we have suggested can make sense biblically, or is it an attempt to get away from the dichotomy felt between what is termed *a rather narrow evangelistic sense* and a *wider area of service?* What is implied in alleging that *verbal evangelism* means largely *ineffectual evangelism?*

If the joining of terms as stated refers only to a *method of mission,* a new theological direction is not necessarily taking place. But where the inference that "verbal evangelism" is ineffectual or "evangelistic effort" is narrow is drawn from a change in the *message of mission,* then the course is sharply set in a new direction. What happens then can be seen in at least six propositions we deduce from a presentation by Dr. Pieter de Jong entitled, "The Difference the Gospel Makes."

1. *Evangelism has cosmic implications.*
   "We can regain a sense of urgency only if we are clear about the difference the gospel makes in every area of life. Evangelism has cosmic implications."

2. *Man under God is the master of nature.*
"Where the good news of creation and redemption is proclaimed the world becomes w-o-r-l-d. Thus, it is no longer regarded as a divine reality which must be influenced by magic or religious practices. Instead, there is born a true secularity in which man under God is the master of nature."
3. *Man is called to become co-creator with God and to help Him in leading the world to its final goal.*
"The right interpretation of the doctrine of creation leads to the de-deification of the world and to the sanctification of man's active life. Through the good news, man is set free to make himself and his own world. Through the gospel man is called to become co-creator with God and to help Him in leading the world to its final goal."
4. *The gospel with its concern for one's neighbor becomes a penetration of this value into other cultures and religions.*
"Under the influence of the good news a human life is considered worth more than before. The gospel demands concern for one's neighbor; and we can almost speak of an 'osmosis', or penetration, of this value into other cultures and religions. This remains a fact even if Christians themselves have often disregarded this principle, both as individuals and as groups. . . ."
5. *The gospel is the impetus for a converging trend.*
"The United Nations would be inconceivable apart from the fact that there is in the human race a converging trend of which the gospel is the impetus and Pentecost the beginning."
6. *The Lord of the Church is the Lord of the world.*
"The Lord of the Church is the Lord of the world. Many people in their daily work serve God without knowing it, and the Church gathered in worship offers thanks to God on behalf of the world."[15]

In this light the case now made for the mission of the church is that it is the process of informing men that they are in fact redeemed by Christ and should start living accordingly. This precludes having to win them to Christ. As Dr. Bernard Ramm, one of the apologists opposing this viewpoint says when he summarizes the position, "The missionary does not bring Christ to India or Africa, for Christ is already there, being the universal Saviour of all men. The missionary comes to announce the universal lordship of Christ and summons men to acknowledge it in their lives."[16]

In the broadest sense the implication is stated by Robert Beach Cunningham:

> Sinners who know that they have been reconciled of God are seeking to tell other sinners, who do not know this, that they too have been reconciled of God.[17]

When it comes to the scriptural demands of the Gospel for salvation and the statement that few will be chosen out of the many who are called (Matthew 20:16), the interpretation of "mission" now affirms concerning this imperative,

> Our Lord is speaking about the movement of the Kingdom which He has come to inaugurate and the few who, at all times, will yield to its pressure and share in the tasks. . . . In this sense "salvation" is actually the experience of the few. But the question still remains concerning the final end of all.[18]

The movement of the concepts of the new universalism in the program of "church mission" now becomes clearer. It goes on to suggest that service becomes the act of reconciliation of the "church in mission." Sin is not *an individual act* which must be dealt with by the message of reconciliation in personal redemption but rather *the corporate deed* by which man is alienated from God. Corporate sin rends the fabric of the human and makes a fugitive. To reweave the torn fabric and have peace restored there must be a coming once more into a right relationship with God. But this coming will be on a corporate and not an individual level.

A further step in the whole process is the belief that all religions may be brought under the beneficent reconciliation of God through a sense of inter-religion harmony. It is but a step to the assertion of Dr. Niles, "But what of those who already have 'faith' to whom this declaration is made? Are there not those who have not consciously accepted God in Christ, but who nevertheless in some measure respond truly to God's action on them? Are there not those who, being outside the Christian faith, still do the truth? (John 3:21). The answer must be 'yes'."[19]

From this position it is but a step to a new universalism of all religions and faiths—a veritable universalistic syncretism of Christianity with other ethnic faiths.[20] A leading journalist has pictured it recently as follows:

> Emphasis in recent years has turned toward the many things which all religions have in common. Announcement was made in Geneva, Switzerland, in July that the Lutheran and Roman Catholic Churches of the world had agreed to make their "first official contacts" in several centuries. Two months earlier, the Roman Catholic Church began conferences with the Protestant, Anglican and Orthodox Churches "centered on unified actions and the ending of competition" This is not a new objective. Thirty-five years ago in India, Bhagavan Das, a noted Hindu scholar, traced similarities of Judeo-Christian doctrines and those of ancient Persia, Arabia and China, comparing the teachings of Moses, Jesus, Mohammed, Buddha, Confucius and earlier spiritual leaders. The concept of a supreme being was dominant in virtually all. He concluded: "If men are led to see that all religions are one and the same—*in essentials*—they will also become one in heart, and feel their common humanity in loving brotherhood."[21]

Here then this particular sense of the *mission* of the church comes to full universalistic syncretistic flower. To those who say, "But without the shedding of blood is no remission of sins," the benign reply can now be given, "True, but who of us can perceive how God in His infinitude will so apply the provision to all?" The issue of the new universalism is no longer "God hath spoken" but "Man hath reasoned."

I am convinced that inherently such a concept of *mission* is the path to a new universalism when followed to its logical conclusion. No wonder that in the light of all this the call to the harvest fields in so many quarters is but a glimmering light, that volunteers are dwindling away, that the sense of evangelism in the Great Commission is no longer one of urgency.

III. *The Church's Worldwide Mission and Neo-Universalism.*

To establish further the "mission of the church" today in the light of the onslaughts of neo-universalism, I suggest four things as necessary.

First, we must reaffirm and relevantly define our belief in the inspiration of Scripture. I have referred to this before.

Second, we must continue and broaden our exegetical study of Scripture relating to eternal punishment and the call to redemption and reconciliation. This Congress should be the starting point for Biblical scholars to give special attention to this area so as to produce up-to-date studies and literature presenting in depth the Biblical exegesis on eternal punishment, hell, the lake of fire and other similar concepts as well as the truths of grace, mercy, redemption, and reconciliation.

Third, we need a renewal in our *preaching* and our *teaching* of the testimony of the Bible that it is painfully clear from the Scriptures that bad news is fundamental to good news. We must, with renewed vigor, stress the awful reality of eternal loss through sin and unbelief for those who are found out of Christ at the cessation of this life.

Despite the grotesque terminology of several decades ago from which so many of us have understandably revolted we must learn to take the reality of hell seriously, for we cannot take seriously the universalist alternative to it.

Fourth, we must acknowledge again that the mission of the church is the proclamation of a harvest. The words of our Lord come incisively down two millenniums: "The harvest truly is great, but the labourers are few. Pray ye, therefore, the Lord of the harvest to send forth labourers into his harvest" (Luke 10:2).

Such a commission will speak not only of the "dimensions of the harvest," and of the "dilemma of the harvest," but also of the "demand of the harvest." The incisive imperative—*you pray!*—will come through with the ringing tones of a commanding Christ.

Let us see it positively. The mission of the Church involves a concern for the poor, the sick, the needy, the oppressed, and the problem of human relations. The mission of the church is to proclaim powerfully the fact of sin, divine wrath, judgment and hell, as well as the grace of God through Jesus Christ that saves men from eternal punishment to everlasting life. This is the grace of a Saviour who delivers men from this evil as well as from all evil.

Let the mission of the church be the proclamation of the dark side of the story so as to proclaim with power the gospel of deliverance.

FOOTNOTES

1. Dr. J. I. Packer has developed this thesis somewhat at length in his first lecture of the 1965 Peyton Lecture Series, Fuller Theological Seminary. As yet these lectures are unpublished, though it is expected they will be published some time in 1966.
2. Dr. Robinson wrote in favor of a new universalism in his article, "Universalism—Is It Heretical?" *Scottish Journal of Theology,* Vol. 2, No. 2 (June, 1949), pp. 139-155. Professor Torrance questioned the position in his article, "Universalism—or Election," *Scottish Journal of Theology,* Vol. 2, No. 3 (September, 1949), pp. 310-318.
3. See J. A. T. Robinson, *In The End, God . . .* and *Honest to God.* Also cf. the rebuttal by Dr. Robinson to Professor Torrance in the article, "Universalism—A Reply," *Scottish Journal of Theology,* Vol. 2, No. 4 (December, 1949).
4. E.g., Nels F. S. Ferré, *The Christian Understanding of God,* see specifically chapter 9, "The Work of God in the Last Things." Also cf. Ferré, *Atonement and Mission* (London: London Missionary Society, 1960).
5. Prior to 1949 the theological writings of Karl Barth indicate a universalistic trend. While Karl Barth denies that he is a universalist, the development of the triumph of grace in the *apokatastasis* point to a greater or lesser degree to the concept of the ultimate salvation of all. See G. C. Berkouwer, *The Triumph of Grace in the Theology of Karl Barth* (Grand Rapids: Wm. B. Eerdmans, 1956), Note particularly:
   Chapter IV—"The Triumph of Election," p. 89f.
   Chapter V—"The Triumph of Reconciliation," p. 123f.
   Chapter VI—"The Eschatological Triumph," p. 151f.
   Chapter X—"The Universality of Triumph," p. 262f.

   On the other hand, Emil Brunner opposed the direction of Karl Barth's thinking in this area. Yet as George Florovsky of the Harvard Divinity School points out, even in the theology of Emil Brunner there is the possibility of *universal salvation* even in the context of taking the possibility of Hell quite seriously. Florovsky states, "Brunner takes the possibility of Hell quite seriously. There is no security of 'universal salvation,' although this is, abstractly speaking, still possible—for the omnipotent God of Love. But Brunner still hopes that there is Hell already. Its existence does not depend upon divine decision. God never sends anyone to Hell. Hell is made by creatures themselves. It is human creation, outside, as it were, of "the order of creation.' "

   "The Last Judgment remains a mystery." George Florovsky, "The Last Things and the Last Events," *The Theology of Emil Brunner* (Charles W. Kegley, ed., New York: MacMillan, 1962), chapter 11,

p. 224, cf. 207-224. Also cf. Emil Brunner, *The Christian Doctrine of the Church, Faith, and the Consummation* (Philadelphia: The Westminster Press, 1962).

6. Cf. the statement on the book jacket concerning Dr. Niles' work which says, "Its arguments and judgments have been thoroughly examined in the Department of Missionary Studies of the World Council of Churches."
7. For the full treatment see D. T. Niles, *Upon the Earth* (New York: McGraw-Hill, 1962), pp. 92-98.
8. For a fuller elaboration of the discussion above see Louis L. King, "New Universalism: Its Exponents, Tenets, and Threats to Missions," *Evangelical Missions Quarterly,* Vol. 1, No. 4 (Summer, 1965), p. 3f.
9. Ferré, op. cit., p. 229. The context to the phrase bears out, the writer believes, the interpretation as given in the setting of the phrase here. See p. 228f.
10. Harry Buis, *The Doctrine of Eternal Punishment* (Philadelphia: Presbyterian and Reformed Publishing Company, 1957), p. 115. Mr. Buis discusses the scriptural implications involved.
11. R. Pierce Beaver, *From Missions to Mission* (New York: Association Press, 1964), p. 108.
12. For the development of this concept by Nels F. S. Ferré, see Ferré, *op. cit.*, chapter 7 and note particularly p. 190f.
13. *Ibid*, p. 191. Dr. Ferré says, "Reference to the Virgin Birth is not found in Paul's letters, the earliest writings we have. It is not found in Mark, the original Gospel. It is not found in the various epistles of the New Testament. It is not found in the Johannine tradition. Mary, we remember, was found pregnant before her engagement to mild Joseph. Nazareth was hard by a Roman garrison where the soldiers were German mercenaries. . . . Hence Jesus must have been the child of a German soldier! . . . If a manuscript would be found, however, proving this as far as a manuscript can, would this invalidate the incarnation of Christ in Jesus? By no means."
14. David M. Stowe, *A New Look At An Old Subject* (Pamphlet), pp. 3-5.
15. *Ibid.*, pp. 21-23.
16. Ramm, *op. cit.*, p. 23. This is an objective analysis by Dr. Ramm and does not in any way express his personal viewpoint and theological position.

    cf. D. T. Niles, *Upon the Earth* (New York: McGraw-Hill, 1962), p. 104: "I have found that for me the most effective safeguard against this obtrusion of the preacher is to keep always in the foreground of my thought the fact that all those to whom I am privileged to speak about my Lord are already one with me within His saving ministry. I believe Him and confess Him, they do not: and yet the essential facts of the Gospel remain true for them as for me.

    God made us.
    God loves us.
    Jesus died for us.
    Our trespasses are not counted.

    When we die we shall go to Him who will be our Judge. "These affirmations are true of all men and for all men whether they know them or not, like them or not, accept them or not. I am able to speak with men who do not yet bear the name of Christ, as those with whom I am one because the wall of partition between us has already been removed (Ephesians 2:14). Faith in Christ they have yet to find; but already they belong with me within the saving facts of the Gospel."

17. Robert Beach Cunningham, "Evangelism and the Challenge of the City," *Evangelism and Contemporary Issues* (Gordon P. Baker, ed., Nashville: Tidings Press), chapter 10, p. 87. This quotation is the position held by the author!
18. Niles, *op. cit.*, p. 94.
19. *Ibid.*, p. 238.
20. In addition to ethnic faiths being involved, even animism may be brought into the picture. An example of this is the declaration from the Consultation on the Evangelization of West Africa Today held in Yaounde, June 23 to 30, 1965:

    "We have felt particularly helped by studying the use of points of contact with the Gentiles found in Apostolic preaching. The start is made from nature and from natural religion, and the following four elements seem commonly to have had a place at the beginning of the Apostles' evangelism: reference to God the Creator, and to the vanity of idols; God's witness to Himself in nature; the universality of man's search for God; and to a kind of discounting of the past in fact of the all-important present offer of salvation. Throughout West Africa a common belief is found in a single, though distant, Supreme Being; our message should therefore be 'Him you worship as distant, we proclaim to you as near." The existence of a hierarchy of gods, ancestors and spirits should not unnecessarily be denied, but Jesus Christ must be so preached as to emphasize its liberating power; God has placed the whole world under the dominion of man, though this must be exercised to His glory. The concept of sacrifice should also be fully used, and reference made to the teaching of the Epistle to the Hebrews in order to explain the relation of African sacrifice to the one, eternal Sacrifice which truly saves. The problem of the fate of ancestors should be squarely faced, not in preaching so much as in replies to questions; Scripture passages like Acts 17:30; 14-16; Ephesians 4:8-10; I Peter 3:19-20 and 4:6 may be used to help Africans find comfort in the thought that their ancestors are in the merciful hands of a God who truly cares for them."
21. David A. Lawrence, A quotation taken from the *New York Herald Tribune*, "Unifying Force" *Readers Digest* (October, 1965).

CHAPTER 11

Mission—And Proselytism

by Dr. Jacques Blocher

consultants:
The Reverend Philip E. Armstrong, Dr. David Gotaas,
Dr. Harold B. Kuhn, The Reverend Lester Westlund

Many of the theologians would no doubt alter the title of this paper and make it to read: *Mission versus Proselytism.* Indeed in our day almost everyone seems ready with a quick condemnation of proselytism.

It is true that when Jesus used the word "proselyte"—and he employed it only once—he used it in a somewhat deprecatory way: "Woe unto you, scribes and pharisees, hyprocrites! for ye compass sea and land to make one proselyte and when he is made, you make him twofold more the child of hell than yourselves!" (Matthew 23:15).

Before going further, let us define the terms. We do not need here to analyze the terms mission and evangelization, but, let us investigate the word proselytism.

The Greek original of the word, *proselytos,* is not used by classical authors. It was evidently borrowed from colloquial speech by the translators of the Septuagint as an equivalent for the Hebrew *ger,* stranger. In this sense the word occurs 78 times as the translation of *ger* in the Septuagint. The Syriac Version frequently paraphrases the idea of proselyte in terms of "he who is converted unto me." The word occurs 4 times in the New Testament, but the term is seldom found in other early Christian literature.[1] The Greek source of the word is the verb *proserchomai,* "I approach," "I come near." In New Testament usage it always signified a Gentile who had been converted to Judaism.

The Jews were very active in their work of proselytizing, as the words of our Lord in Matthew 23:15 testify. Not only the Jewish historian Josephus bears witness to the widespread effect of this action of the Jews throughout the ancient world, but the Roman writers Seneca, Dio Cassius, Tacitus and others.[2]

As the word *proselyte* was almost exclusively used to describe a convert to Judaism, the early Christian church did not apply the word to its own converts to Christianity, they spoke of pagans becoming "disciples," "saints" or "Christians."

Later the word came to be used by the Christians and its meaning was enlarged. Today it has come to be applied in a secular sense to those who come to accept a form of religion or a philosophy or even a political party which they did not previously embrace. Thus we speak familiarly of proselytes to the theories of Kant or of Einstein. But, in general, the word primarily refers to converts to some religious creed. In France, for instance, the Protestants denominate as "proselytes" the Roman Catholics who become members of their churches.[3]

The terms proselytism and proselytization, derived from the word proselyte, commonly connote the practice of inducing people to leave their original religious affiliation to unite with a church or any other religious body of their own choosing.

The analysis of the meaning, both etymological and historical, of the word leads us to say that proselytism includes three major elements: an individual decision (a choosing of a church), a doctrinal persuasion (one church rather than another) and a modification of the social status (the fact of breaking a previous group affiliation to join a church).

We know that today this word more and more has a deprecatory meaning. Here is the statement made on proselytism in the provisional report submitted by the World Council to the member churches as published by the *Ecumenical Review* in October, 1956, and reprinted since:

"The term has taken an almost completely derogatory sense: probably no church and no missionary society involved in the Ecumenical Movement would wish to call itself a 'proselytizing body.' It does not seem possible, in practice, to restore the good connotation which the word 'proselyte' once carried. Thus 'proselytizing' has come to be set over against true obedience to the Great Commission."

Later, after having defined what it regards to be the true nature of Christian witness, this report adds:

"Proselytism is not something absolutely different from witness: it is the corruption of witness. When cajolery, bribery, undue pressure or intimidation is used—subtly or openly—to bring about seeming conversion; when we put the success of our church before the honor of God; when we commit the dishonesty of comparing the ideal of our own church with the actual achievement of another; when we seek to advance our own cause by bearing false witness against another church; when personal or corporate self-seeking replaces love for every individual soul with whom we are concerned; then witness has been deformed into proselytism. . . . since the difference between witness and proselytism is a matter of purpose, motive and spirit, as well as of means, objective criteria alone cannot distinguish adequately between the two."

Certainly we condemn the evil of forced conversion. In my own country, France, the Church of Rome has constantly sought, by all means to convert Protestants to Roman Catholicism. An ancestor of mine was for several years a galley-slave of the king Louis XIV, in the XVIIth century, because he refused to attend mass. Such forced conversions cannot openly be secured today, but I know of several cases in France, Italy and Spain, where economic and political pressure, intimidation and bribery have been used to force evangelicals into the papal fold.

Although history and experience show that this kind of religious pressure has been exercised largely by the Church of Rome and some of the churches which are members of the World Council of Churches,[4] we must frankly recognize that on our mission fields our evangelical missionaries have not always been above blame in this regard. Some of them have sometimes offered to converts, at least by suggestion or by implication, money or goods or social advantages in a manner very similar to bribery. Cases have been alleged of certain missions offering higher salaries than those being paid by other missions if national pastors would leave their mother churches and unite with the new church.

Naturally, we solemnly affirm that such practices are contrary to the Gospel of Jesus Christ and to the teaching of the apostles. It is the love of God which constraineth us and which must attract those to whom we preach.

When speaking of another church, we must remember our own shortcomings and always be fair. We must respect the church loyalty of those to whom we speak. We must be careful not to preach ourselves, or our church, but our Lord Jesus Christ and Him crucified, the risen and living Saviour.

But in condemning such practices, we do not accept the implication that this is or should be the true use of the word "proselytism." No one has the right to corrupt the meaning of a word which does not signify in its etymology a criminal action bringing about forced conversions.

Although we recognize that the New Testament writers did not apply the word "proselyte" to those who became disciples of Jesus Christ, we believe that the apostles were in the best sense of the word those who proselytized Romans, Greeks, and Jews to the Christian faith. In this light the New Testament very clearly indicates what true Christian proselytism can be. We know that we are undertaking a usage of the term upon which all may not agree and which requires clear definition. We do this in light of the allegations by ecumenical leadership or theologians that to attempt to win men to a knowledge of saving grace in Jesus Christ when such men are already members of any denomination or ecclesiastical body is proselytization. This we deny, and thus we study the word.

To approach the question analytically, let us note carefully three basic propositions which may serve to clarify the question. In the apostolic missionary methods let us note the three aims we found in the meaning of the word proselytism: (1) an individual decision; (2) a doctrinal persuasion; (3) a change of social situation.

1) When the apostles proclaimed the Gospel to all men, they did not expect, as a rule, a collective response. They called everyone to repent and believe in the name of the Lord Jesus

Christ. Every man and woman to whom the Gospel is preached is sorted from the mass and stands alone, as it were, before God, who says, in the words of Proverbs 23:26, "My son, give me thine heart."

God requires a personal answer, a definite decision upon the part of every individual to whom He speaks "Whosoever shall call upon the name of the Lord shall be saved" (Romans 10:14), "Whosoever," "every one," "thou"! These are the words used typically by the apostles everywhere in their preaching. These words have been used in true Christian evangelism from apostolic times until today. It is a call addressed to individuals and requiring a personal decision, even when many individuals give the same answer at the same time.

2) Salvation demands a personal decision of repentance and faith. Faith needs a foundation. "Faith comes by hearing, and hearing by the word of God" (Romans 10:17). In order to believe in Jesus Christ one must know some facts about Him. One must hear His Word and know His claims.

Everywhere in the New Testament we see the need for a basic doctrinal knowledge. A man has to be convinced of the truth of the Gospel before he can believe it. King Agrippa saw this when he said "Almost thou persuadest me to be a Christian" (Acts 26:28). To become a Christian one must be persuaded doctrinally, one must hear effectively the Word of Truth.

3) If one becomes a child of God, he is no more a child of the Devil. Salvation brings a radical change into his life. Even if Nicodemus did not understand or like it, Jesus insisted that "except a man be born again he cannot see the kingdom of God" (John 3:3). This new birth means a complete change of conduct. The new convert must leave his old way of life. Sometimes he must even forsake his family. "He that loveth father or mother more than me is not worthy of me" said Jesus (Matthew 10:37). The idol worshippers of Ephesus left their pagan temples and the Jews of Antioch or Corinth left their synagogues when they became Christians and followed the apostle Paul, as he formed groups of believers into congregations and local churches.

Throughout the New Testament one sees that these three basic elements of proselytism were present in the apostolic missions.

The early Church was, in fact, "a proselytizing body." There is then a proper and legitimate form of proselytization, which has been obscured by a wrong and often pejorative use of the term.

A question thus arises in our mind, if this be the case, how can we explain that this word 'proselytism' has taken an almost completely derogatory and pejorative connotation for so many Christians and for much of the Church? Why has its etymological and historical use been forgotten? Why has this word taken a different meaning altogether?

In my opinion, it is due in large measure to theological reasons, in reaction to the three points we have just emphasized. Too often church leaders may inveigh against proselytism as such, because they do not desire this type of apostolic evangelization. As we say in French, "When a man wants to get rid of his dog he declares it mad." They present a caricatured picture of proselytism and then war against this straw-man they have created. Consciously or unconsciously they refuse to admit as valid the apostolic methods of evangelism.

The so-called *liberal* approach to Christianity (whether in old or new garb) dislikes any radical and thorough form of Christian conversion, and thus uses the wrong sense of the term "proselytism" to implement its dislike of clear-cut conversion.

First, these theologians have an inveterate dislike for *individualism.* They deny the need of a personal decision for Christ, they think that one becomes a Christian by a process of slow evolution within the frame of the social community in which one is born, or as a result of some vague type of mass action.

This view is contrary to the Bible which clearly teaches that one becomes a Christian by regeneration, and not through natural birth. The Christian is a new creature, born of the Spirit, dead to sin and risen to a new life in Christ.

Secondly, they deny the need for *doctrinal persuasion.* They do not believe in the uniqueness and final absoluteness of the Truth. Truth, they say, is only confusedly seen by man, it is as bright, but as rare and short-lived as a flash of lightning. One can never be sure of it, even if it strikes him. It is contended that one is thus bound to admit that there is no final truth, fixed and capable of being personally apprehended. The best one can do is to search for it and perhaps to catch a glimpse of it.[5] So it is with my brother. Even if he does not hold the same part of the Truth as I hold, he may possess relatively as much of the Truth as I do. The result is a great laxity in doctrine, which becomes relative and uncertain. I have no right to persuade my neighbor of my truth: he has his own little chip of the unseen block of the unsearchable Truth.

This philosophy is contrary to the Word of God. We know that the truth of God is infinite, and that we will never be able totally to comprehend it; but God has revealed His truth to man. He has sent His Son into the world as the Way, the Truth and the Life. Our Lord is the Truth. God has spoken. His word is the Truth. The incarnate and the written Truth are one. We can reach a clear and saving knowledge of Truth in spite of our limitations because God has come to our level, and has expressed His thoughts in our own humble and limited words.

We confess our limitations, and even if we know that we are unable to understand God as He is, we are certain that the word He has spoken to us is objectively the Truth: we can rely on it, as the Bible rightly says "thy word is truth!" (John 17:17)

Thirdly, these theologians believe that a Christian *should not be different* from the persons belonging to the *social group* in which he lives. The Word of God teaches that conversion involves a separation from the world. The Gospel implies a call to break with the old life. The preaching of salvation will inevitably bring about radical changes in the lives of these concerned. Thus this objection made to proselytism that it makes for social and ecclesiastical division is in fact made against the very message of the Bible. God said to Abram, "Get thee out of thy country" (Genesis 12:1). All of us are called to leave "our old city" to start as a pilgrim. We are foreigners who have left our country, who are separated from our fellow-citizens, to come near the cross of Calvary. We are thus exactly *proselytes*, those who did approach Christ.[6] That was the main theme of the preaching of the apostles: "Ye are no more strangers, but fellowcitizens with the saints!" (Ephesians 2:19). A Christian is one who has left his old way of life.

Thus the so-called *liberals* dislike proselytism because they dislike any radical form of Christian conversion, but today the most violent attacks against proselytism come from those who believe that the only hope for the world is the *visible unity of the Church.*

In the eyes of most members of the Ecumenical Movement proselytism is a deadly sin against unity. Here is a statement of the Department of Study on Evangelism of the World Council of Churches as translated from the French text published in the acts of the Assembly of New Delhi: "During these last years, the churches have understood clearly . . . that there is no brotherly love, no true unity between local communities, as long as they have not ceased to 'make proselytes' among members belonging to other churches. More than once the World Council of Churches has drawn the attention of its members to the fact that ecumenism and proselytization are excluding each other."[7] Professor Karl Barth has written these words, ". . . In general, I do not like conversions, the passage from one church to another. First these converts manifest an unbearable zeal . . . and these conversions deny the invisible unity of the Church, which is a fact to deplore."[8]

The ecumenists say that we must be one, at all costs. It is held to be sinful to stress the differences between or among churches which will inevitably come together soon. To proselytize, you must steal souls belonging to others. It is a sin. Many so-called Christian churches, which claim almost the totality of the population of one country, as it is the case of the state churches of Europe and of Latin America, deem that they actually possess the souls of everyone who is born in the land.[9]

To proselytize, in the eyes of many ecumenists, is not only sinful, it is an absurdity. At this point we must remember what was said yesterday about Neo-Universalism. Anybody and everybody is held to be saved anyway! Let them keep their church affiliation since it does not matter of what church or denomination they are communicants. As an example, we would quote the leader of a French Protestant Monastery which has become known far outside our borders, the Community of Taize. Pastor Schultz, their Prior, has many times been to Rome to visit the Pope, and claims to be, in Western Europe, the spearhead of the Ecumenical Movement. He has recently written a book in which he states it is wrong for a Roman Catholic to leave his church. He argues thus: "Of course, at first, such a breaking away may seem beneficial, but it is exactly as a divorce: the wedding ties are broken, and sooner or later the result of such a sin will be detrimental." [10] A Catholic bishop said recently that Pastor Schultz had told him and other bishops that he had warned the Pope against the Evangelical Missions working in South America, because he thought that their proselytizing spirit was a real danger for the Church.[11] This seems to me a tragic example of the spirit of many Protestant leaders today, at least in Europe.[12]

Some ecumenists, through their pro-universalist spirit, go farther still. They believe that all men are saved, even if they are Muslims, Hindus, or atheists. All kind of proselytism is therefore absolutely useless. Thus *Newsweek* magazine reported on the Mexico Missionary Conference, sponsored by the World Council of Churches: "Old-styled churchmen held that the benighted pagans were fortunate to have missionaries. Now the right to proselytize is being challenged by some church leaders. . . . The Christian bears witness to his faith not by trying to convert the heathen to the true belief but by helping them in material ways." [13]

Another dangerous claim of some ecumenists is that almost all differences between churches are *adiaphora,* that is meaningless or without importance. They generally include doctrinal differences among them. We agree that many differences between denominations or missions can be considered as important but non-fundamental. These can be overlooked in interdenominational efforts, but they must often be preserved locally. But we strongly emphasize the fact that churches may become apostate even if they retain the name of a Christian Church.[14] In some of them the teaching of the Word of God has been adulterated to such an extent, that a born-again Christian can scarcely be expected to grow in grace and prosper and serve, if he does not break away and unite with a church in which God's Truth is effectively proclaimed.

The church of which the writer was pastor for many years in Paris has a majority of its membership composed of former Roman Catholics. For many of them it was very difficult to leave their old church, but they could not do otherwise. I am certain that there are some real Christians within the Roman Church, but their difficult struggle for survival is a proof that their position is to be regarded as exceptional. Our statement remains valid: the Roman Catholic system hinders the spiritual growth of a born-again Christian. And it is to be feared that Rome is not the only Church of which this is true.

A very well-known French Reformed minister, who has been director of the Macall Mission in France, has written a booklet with the title: *Ecumenism, a Danger for Evangelism.*[15] We know that from the apostolic time until today proper missionary evangelism will inevitably involve change of religious adherence, and this fact brings a negative reaction from liberal churchmen as well as from the ecumenical leaders.

These reactions lead such churchmen to hold a very restricted view of the *true nature of mission and evangelization.* They say that an evangelist is merely a witness, a herald. They insist upon the fact that the apostles did proclaim a message, the saving power of the Person and Work of Jesus Christ, unto whom they were witnesses, and would minimize other phases of their ministry. They remind us that the Gospel which we have embodies the essence of the message proclaimed by the early church, the *Kerygma.* This is true, but that is only the beginning of the apostolic evangelism. The early Christians also took care of the converts and led them to become a teaching and a serving community. They did not act as the cuckoo which is accused of laying its eggs in any nest without any care for the babies. It was not so with the Apostle Paul, who declared himself to be a loving father caring for his children in Christ.

A missionary or an evangelist is primarily a herald of Jesus Christ, a minister of the Word. His task is to preach the Cross in such a way that all men may be drawn to Christ and will commit their lives to Him, the risen Saviour. But the evangelist is also a servant of his fellow man, he must serve Jews and Gentiles alike. He must take care of his new-born Christian brother or sister and must bring them to a place in which they will grow and thrive.

This is the apostolic pattern of evangelism as it appears in the New Testament.

First stands the proclamation (*Kerygma*) to all men of the Person and Work of Jesus Christ, and the need for a clear decision and commitment, bringing a separation from the world, a passing from death unto life eternal "Save yourselves from this untoward generation" (Acts 2:40).

Second, as soon as possible, the new disciples must be led into a teaching and witnessing community. When men and women have become living stones, they become part of the order in which Christ is building His Church.

This is apostolic evangelism and a high order of proselytism, which are two inseparable elements of the same reality.

The history of the church teaches us that when this example is forgotten the church dies and deserves no more to be named a Christian church. For instance, when the Coptic Church in Egypt and in Abyssinia, surrounded by Muslims, were prepared to live without this spirit of proselytism, in order to win others to Jesus Christ they became for this very reason mummified bodies, a fossilized institution.

May we suggest that in analyzing the relation of such a proselytizing to evangelism, we discover that the former is a secondary and derivative aspect of the latter. Evangelism refers to the proclamation of Christ, the Redeemer, the Lord who gives himself to men. Proselytism refers to the *response of man,* who through repentance and faith accepts Jesus Christ as a personal Saviour and becomes a member of His body, the true Church.

Far from being "against true obedience to the Great Commission" as the provisional report of the World Council of Churches would have it, such proselytism is a necessary part of all true missionary enterprise. It is the inevitable consequence of the Great Commission: "Go ye therefore, and teach all nations, baptizing them in the name of the Father, and of the Son and of the Holy Ghost: teaching them to observe all things whatsoever I have commanded you: and lo, I am with you alway, even unto the end of the world."

Every Christian has the duty to proclaim the Gospel of Jesus Christ to every man and woman in the world in such a way that whosoever believes in the name of our Lord Jesus Christ has everlasting life. Whenever an individual has come to a new personal relationship with Jesus Christ through faith, his right and his duty is to choose freely a Christian group which will give him the best opportunity to grow in grace and bring his spiritual life to a full maturity. No pressure, be it psychological, financial, social or legal should be used against such an individual to keep him in or attract him to any particular church or movement. The preaching of the Gospel implies a full freedom of choice.

We need in our time to return to an apostolic pattern of evangelism in which a method of proselytism (properly understood and in the real etymological use of the term) is employed, particularly in missionary endeavor.

Thus after having seen the renewed meaning of the word proselytism we claim that every missionary and evangelist, yea, that every Christian has the right and the duty to so witness. Christians are under the authority of Jesus Christ and His Great Commission. Christian witness is to present Jesus Christ by the power and grace of the Holy Spirit and to demand a verdict. The purpose of witness is to persuade persons to accept the supreme authority of Christ and to commit themselves to Him. In this light any action taken against evangelistic proselytization may in fact be an attack against the very essence of evangelization. Indeed missionary work must include such seeking to convert.

On the other hand, to proselytize so as to bring about a conversion by the use of pressure is wrong scripturally and ethically whether it applies to economic pressure, political pressure, physical pressure, or undue emotional pressure.

May all our evangelical churches preach the Gospel of our Lord Jesus Christ to every creature under heaven in such a way that a great multitude of men and women, believing in His name, may come out of the world to find that place of worship where in the fellowship of true believers, they will hear the Word of God, grow in grace and serve their fellowmen to the glory of God, the Father, Son, and Holy Spirit.

FOOTNOTES

1. *New Schaff Herzog Encyclopedia* (Vol. IX), p. 280.

2. ***International Standard Bible Encyclopedia,*** **"Proselyte."**
3. *Liturgie de l'Eglise Reformee de France,* "Bapteme des Proselytes." *Revue Reformee* (No. 51 et 53), articles "Proselytes."
4. The Orthodox Church in Greece in its action against the small Protestant minorities in this country.
5. This is the teaching of many French Protestant philosophers, among whom we may mention Professor Gusdorf of Strasbourg University.
6. Hebrews 12:22. Proseleluthate . . . you have drawn near.
7. *Manuel de la Troisieme Assemblee de New Delhi,* p. 128. See also Monthly Letter on Evangelism published by WCC, No. 6-8, 1960.
8. *Revue Reformee* (Vol. XIV, p. 53; 1963/I), p. 30.
9. Rudolf Obermueller, *Evangelism in Latin America* (WCC, London, 1957), pp. 14-15: "These souls belong to me," said a priest in Ecuador to a young missionary of the Moravian Brethren. "These people are not pagans, they have all been baptized. You have no business here." Although Obermueller does not agree with the priest's viewpoint, he does not condemn it either.
10. Roger Schultz, *L'Unite, Esperance de Vie* (Taise, 1962), p. 80. The same opinion is held by the Vice-Prior, Max Thurian, in several books.
11. *Le Chretien Evangelique* (Paris, 1964, No. 530).
12. Frederic Hoffet, *La Demission des Protestants* (Paris, 1962), p. 152: ". . . The Protestant pastors used to welcome proselytes from Roman Catholicism among whom one did often find priests . . . This form of missionary work has become practically impossible through Ecumenism . . . A number of Protestants, and many ministers among them, under the impact of the ecumenical spirit receive with sore feelings people coming to them from the Roman Church . . ."
13. "The Missionary's Mission in the World Today," *Newsweek* (December 30, 1963), pp. 36-37.
14. Bishop Lesslie Newbigin said to the writer of this paper at Geneva in 1963 in a private conversation, that no church could really become apostate, in his opinion.
15. Emmanuel Chastand, *Oecumenism, danger pour l'evangelisation,* (Anduze, 1962), *Revue Reformee, Articles on Proselytism,* Vol. XIII (1962/1963), p. 51, Vol. XIV (1963/I), p. 53.

CHAPTER 12

Mission—And Neo—Romanism

by Dr. Vernon Grounds

consultants:
The Reverend Stuart P. Garver
The Reverend Francis J. Keida
The Reverend Ruben Lores

I.

Our 20th century world is writhing in the throes of revolution. Very perceptively Abbé Francois Houtart has underscored and highlighted today's situation in his book, *The Challenge to Change: The Church Confronts the Future.* He points out that we are now facing a "planetarization" of our globe. "The world," he says, "is becoming a unity from the technological point of view, from the point of view of scientific discoveries, of geographical distance, of communications, and especially of telecommunications, which is only beginning."[1] He also points out that "not only are we now living in a state of transition, in the process of changing from a pre-technical to a technical society, in the passage from one type of civilization to another, but *we are reaching the point of living in a rapidly and perpetually changing society,* and most probably this will continue until the end of the world."[2] Living, consequently, "in a state of perpetual mutation we are faced with all kinds of new problems,"[3] problems of staggering complexity and overwhelming magnitude.

Indeed, as Roman Catholic missiologist Ronan Hoffman asserts, these problems are "so complex that they can only be referred to as 'human problems.' Such are world poverty, hunger, population growth, world peace and disarmament." These problems, he insists, are not merely Christian problems or missionary problems; no, they are problems which affect all mankind. And what is "the practical implication" of this?

> Catholic missionaries must collaborate not only with each other, but with other groups within and without the Church, including Protestant missionaries, national governments and international organizations. Our thinking and planning must take them into account, since it would be senseless to take unilateral action without knowledge of the plans and activities of these other groups.[4]

Adding to the complexity of our situation as viewed from a Christian perspective is the surprising resurgence of non-Christian faiths. In the words of Norman A. Horner:

> Among the world religions, Hinduism, Buddhism and Islam are showing signs of new life. This is partly in consequence of political revolution, because nationalism often seeks traditional religious bulwarks for its own purposes. Thus it is safe to assume that not all of the new vitality is authentically spiritual. Nevertheless the fact remains that strengthened religious opposition now confronts both Catholic and Protestant expansion. This situation is in marked contrast to a century ago when to a large extent the religions of the Orient and Middle East were degenerate if not moribund.[5]

In a revolutionary world, where Protestants no less than Catholics are dismally failing to meet the challenge which confronts all of Christendom, we must forget our traditional animosity, so Horner asserts, and join hands in an effort to solve the human problems of our era. In a revolutionary world, Horner likewise asserts, "Catholic-Protestant differences seem less impressive than they once did. No branch of Christendom can any longer afford the luxury of isolation."[6] Catholics and Protestants, abandoning their "senseless" and "damaging" antagonism,[7] must take more than a "marginal interest" in the world around us.

II.

The Roman Catholic Church has changed, incontestably so, since Pope John XXIII began his *aggiornamento*. The Second Vatican Council, which ended four years of grueling work on December 8, 1965, served as a catalyst for reform and ferment to an extraordinary degree. We shall not here discuss the sixteen major documents which it produced. Instead of doing that suppose we notice some appraisals of the Council which come from qualified observers and interpreters.

With a touch of humor Thurston N. Davis, editor-in-chief of *America,* describes the turmoil produced, paradoxically, by one of the mildest pontiffs in history, John XXIII.

> Some Catholics, knocked slightly ajar by the *aggiornamento,* are trying to puzzle out where all this is going to end. How many other familiar things, besides the altars in their churches, are due to be turned around? When Pope John opened the windows to let in the fresh air that was to ventilate the Church, they asked, did he realize how much of the furniture might start blowing around the room? . . . All of a sudden, we are experiencing not one or two changes, but a whole battalion of them. There is a reform of the liturgy, and we hear talk of a reform of canon law. We have a crisis of obedience and of authority, seminary training is being pulled apart and put together again. There is a great wave of ecumenical activity, an important decree on religious liberty to be assimilated, much discussion about the meaning of collegiality, and an emerged and newly vocal laity. What in the world has happened to the old, unchanging church of yesterday? [8]

A sympathetic Protestant, Robert McAfee Brown, while recognizing that the conciliar achievements were not all one might have wished for, insists that they were nevertheless tremendously creative.

> • It counts for a great deal that hundreds of bishops go back to their dioceses with new ideas, new courage, new liberation, and with a wide range of new freedom to do things that do not have to be cleared in advance with Rome.
>
> • It counts for a great deal that ecumenical encounter is moving with unprecedented speed and that possibilities of ecumenical relationships increase in almost geometric proportion.
>
> • It counts for a great deal that a whole generation of bishops has met with, listened to, and learned from the

periti of the Council—men like Küng, Congar, Schillebeeckx, Danielou, Phillips, de Lubac, Diekmann, Häring, Murray—and that they will never be the same again.

- It counts for a great deal that hundreds more have seen, and measured, the type of tactics often employed by Curia officials, and are thereby forewarned for the future.
- It counts for a great deal that the principle of collegiality is established (even though the outworking may take a long time). . . .
- It counts for a great deal that bishops can now vigorously and even violently disagree. . . .
- It counts for a great deal that a new spirit of discussion and responsible criticism has entered into the contemporary Catholic Church as a result of the Council.[9]

At the same time, though, the Council has spawned a swarm of problems for Rome. So Albert V. Fedders, Rector of Maryknoll Seminary, can almost casually remark, "The Church itself is questioning the most sacred things and there are great changes of policy going on throughout the world within the Church."[10] Yes, with some justification the traditionalists are flinging at the progressives within their church such charges as relativism, secularism, liberalism, modernism, ecumenism, rationalism, and utopianism! In reply, the progressives are accusing the traditionalists of isolationism, medievalism, clericalism, triumphalism, and obscurantism! The Catholic Church is therefore in a seething state of crisis. Accordingly, G. C. Berkouwer speaks frankly of "the common concern that Protestants and Catholics exercise together for the very real problems of theology today."[11] Protestants, no less than Catholics, he reminds us, are haunted by critical and scientific problems and especially by semantic problems.

Granted that Rome has placed itself in the midst of a drove of problems "by permitting" the new methods of Biblical research. Granted, moreover, that in so doing Rome "has reached a point of no return." Granted, yet again, that "The kerygmatic approach to the Bible is, in the view of its critics, irreconcilable with the historical truth of the Scripture." Granted all this. Common honesty forces Protestants to confess that these are "very real problems" and that they also concern "Reformation theology in a very urgently real way."[12]

No wonder, then, that Boelo Boelens, a thoroughgoing evangelical, is constrained to inquire as he addresses his own religious community, the Christian Reformed Church:

> Is a contemporary expression of the Gospel message simply not possible? Does the Bible forbid us ever to deviate from *its* language on penalty of losing its message. This, is seems to me, is the crucial question to which we must increasingly address ourselves—fearlessly, and without hidden prejudices, for an honest proclamation of the Gospel is at stake, and the salvation of the world (I Peter 2:9). And as we face this crucial question, we should not deny that in the proclamation of the Gospel to an unbelieving world Protestants and Roman Catholics need each other badly.[13]

III.

How does all of this impinge on the missionary task? Does it mean that the day of Christian expansion is over and that in the future little can be hoped for except perhaps the maintenance of the *status quo*? Cyrus L. Sulzberger, columnist for the *New York Times*, wrote a dispatch from Uganda in 1964 under the headline, "As the Missionaries' Era Ends." He said:

> Historically speaking, the age of the missionary is drawing to a close. That is why so many brave, self-sacrificing Christian churchmen are experiencing troubles in Africa and Asia. In the collective mind of new Afro-Asian nations, the white missionary is associated with white colonialism.

And Sulzberger quotes Milton Obote, Uganda Prime Minister, as stating, "We don't even like the word 'missionary.' We would avoid difficulty by having more African clergymen; after all, churches are international. White missionaries have done good work, but their era is finished." [14]

Is Sulzberger's pessimistic verdict correct? Or does Richard Cardinal Cushing see the situation much more clearly?

> There is, it would seem a tide in the affairs of God, as of man, a season when though the elements rage, all is Spring. The season is here, I do believe. For—as if the gains of the last century were not enough—the Church has now been

given a bright new vision of her mission, one that will inspire the faithful to new heights of participation, the missionaries to new heights of achievements, perhaps even, make the next half century the greatest Age of the Missions.[15]

Who is right, the pessimist or the optimist? But if the missionary cause is to prosper, a number of things must be done.

(1)

First, a profound reappraisal is essential. Ronan Hoffman, for instance emphasizes this. Nothing will suffice save a radical rethinking of the nature of the Church's mission. It is necessary for the Church "to look to the present, the new conditions, and new forms of life introduced into the modern world." [16] Edward L. Murphy, for another, emphasizes this need: We must engage in the reassessment of our works. Reassessment must proceed from a solid knowledge of the mystery and function of the Church and a clear understanding of both world movements and religion societies.[17]

(2)

Secondly, an adequate missiology must be developed, a missiology which properly interprets the nature of the Church's planetary task. And what is missiology? This is the definition which Hoffman proposes: "Missiology is the scientific specialization which studies the work of the establishment of the Church in its doctrinal principles, in its practical norms, and in its historical development both past and present. As such, it pertains to theology and has the following branches: scriptural, dogmatic, patristic, pastoral, mission law, mission history, and missiography." [18] "Nothing will offer greater hope for mission success than the development of the theology of the missions. . . . It is necessary to stress the priority of theology if error is to be avoided. . . . If one neglects the normative character of theology, there is danger of being submerged in these other fields."[19]

(3)

In the third place, certain controversies may be resolved, especially the far-reaching debate among Roman Catholics concerning the very character of "missionary activity." Eugene Hillman in *The Church As Mission* says a new theory has been gain-ing ascendency in his church. It is a theory which virtually equates pastoral care with missionary activity.[20] It seeks to obliterate any distinction between home and foreign missions.[21] It maintains that "to stem the ominous trends toward sectarianism and communism" in a nominal Christian country is as much a valid piece of missionary activity as establishing the Church in a non-evangelical culture. But this new concept, Hillman holds, is mistaken. "The traditional concept needs to be radically reconsidered in the light of modern world problems. But in seeking to renew the missionary spirit, we cannot afford to ignore all that this has meant to the Church up to now." [22]

For a second thing, the new theory of mission ignores the Biblical teaching that now "The Church has an eschatological work to do in the world. . . . The Church is Christ sacramentally bringing salvation to visibly and corporately signified realization among the distinctive ethnic-culture units of people who make up mankind." [23] The new theory, accordingly, confuses the two functions of the Church. The first "consists in the activity of raising up the sign of salvation among a people who have not yet believed." This, obviously, is prior in both the order of time and the order of urgency. The second consists in the activity of maintaining the clarity of this sign once it has been raised up among a people, so that it will be something meaningful and salutary for all who live in the nation." [24]

For a third thing, this new theory is spiritually baneful. In Hoffman's words, it results "in a certain loss of interest in the foreign mission apostolate," [25] but that is by no means the worst effect. For whenever "the Church is exclusively absorbed in the care of herself—whether in a mission area, a parish, a diocese, a region, a nation, or a religious community—there she signifies nothing but her own death." [26] In short, the Church's vitality depends on the strength of "her missionary commitment to the remaining non-evangelical peoples of the world." [27]

(4)

In the next place, a proper missiology will tend to correct any excess or deficiency in social emphasis. On the one hand, there is the danger of an overemphasis. Edward L. Murphy therefore inquires: "Can we lose ourselves in improving economic and cultural conditions of the peoples to the detriment of our direct apologetic? We are here in an area not of doctrine, but of strategy."[28] Rare wisdom is required to sail between the Scylla of over-emphasis and the Charbydis of underemphasis.

(5)

In the fifth place, the role of the laity must be thought through theologically and pragmatically. Abbé Houtart suggests that only by utilizing laymen can his Church break through the bottleneck created by a shortage of priests especially in rural areas.

> At present a layman can baptize or witness a marriage while awaiting the arrival of a priest. This authority is subject to certain dispositions according to the different localities in Latin America. However, where the community is judged to be sufficiently prepared, why not give laymen the authority to distribute Holy Communion? This has already been authorized in certain exceptional cases when the great majority of the population does not have access to the sacrament of the Eucharist.[29]

Can the laity participate even to the degree which Houtart suggests and the Church still retain its traditional concept of the priesthood? This is one of the problems which Roman Catholic missiology must solve.

(6)

In the sixth place, what about an ecumenical approach to the non-Christian religions? Are pagans wholly destitute of saving knowledge and grace? Murphy thinks that old missionary motives and attitudes "neglected a very important dogma, the universal Providence of God over His human creation . . . God has been active throughout history before the missionary arrived."[30]

So eminent a Roman Catholic theologian as Karl Rahner contends that redemptive grace may—undoubtedly does—reach people who have never heard the Gospel. Adhering to the position taken by Rahner, Hillman asserts this about God: "In His own ways of saving faith He reveals Himself as an option offered to every man who comes into the world, and with due respect to the particular time and historical context in which each man is providentially placed."[31] This means, as Rahner puts it, "That there are many who are Christians without explicitly knowing it, that grace is more widely accepted than is recorded in the Church's statistics."[32] It means likewise that a man can be saved "though he may have no historically explicit knowledge of Christ."[33] In short, we may legitimately anticipate "salvation for—the words are those of Jean Danielou—'that immense body of pagan humanity' (the vast majority of redeemed mankind), living both before and after Christ."[34]

Last of all, if the Church is to become truly catholic, raising a witness in every land, a new breed of missioners is called for. Tomorrow's missioner must not be like today's missioner. Why not? Today's missioner has been too much like yesterday's missioner—"a man of Trent!" Tomorrow's missioner must follow the apostolic model so ably delineated by Joseph A. Grassi in his book *A World to Win: The Missionary Methods of Paul the Apostle.* If he is like Paul, he will be a man of flexibility,[35] who knows how to function as a team member,[36] a man who will know how to accommodate himself to every situation,[37] a man whose objective will be that of developing a church marked by self-government, self-support and self-extension.[38]

IV

Our specific concern, however, is the relationship between Protestant missions and their Catholic counterpart. How, then, does the post-conciliar Church of Rome view evangelicals who are striving to obey the Great Commission? And what is likely to develop in the future as that changing Church in a changing world encounters Christians who do not acknowledge its claims or embrace its dogmas?

One thing seems sure. Ecumenism is here to stay, not only Protestant-Orthodox ecumenism but likewise Protestant-Catholic ecumenism; and this will have repercussions that ultimately are going to be felt on even the remotest overseas station. Revolutionary indeed was the decree on ecumenism adopted by the Second Vatican Council. This declaration, Eugene C. Bianchi writes, opens many doors and leaves others unlocked and ready for exploration by future generations. . . . The decree opposes triumphalism at every turn . . . Nor does the decree merely salute

Protestants as *bona fide* members of the Christian family. It likewise declares that their churches, though defective and deformed, are vehicles of redemption. . . . And, in addition, the decree states that Protestant worship, even its degenerate equivalent of the Mass, has value—if not validity! "When they commemorate His death and resurrection in the Lord's Supper, they profess that it signifies life and communion with Christ and look forward to His coming in glory."[39]

Typically, therefore, the Reverend George Mejia of Buenos Aires, is hopeful concerning the future relationship of Protestants and Catholics on his continent.

One can say that the Latin American public is better disposed to our separated brethren after the Council. It is better prepared to understand ecumenical action and to work for unity.[40]

Ecumenicity implies a transformed attitude toward Protestants; and such a transformation requires a new approach to them. With irenic magnanimity Cardinal Bea, addressing his coreligionists, pleads that they labor to mitigate the bitterness of "historical memories," overcome "positive aversion," and steadily neutralize the corrosive acids of—these are his own terms—ignorance, prejudice, misunderstanding, calumny, distrust, and hatred. This, however, cannot be done, he insists, unless Roman Catholics exhibit—these, too, are his own terms—compassion, humility, frankness, courtesy, respect, and love. Truth cannot be compromised, needless to say, but fullest loyalty to truth is entirely compatible with a non-judgmental spirit. After all, on the Cross, the common Lord of both Catholics and Protestants pleaded, "Father, forgive them; they know not what they do."

St. Augustine put it in a nutshell: "We must hate error but love those who err." So nothing forbids us to practice in their regard *the sublime and profound teaching of the New Testament on mutual respect.*[41]

Fullest loyalty to the positive truth, Bea keeps on insisting, is entirely compatible with genuine love, a genuine love which inspires penitence and prayer, sanctity and sacrifice.

Each of us who meets non-Catholics in his everyday life can do much to prepare them mentally for union by a wholehearted attitude of *charity*. . . . An effort of this kind would

> be a practical way of showing our separated brethren that, though the Catholic Church carefully guards the integrity of the dogma and faith of her own children, she is a loving mother for them also, and now anxiously wonders whether this terrible quarrel of the past may be made up today, through greater sanctity, prayer and sacrifice.[42]

Such, then, is the new attitude toward Protestantism which prevails more and more among informed Roman Catholics. What its ultimate results will be who can foretell. Vittorio Subilia, the distinguished professor of the Waldensian Seminary in Rome, speculates about the course of future events:

> By a slow and seemingly imperceptible change of levels on both sides, there could creep in a spirit of humble quest in place of prejudice—in the theological sphere it is largely already there; in place of scorn, the desire for colloquy; in place of patterns already fixed, an interest in something that suddenly is realized to be an unknown quantity. . . . It is now admitted that there may be, imperfectly and incompletely, Christians outside Catholicism, not "despite" their own confession, but "precisely by means and virtue of" their own confession.[43]

Another salutary transformation is Rome's new stance with respect to Scripture. Hermann Sasse says:

> In the beginning of this century . . . the Church . . . established the Pontifical Biblical Institute in which the best scholars tried in many years of hard work to find a solution to the problems of Biblical research. After two generations the fruits of these endeavors were ripe. While the Protestant churches are disintegrating under the effects of a Biblical scholarship which was separated from the life and the faith of a living church, Rome is becoming more and more the church with the Bible. The Roman Church can never give up the dogma defined at the First Vatican Council (which is actually the doctrine of the entire Church of all ages), that the Bible is the divinely inspired Word of God and as such given to, not made by, the Church.[44]

Not only has Rome rediscovered the Bible: in many places it is assiduously distributing the Bible and encouraging its study.

Consider just one instance, that of Latin America. Vergil Gerber, a missionary who has an insider's knowledge of the situation, and who is no stranger to this Congress, asserted last year in a public lecture at my own seminary:

> Today not only is the layman permitted to read the Scriptures, but there is a vigorous movement in all of Latin America to promote the sale and use of the Bible. . . . Today bookstores in Mexico City realize some of their greatest profits from the sale of Roman Catholic Bibles. In San Jose, Costa Rica, posters urge, "Catholic: Read your Bible." . . . the most thrilling result of these new versions of the Scripture is the fact that the Word itself is finally getting through to the masses. . . . Millions of Catholics are now reading this sacred Book in the privacy of their own homes—millions, who never before have had any direct contact with God's Word, both humble and erudite.[45]

At this juncture, however, let us turn on a red light. Some roadblocks loom ahead, and they seem to be immovable. While Rome has changed and is changing, it has not modified nor will it modify essential dogmas. Take an authoritative spokesman like Augustin Cardinal Bea who stands at the forefront of Catholic ecumenicity, an erudite, irenic, persuasive apostle of unity. Himself a devoted ecumenist, the Cardinal has pulled no punches and offered no concessions with respect to the crucial issues of theology. Instead he has repeatedly—courteously, to be sure, yet with the flattest kind of finality—affirmed that in this area there can be and will be no change. Thus at Harvard University in 1961 he uncompromisingly stated:

> First and foremost the fundamental teaching of the Catholic Church will not be changed. Compromise on points of faith which have already been defined is impossible.[46]

Bea also has lucidly differentiated between the doctrines of his Church and its practices: forms and rites may be changed, but dogmas are infallible truth and consequently beyond amendment. In *The Unity of Christians,* he brings out this vital distinction:

> Practice concerns discipline, Canon Law, liturgical rules, forms of piety, traditions. In this sphere, as we know, the Church teaches that her Founder has left her a much wider

margin and far greater freedom. . . . On the doctrinal level it is quite different. . . . In this sphere, then, there is no room for concessions. The reason for this is very simple. The Church is not the mistress of the doctrine received from Christ. She has received it as a deposit and she is bound to teach it and hand it on intact.[47]

In other words, the practices of Roman Catholicism possess a reformable fluidity. Circumstantially they have been frozen into various shapes which are fixed and firm; but they can be thawed out and refrozen in a surprisingly different mold. Doctrine, however, is akin to petrified wood: once it was a living thing, but now it is as hard as granite, incapable of being changed without being destroyed.

Suppose we revert now to some other directives which Prudencio Damboriena gives to his fellow missioners as they "in the midst of an ecumenical movement" strive to achieve a new orientation toward Protestants. His first directive, it will be recalled, was that doctrinal compromise of any kind be avoided. He then offers this fourfold counsel:

Second, steps should be taken not to cause scandal to our young Christians or give them the impression that "more or less we believe the same thing." This is a much greater danger in the missions than some of our European theologians might think.

Third, nothing should be done by priests or the faithful against the laws of Christian dignity in regard to our separated brethren. I do not mean physical harm, but even in our written or spoken remarks, our criticism should be objective and fair. Ridicule leads nowhere and this applies to Pentecostals and Jehovah's Witnesses. . . .

Fourth, so far as doctrinal contacts are concerned, the general rules laid down by the instruction of 1949 apply also to our mission lands. Responsibility here falls primarily on the bishops, both in the care of lay Catholics and priests. The selection of speakers has to be made in a careful way. . . .

Cardinal Suenens, in one of the sermons at the Vatican Council II, has insisted that it is extremely important that this ecumenical and irenical spirit, which we must foster in our mission lands, does not become an impediment to the spread of our faith.[48]

Damboriena's guarded language must not deceive us. He speaks about "efforts to attract our separated brethren to the church." In plainer language, he is alluding to proselytizing. And we must bear in mind that, for all its sincere ecumenicity, Rome has not renounced the right and responsibility of proselytizing—any more than we have!

Recognizing that a conscientious Protestant is truly a Christian, C. F. Pauwels avers: "The Catholic work of making converts, even when directed to members of the Christian churches, can never by Catholic standards be called in itself proselytism."[49] Perhaps not. But if Rome is indeed the one true Church of God, then it ought never abandon its "will to proselytize." And the same is true with any convinced Protestantism, *mutatis mutandis*.

What, then, must we do as we grapple with the problems and utilize the opportunities created by what Berkouwer calls "the new Catholicism"? Without compromising our own convictions in the slightest, we can engage in much more open and extensive dialogue, seeking to share that understanding of the Gospel which the Holy Spirit has given us.

But that is by no means all that we can and must do. As Evangelicals, entrusted with a global mandate, we can and must collaborate with one another across organizational lines to solve persistent and emerging problems.

We can and we must urge our seminaries and societies to devote sustained attention to the preparation of missionaries. Here we ought to learn from the emphasis of the new Catholicism on the training and formation of its future missioners.

We can and must keep abreast, if only through magazines, of the enormous literature which the new Catholicism is proliferating, much of it biblical and much of it geared to the interests of contemporary man. Not only that, but we can and we must strive to produce a comparable and, as God enables us, an even superior literature. As Ruben Lores of Latin America Mission inquired in a personal communication, "Is it not time for a great coordinated step forward in the printing and distribution of literature?" And this literature cannot be a rehash of tired polemics: something fresh, relevant, and above all Biblically oriented is required.

We can and we must discuss a strategy for our planetary campaign comparable to Rome's master-plan for missions, a master-plan which includes objectives, personnel and finances. Merely to pass resolutions will not do: we must formulate and implement a unified program.

Finally, with less and less inhibition we ought to acknowledge in practice a truth to which we subscribe theoretically: the Holy Spirit moves with unpredictable sovereignty and freedom where and how He chooses. If He is choosing to move within Roman Catholicism, let us be eager to detect His gracious operation, and, whenever we detect it, let us sincerely rejoice.

FOOTNOTES

1. Francois Houtart, *The Challenge to Change* (New York: Sheed and Ward, 1964), p. 8.
2. *Ibid.*, p. 94.
3. *Ibid.*, p. 206.
4. Ronon Hoffman, "Problems in Mission Work Today," *Reappraisal: Prelude to Change*, (William J. Richardson, ed., Maryknoll, New York: Maryknoll Publications, 1964), pp. 30, 31.
5. Norman A. Horner, *Cross & Crucifix in Mission* (New York: Abingdon Press, 1965), p. 125.
6. Horner, *op. cit.*, p. 126.
7. *Ibid.*, p. 223.
8. *America* (March 20, 1965), p. 377.
9. Robert McAfee Brown, Letter to the Editor, *Ramparts* (December, 1965), p. 14, 16.
10. Albert V. Fedders, "The Maryknoll Major Seminary," *The Modern Mission Apostolate* (William J. Richardson, ed., Maryknoll, New York: Maryknoll Publications, 1965), p. 48.
11. G. C. Berkouwer, *The Second Vatican Council and the New Catholicism* (Grand Rapids: William B. Eerdmans, 1965), p. 73.
12. *Ibid.*, pp. 77-143.
13. Boelo Boelens, "The Changing Climate in Roman Catholicism," *The Reformed Journal*, Part II (November, 1965), p. 20.
14. Quoted by Albert J. Nevins, "The Reappraisal of the Mission Vocation," *Reappraisal: Prelude to Change* (William J. Richardson, ed., Maryknoll, New York: Maryknoll Publications, 1964), p. 13.
15. Quoted in J. Gerard Grondin, "Toward a Complete Mission Program," *The Modern Mission Apostolate* (William J. Richardson, ed., Maryknoll, New York: Maryknoll Publications, 1965), pp. 34, 35.
16. Ronan Hoffman, "The Council and the Missions," *Vatican II: The Theological Dimension* (Anthony D. Lee, ed., Washington, D. C.: The Thomist Press, 1963), p. 544.
17. Edward L. Murphy, "A Reappraisal of Mission Theology," *Reappraisal: Prelude to Change* (William J. Richardson, ed., Maryknoll, New York: Maryknoll Publications, 1964), pp. 66, 67, 79.
18. Hoffman, *op. cit.*, p. 550, n. 19.
19. *Ibid.*, pp. 540, 541.

20. Eugene Hillman, *The Church as Mission* (New York: Herder and Herder, 1965), p. 40.
21. *Ibid.*, p. 27.
22. *Ibid.*, p. 37.
23. *Ibid.*, pp. 37, 38.
24. *Ibid.*, p. 39.
25. Quoted in *ibid.*, p. 30.
26. *Ibid.*, p. 65.
27. *Loc. cit.*
28. Murphy, *op. cit.*, p. 62.
29. Houtart, *op. cit.*, pp. 150-152.
30. Murphy, *op. cit.*, p. 62.
31. Hillman, *op. cit.*, p. 75.
32. Quoted in *ibid.*, p. 84.
33. *Ibid.*, p. 87.
34. *Ibid.*, p. 96.
35. Joseph A. Grassi, *A World to Win: The Missionary Methods of Paul the Apostle* (Maryknoll, New York: Maryknoll Publications, 1965), p. 119.
36. *Ibid.*, pp. 81-83.
37. *Ibid.*, pp. 93-95.
38. *Ibid.*, pp. 135-153.
39. Eugene C. Bianchi, *et al.*, "Three Giant Steps," *America* (December 12, 1965), p. 776.
40. George Mejia, "The Ecumenical Situation in Latin America," *Documentazione Olandese Del Concilio* (No. 129), p. 4.
41. Augustin Cardinal Bea, *The Unity of Christians* (New York: Herder and Herder, 1963), p. 57.
42. *Ibid.*, p. 149.
43. Vittorio Subilia, *The Problem of Catholicism* (London: SCM Press Ltd., 1946), pp. 77, 78.
44. Hermann Sasse, "How Has Rome Changed?" *HIS*, December 1965, pp. 30, 31.
45. Augustin Cardinal Bea, "The Second Vatican Council and Non-Catholic Christians," *Ecumenical Dialogue at Harvard: The Roman-Protestant Colloquim* (Samuel H. Miller and G. Ernst Wright, eds., Cambridge, Massachusetts: Harvard University Press, 1964), pp. 63, 64.
46. Bea, *The Unity of Christians*, pp. 200, 201.
47. Prudencio Damboriena, "Protestant Missions Overseas," *The Modern Mission Apostolate* (William J. Richardson, ed., Maryknoll, New York: Maryknoll Publications, 1965), pp. 182, 183.
48. C. F. Pauwels, "Ecumenical Theology and Conversation," *Vatican II: The Theological Dimension* (Anthony D. Lee, ed., Washington, D. C.: The Thomist Press, 1963), p. 592.

CHAPTER 13

Mission—And Church Growth

by The Reverend Melvin Hodges

consultants:
The Reverend Ralph Cox, The Reverend Norman Cummings, Dr. Donald A. McGavran, Dr. George Peters

The time has come to "sound the trumpet in Zion" and once again call the Church to the fulfillment of its mission: To reconcile men to God and plant vital New Testament churches that will in turn multiply and replenish their section of the earth.

Ours is a world of change. Total scientific knowledge has doubled in the last 50 years. A rampant nationalism has risen as the earth's little and forgotten people demand that their own voice be heard among the nations of the world. Communism takes advantage of every disturbance and every difference between nations and among people.

Social changes contribute to this kaleidoscopic background of the world of the twentieth century: the population explosion, the rush of rural populations to the cities, the resurgence of non-Christian religions.

To the above pressing issues may be added modern theology's new concept of the mission of the Church basically derived from theological and social universalism. In this concept, the mission of the Church is not primarily evangelism but social action. Men without a personal knowledge of Christ are not seen to be totally and irremediably lost.[1] Thus the sharp cutting edge of evangelism is dulled.

Dr. G. W. Peters suggests four reasons for liberalism's confused thinking:

1. An unscriptural view of the nature of the Church;

2. Ignorance of the purpose of God for our age;
3. Ignorance of the nature of the Gospel of God; and
4. An unscriptural universalism.[2]

The Church is the present manifestation of the kingdom of God in the earth, or at least, the agency that prepares the way for the future manifestation of the kingdom. Its mission therefore is the extension of the Church throughout the world. Liberalism does not accept this view. So a new approach is offered. A defeatist attitude is taken toward biblical evangelism, and church growth is held to be relatively unimportant. God, it is said, is working *in history* to bring about His kingdom.

Social revolution is part of the preparation. The Church is only one of several agents for the coming kingdom. The Church therefore must cooperate with God's movement in history and make its contribution to the social revolution. Evangelism, as it has been known historically, is no longer the prime responsibility of the Church. In fact, evangelism which calls for personal conversion from the world and uniting with the Church is frowned upon as irrelevant. The emphasis is on social action. Salvation history formerly confined to the Church has been universalized and made all-inclusive.[3]

This new concept of the mission of the Church changes the very content of the Christian message.[4] Rather than urging individual repentance and conversion, men are seen as redeemed and needing only to be made aware of that fact. Repentance is emphasized as something which society must do, rather than the individual. When an individual repents it is as part of, and in the name of, society.[5]

This change of emphasis is characterized by the changing of the term "missions" for mission. Dr. Clyde Taylor explains the significance of this change of emphasis.

> Moreover, this "mission" includes all united Protestant bodies functioning in their total impact on world society. This involves the Church in economic, social, legislative, administrative, education of youth, welfare, and religious matters. Hence, it can well be said that the mission of the Church is not only to get the "uncommitted" in the Church

"committed," but its business includes every possible impact that the Church can have in and upon society.[6]

This concept that the mission of the Church is to society first, and to individuals second, is a reversal of the biblical order. Evangelicals protest this as a departure from the message of the Gospel. However, we cannot lay all the blame for lack of success in the Christian mission on the liberals. The missionary program of many orthodox evangelical churches has ground to a standstill. What is hindering the vigorous advance of the Church? What are the sins that are obstructing the flow of the Spirit? Where are we using the wrong approaches? In short, where are we failing? We shall attempt to mention some of the more obvious reasons.

First, a failure to translate theology into life and action. Too often the spiritual life of our churches has been self-centered, failing to recognize that the Church is the army of the living God, called to make Christ known everywhere. Second, the failure to keep the true goal *primary*. Sometimes our efforts have found a substitute channel in institutional work that ministers to the physical and intellectual needs of the people, with little or no church planting as a result.

Third, too often the evangelical community has the stamp of foreignness on it. This is seen in the architecture, in the forms of worship, and sometimes in the manner of dress. Such foreignness can well be the "kiss of death" to the life of an indigenous church. Fourth, failure to perceive and employ methods that produce church growth. The reasons for the lack of fruit must be exposed, whether it be that sin in the Church is hindering the work of the Holy Spirit, or that methods are being employed that spring from human reasoning and ingenuity rather than being the product of the Holy Spirit.

The Mission of the Church: Evangelism and Church Planting.

"The Church is, at one and the same time, the community of the redeemed and the redeeming community."[7] The Church is God's agent in the earth. The true Church is the present manifestation of the Kingdom of God. The Church is Christ's body—the medium through which He expresses Himself. Evangelism historically understood is the God-appointed mission of the Church to the world and must remain primary.

It was to representatives of the early Church that the commission was given. The Church, which is the body of Christ, must "make increase of the body unto the edifying of itself in love" (Ephesians 4:16). This means that every true Christian everywhere has a part in church planting.

Factors in Church Growth.

Prominent religious leaders are insisting that the former emphasis of evangelism in pressing for individual decision on the part of each person to accept Christ is not a proper emphasis for today.

Most certainly we welcome movements where whole tribes or communities move as a body toward Christ, but we hasten to declare that the ultimate validity of such movements depends on the individual's understanding and response to the Gospel. Thus to the extent that persons who have had no personal experience of God are brought into the Church in such a movement, just to that extent is the Church weakened and the seed for failure is sown.[8]

There is no pattern in the New Testament except that of genuine individual conversion. When Jesus gave His disciples the command to teach all nations (Matthew 28:19, 20), He did not imply that the nations as such were to be made disciples, but rather He referred to the individuals that composed the nations. The gender of the pronoun *autous* (Baptizing *them* . . . Teaching *them)* does not correspond to the noun *ethne* translated *nations* and must refer to individuals. The apostle Paul followed the same procedure. We insist that in the final analysis the individual is required to demonstrate his primary allegiance to Christ even at the cost of all else besides.

This insistence on individual conversion does not minimize the importance of winning families to Christ. We agree with Dr. Donald McGavran that we should aim at winning the family unit to Christ. It is extremely helpful in the propagation of the Gospel when a sufficient number of families in the community can be won so that the individual is not isolated from his society.

Conversion normally does not require complete cultural dislocation.[9]

In a society organized principally on the basis of clan or family authority, it is foolish for the Church to ignore those men that normally make the decisions for the family group. Usually when the head of the family accepts Christ, the door of Christian obedience is open to the whole family. We have known of a head of a small jungle tribe accepting Christ because of a contact made outside his area, and then inviting the pastor to visit his people. Upon arrival he called in seventeen of his men and presented them to the pastor. "These are my men," he said, "They are going to accept Christ." They did so formally that day.

This does not eliminate the need for the Holy Spirit to do His work individually. Not all would accept Christ in such a situation with the same faith and spiritual hunger. But it does highlight the fact that when the head authority of a clan or family accepts the Gospel, the opportunity for evangelism and church planting is immensely increased.

It is important that a missionary understand the social structures of the community he is trying to win and endeavor to use this knowledge as an instrument of evangelism ("Bridges of God," McGavran would call them), rather than ignoring the social structure and blindly following "the American way."

All of this does not in any sense minimize the fact that the Holy Spirit is sovereign and must direct His messenger according to His sovereign will. He must also convict the individual and impart saving faith. However, our lack of success does not stem from having followed the Spirit's leading, but from our inflexibility and failure to be guided by the Spirit in such a way that each situation is met under His divine direction. The Holy Spirit is not unaware of the anthropological implications of missionary work, and His servant should not be ignorant of the doors that may be found ajar to him and his message through an understanding and correct approach to the culture of the people.

The Role of the Church.

Church growth requires a partnership between God and man.

The first partner is the Holy Spirit. The second partner is the redeemed community, the Church of Jesus Christ. The Church must commit itself to the carrying out of God's purposes, so that God's work becomes the work of the Church and of each of its members.

Some fallaciously think that the Church brought into being on the mission field is not quite the Church in the same sense that it is at home. We must re-emphasize that the Church is the Church anywhere and everywhere. It is the Holy Spirit that gives life to the Church and imparts gifts and ministries as well as power for their performance. So the Church in each area is just as responsible for its maintenance, extension, and spiritual growth as is the Church in any other given area. The one sure sign that the Church in any land is in truth functioning as *a Church* is in the manifestation of a *sense of responsibility*.

It is well recognized that the Church in every land must propagate itself if the Gospel is to be preached in all the world. It is normal, not extraordinary, for converts to witness to their faith in Christ and to the profound change that has been wrought in their lives by accepting Him. This normal spiritual quality, inherent in all true believers, needs to be encouraged. There is usually far more potential for propagation in most churches than is being realized.

The organized evangelistic activity of a local church may include street meetings, preaching in the homes of believers and friends, branch Sunday schools, and literature campaigns. This procedure not only reaches the unevangelized, but at the same time develops Christian workers; for such a church is not only a center for evangelism but also a "seed-bed" that produces new workers.

"Dependence is natural to the child, but it is not to the Church; the Church is often most virile in its infancy whilst the former is always feeblest then."[10] If the Church is to fulfill its role as the living body of Christ it must be free to make its own decisions under Christ without the smothering, limiting, and sometimes embarrassing dependence upon a foreign entity. This includes the management of property and church affairs as well as maintaining the discipline of the Church in regard to members that may need exhortation or correction. No one else can be permitted to do these tasks for the Church if it is to develop spiritual vitality.

Financial self-support in each congregation should be initiated from the beginning. It is a crippling and deadening experience for the new church to have its advances dependent upon outside finances and to have decisions for its progress made by the people who control the finances.

Missionaries often introduce practices, methods, and standards of living which are not compatible with the local economy and consequently sentence the budding church to a life of financial dependency. What is needed is a clear vision that the Church of Jesus Christ exists as a result of faith in the Word and the operation of the Holy Spirit in the lives of the believers, and that the Church may truly exist in each culture on the level of its own economy and be as much the Church of Jesus Christ as any other church anywhere in the world.

It goes without saying that the new church is responsible for the conserving and propagating of Christian truth. Only if a solid biblical foundation is laid will there be any surety that the house will not fall when the winds blow and the rains descend. Proper instruction in the beginning sets the pattern for church life and multiplication.

To perpetuate Christian truth it is also necessary that the Christian leaders be prepared by proper biblical training. Leaders thus taught will be in a position to "teach others also," as Paul said to Timothy. It is just as incumbent on a missionary to raise up spiritual leaders for the churches as it is to found the churches. Risk is involved, yes! But there is also tragedy involved if we fail to make them responsible for their God-given task. When such is the case, heartbreak comes from other sources—in the spirit of a static dependent church; or perhaps it will come in rebellion against the missionary as the only way left to them to find fulfillment.

All too often the missionary makes the mistake of believing when he is no longer prominent in administration that he is no longer needed on the field, when in reality the main missionary ministry is not administrative but in the realm of evangelism, teaching, intercessory prayer and as an example of the power and grace of God in ministry.

Role of the Missionary.

The greatest factor in missions is the *man* who is sent. The missionary creates the climate in which a church can grow. If he is a man of vision, he will impart his vision; if he is sacrificial and self-denying, his converts will learn the meaning of the cross from his example; as a man of faith, his faith will be communicated to those that surround him.

The missionary must understand that his task is to plant churches and help them grow. Since this is our goal, evangelicals must emphasize those methods that produce church growth. We cannot use a large proportion of our finances, strength, and personnel to pursue secondary aims when the primary task is so far from completion. The Institute of Church Growth in Pasadena, California is helping Christian missions by analyzing areas where the Church has prospered in foreign lands in order to ascertain the reasons for growth. Many missions would profit by such a study of their own mission work to see whether or not changes might be initiated which would produce more favorable results in their own area of activity.

The missionary must identify himself with the people he serves. Often his contact with the life of the people is superficial. He makes an occasional visit to a church in his car and hurries back to his "little America" after the service. Even more hurtful, perhaps, is the way he depends on America for decisions and finances, instead of helping the church to develop its own resources and patterns of Christian living. So he inevitably leaves the stamp of foreignness on the church he establishes.

The missionary who seeks to identify himself with the people will be quick to appreciate the good things he observes in the culture and seek to make them bridges of contact for the presenting of gospel truth. Above all, this identification will not be superficial nor professional, but profound and practical. He will not only "love souls," he will *like people.*

The Factor of Responsive Fields.

There are some areas of the world's population that are particularly ready for penetration. Cultural, political, and spiritual factors have been at work to make a people receptive for the message of the Gospel. We must be spiritually wise and sufficiently alert spiritually, and sufficiently mobile practically, to work where the Holy Spirit is working in order not to lose a great potential harvest. This may call for a new approach to the strategy of missions, a possibility that we need to consider prayerfully.

Above all, we must recognize that the work of missions is spiritual in character. The extension of the Church of Jesus Christ will not be brought about by material means. The Holy Spirit is the life of the Church. Before the disciples could go out to fulfill the great commission they must wait for the promise of the Father, the Holy Spirit, for power and guidance.

It Can be Done!

The history of the Apostolic Church gives ample proof that the Church has within it the divine vitality necessary to overcome every obstacle and establish itself in every climate once God's people have met the conditions for the manifestation of divine power. We are firmly convinced that God's ability to overcome modern obstacles is not one whit less than in the beginning.

While we lament the slow progress of the Church today in the extension of vital Christianity throughout the world, there are encouraging exceptions which reveal that evangelism and church planting according to the apostolic pattern are by no means a thing of the past.

The Call to the Unfinished Task.

We come to this hour with a sense of destiny. The task of world evangelism is ours. The task of establishing the Church in every neighborhood, in every tribe and nation is ours. The night is coming when no man can work. The "go ye" of the Great Commission is just as binding on the Church today as at the beginning. Basically we go because He commands, and we will enjoy success because He goes with us "even unto the end of the world." We are called to *pray*. Jesus said to His disciples, "The harvest truly is plenteous; but the laborers are few; pray ye therefore the Lord of the harvest, that He will send forth laborers into His harvest" (Matthew 9:37, 38). Prayer is the key to supplying laborers. Jesus indicates that He will send them forth as a result of believing prayer. The word "send forth" in the Greek is a strong word, *ekballo*. It means to *cast them out* or *thrust them out.*

If we will pray, God will call men who never intended to dedicate their lives to the ministry. Through them He can raise up thousands of local churches and their leaders. Surely, the call to the fulfilling of the mission of the Church today is the call to learn the meaning of real prayer as we never knew it before.

We are called to *united spiritual action.* There is a sense in which our ecumenical brethren are right. God does want united action on the part of His Church. We do not disagree with them in the thought that God desires His people to be united. We do strenuously object when truth must be sacrificed for unity and when social service becomes more important than biblical evangelism. True Christian unity is the unity of the *Spirit,* not necessarily of organization. Our plea is that all of us may get close to the heart of God, since the Holy Spirit has shed His love abroad in our hearts and enables us to enjoy the unity of the Spirit for the great task that He has placed before us.

Finally, God is calling all of us to *personal dedication.* He is looking for a nucleus of committed men who will love Him and His kingdom more than anything else in this world.

The clarion call comes to all of us: pastors, laymen, missionaries, and nationals—soldiers in the army of the living God. Let us go forward until every soul hears that Jesus is Lord and Saviour, and until the Church is established in every village and town, in every country and tribe.

FOOTNOTES

1. V. E. W. Hayward, *International Review of Missions* (April, 1964), pp. 205-208: "Do we invite people into the Church because it is only within the believing community that the effects of the Gospel can be enjoyed? Or are Christians commissioned to preach to all and sundry the good news that, whether they believe it or not, they now live within a world for which the Son of God died and which God is even now reconciling to Himself? . . . When we preach the Gospel do we tell men only of a personal salvation offered to those who have faith, or do

we declare to them that in Christ, God has already performed the mighty act to win back this fallen world into the joy of His purpose?"

2. G. W. Peters, Professor of World Missions, Dallas Theological Seminary, in a letter to the author.
3. Bruce Morgan speaks of the "frustrating view of the Church . . . that the Church consists of a voluntary association of individuals who are Christians who have decided to cooperate in some common enterprises, such as worship, education, social service and the support of missionaries somewhere else in the world. Those missionaries are inviting other individuals, one by one, to accept the Gospel of salvation through Jesus Christ . . . and urged in turn to join other voluntary associations, to organize churches." In *Called in Revolution* (Student Volunteer Movement of Christian Missions), p. 55.
4. Paul Tillich, *The Theology of the Christian Mission,* p. 283-284: "One should not misunderstand missions as an attempt to save from eternal damnation as many individuals as possible among the nations of the world. Such an interpretation of the meaning of missions presupposes a separation of individual from individual, a separation of individual from the social group to which he belongs, and it presupposes the idea of salvation, and gives hope for salvation only to a few—comparatively few, even if it is millions—who are actually reached by the message of Jesus as the Christ. Such an idea is unworthy of the glory and of the love of God and must be rejected in the name of the true relationship of God to His world."

   And again: "Therefore, we must say that missions is neither the attempt to save individual souls, nor an attempt at cultural cross-fertilization, nor an attempt to transform the latent Church—which is present in the world religions, in paganism, Judaism, and humanism—into something new; the New Reality in Jesus as the Christ."
5. Morgan, *op. cit.,* p. 65.
6. *Ecumenical Strategy in Foreign Missions,* Evangelical Foreign Missions Association.
7. Peter Beyerhaus, *The Responsible Nature of the Church and the Foreign Missions* (Grand Rapids: Wm. B. Eerdmans), p. 110.
8. *Ibid.,* pp. 140-141: Here Peter Beyerhaus confirms the validity of this observation even while protesting against the Pietist concept that the true Church is composed only of individuals that have had an experience of personal conversion. "We saw unmistakably in the Batak missionary history that, although rarely nowadays, there can be a call to conversion which fails to become a matter of personal challenge to the individual member of the group. Yet . . . whenever the horizontal line of natural ties was not crossed immediately after conversion by a breakthrough of God's Word; where, that is, the individual was not affected and the natural social ties not integrated into the new life, an adverse development was found to follow."
9. Harry R. Boer, *Pentecost and Missions* (Grand Rapids: Wm. B. Eerdmans, 1961), p. 165: "The Church was not built up of so many individual Christians but of basic social units, of organic wholes, were the fundamental cells of society, namely families.
10. J. W. Clark, quoted in *The Responsible Nature of the Church and the Foreign Mission* (Grand Rapids: Wm. B. Eerdmans, 1964), p. 108.

CHAPTER 14

Mission—And Foreign Missions

by The Reverend R. P. Chavan

consultants:

The Reverend Erik Barnett, The Reverend James Bolarin,
Dr. Raymond Buker, Sr., The Reverend Francisco Lievano

The younger church today is the outgrowth of the great movement of missionary evangelism of the Western countries in the nineteenth century.

In the beginning, missionaries adopted operational policies to fit the colonial context of those days. They controlled everything including the supervision of and planning for the church and institutions, and the use of finances and property. The church had no voice.

Now the situation has changed. The new church has grown to maturity. The transition to indigenousness has been a painful process with the outcome sometimes happy, sometimes tragically unhappy. But it is accepted the world over that the indigenous church must be the norm.

There has been an urgent need to re-examine missionary methods and church-mission relationships. The burning questions before the mission and the church leaders are: What is ideal for the development of the church? Should there be an integration of church and mission or should church and mission be organizationally distinct? How self-sufficient should the church be? How should foreign money be used? How can spiritual fellowship between nationals and foreigners be cultivated? How ought property to be managed? Who is responsible for the administration of institutional work? What is the place of missionaries, and what are their responsibilities in the indigenous church, and how ought their assignments to be made? To these questions we address ourselves.

Amalgamation or Separation?

There are two schools of thought regarding church-mission relationships. One believes in the union of church and mission without distinction between the two. The other believes the church and mission should be separate organizationally.

The advocates of union say that the church has "married" the mission and the twain have become one flesh. Others think that the mission and church should remain separate. Neither should absorb the other. Although separate organizationally, church and mission should be one in Christian love and cooperative evangelistic work.

Those favoring union of church and mission base their argument in part upon the phrase in John 17:11 "That they may be one." In fact, on this phrase some are trying to unite all churches into one super church. But we should read the complete verse. Jesus says, "That they may be one *as we are*." The second part of the verse is by far the more important. The unity Christ speaks of is applicable to all real disciples, to all those who have entered the Kingdom of God by the new birth. John 17 does not speak of organization but of those who have become children of God through regeneration. Christian unity is a spiritual unity which we acknowledge by positive action. This spiritual unity brings all under one church in India, Africa, Europe, America or elsewhere. It does not rely on external or ecclesiastical organization.

Proponents of two distinct organizational structures argue the headship of Christ and His purpose for the Church. In the New Testament we do not find anything about amalgamation of mission and the emerging church. Thus one mission leader concludes:

> The criterion by which the mission-church relationship should be judged is therefore functional and practical rather

than theological. It should be a relationship that allows the Church as church to develop and express its life in Christ.

In my opinion, the emerging church can better develop if it stands organizationally separate from the mission which brought it into being. The church of which I am a minister started in India in 1885, but until 1955 the work was largely done by the missionaries. The church and the secular schools were under the direct management of missionaries. The teachers, pastors, evangelists and Bible women were all paid by the Mission. The church had no burden, no vision, no sense of responsibility. It was fully dependent upon the mission. People had no reliance on themselves or on God.

In 1927 the Christian and Missionary Alliance officially stated that the mission and church should remain organizationally separate.

> It is recognized that church and mission are essentially distinct. The mission is an organization composed of representatives from the homeland supported by or through the Society and functioning under the direction of the Society.
>
> In the delicate and essential problem of partnership with the national church, the Society makes a distinction between the foreign mission and the church; and this distinction should not be ignored. The mission is not a church, and it exercises no ecclesiastical powers. In its relation to the indigenous church, the mission is an organized body of friends who stand ready to help when needed. Beyond the ministry of the local church, the mission must continue to function in a widening outreach. The development of the church, often beginning as a relatively small body of believers in any country, should not hinder the initiative of the missionary body composed of men and women who have been called of God to preach the Gospel to every creature. This continuing program shall, when possible, be undertaken in partnership with the established church.

Thus mission is not to regulate church activities and the church is not to regulate missionaries' activities except in those cases where missionaries have been assigned to some form of church-related work by the field conference and at the request of the church.

Missionaries were slow in giving control to the church. They pleaded the ignorance, illiteracy, poverty, and backwardness of the people. And Christians themselves were also slow or reluctant to take on the responsibility of an indigenous church, especially in regard to finances. Twenty-eight years later in 1955, the C&MA called a conference of all mission chairmen and all national presidents in its Asian fields. The theme of the conference was the development of the church and of national leadership.

In India, at my request, all mission subsidy for church workers was discontinued. As a result, the people have learned to give. Church workers are no longer regarded as "agents of the mission or of imperialism."

There has been corresponding growth in evangelism, and we now have the Evangelism-in-Depth program in operation.[1] Our leadership is becoming strong and efficient. Laymen are catching the vision of witnessing. A foreign mission board has been established, and a national couple has been prayerfully separated to go to a foreign land.

Our church is in the central part of India, and the action we took has been observed by surrounding churches. The C&MA of India, has become a pioneer in self-support in India, and many are watching our work. I say again that the church must be indigenous, preferably from the beginning, and in the interests of indigenousness, the mission must remain organizationally separate.

Spiritual Fellowship Between Nationals and Foreigners.

Although church and mission are two separate organizations, associations between missionaries and national workers continue. It is just human that there can be conflicts because of cultural differences, ignorance and misunderstanding.

The withdrawal of financial aid or support for pastors and evangelists can distress, disgruntle, and burden the national church. At first it looks like a cruel policy, with the missionaries at fault. The church is thrown into deep water. But she will not sink. In fact, very soon she will learn to swim. As Le-van-Thai, formerly president of the Evangelical Church of Vietnam has said, "the church is the Lord's church and it belongs to God alone. The nationals and the missionaries should be the best of friends together in their cooperation with God."[2]

How can we have this friendly cooperation? The cross is the basis of our relationship. In the cross there is both vertical and horizontal fellowship. It is the symbol of the love of Jesus Christ. "Love begets love." This fellowship of love should be on both an individual and on an organizational level. If there is no love of God in the heart there is hatred, darkness and death. (I John 3:14)

The Reverend P. N. Potu, an Indonesian, said to a group of missionaries:

> According to my understanding there will be no real problem except it arises with us; that is, members of the national church and mission. If each of us knows how to govern himself with due regard for the other, there will be no problem.[3]

The Joint Committee.

Although the association of churches and the mission are two different administrations, yet there must be a link for mutual consultation. A united, or joint committee provides such a link.

The church and mission executive committees should meet at stated intervals. The functions of the joint committee should be to foster spiritual unity through praise and prayer, to keep fellowship, to share common problems, to clear misunderstandings that could cause a rift of any kind, to reach joint agreement for evangelistic effort, missionary vision, Bible teaching, spiritual retreats, literacy and literature programs, and such other ministries as the two organizations may determine to carry out. There should be no recording of minutes in such a joint committee. Moreover, it is quite essential that all the missionaries and national workers meet together occasionally for a day of prayer and praise.

Property Management.

The chief problems in the church are pride, pleasure and

property. "Properties constitute a very thorny problem," said C. A. DeBruin.[4]

If all the church property and buildings are held by the mission "there may arise no small strife over the administration of this money and the ownership of the property."[5] Complications with government are also likely. The missionaries should solve the problem of property amicably, lest it become a bone of contention between missionaries and nationals. A property argument should not be allowed to hinder the development of the church.

As a result of the missionary movement, almost all of the property at the beginning was bought and registered in the name of the mission. Most of the buildings carried the name mission, as for instance, mission house, mission school, mission hospital, mission compound. This created a "mission mentality," and made mission much more prominent than church in the eyes of Christian and non-Christian, though this of course was not intended.

The indigenous movement and political changes in various countries have caused the mission and the church to face today serious questions regarding property problems. Should all property be transferred to the name of the church? Should there be a division of property for missionaries and mission projects and for church work? How can mission property be transferred without the imposition of government taxes, often high?

Although missions have been turning over properties to national churches from time to time during the past few years, there has often been considerable delay because of the tax costs involved. Expert legal advice should be sought. If all properties except missionary residences are turned over to the church, there arises the difficulty of upkeep and repair. With the church taking the burden of support for pastors and evangelists, the extra cost of property upkeep could be too heavy if imposed immediately.

I feel that all properties except missionary residences should be transferred to the name of the church. Someone may ask, "Why not missionary residences?" Missionary residences are for the missionaries. If the missionaries are transferred to other towns or to some other country, the amount recovered from the sale of the house is needed for renting or constructing new quarters elsewhere.

In the event of the mission's transferring the properties, it would be best if the church would take over complete responsibility for the churches, chapels and parsonages. In the case of other properties such as institutions, it would be well if an arrangement could be worked out whereby the church would gradually assume the care of such large buildings. Even if the mission can buy property at present in independent countries, because of the uncertain circumstances, experience would indicate that such property should be purchased in the name of the national church. In the case of missionary residences or other properties for strictly mission projects, they can be purchased in the name of the national church with the clear understanding between mission and church that these properties are to be administered by the mission with no interference from the church.

The national church should build its own chapels. The value of this is intrinsic rather than extrinsic. The little bamboo chapel which the church builds with its own money and labor, is infinitely more valuable than a beautiful brick and cement structure built with foreign money. The church must learn the spirit of sacrifice and labor. If the church is not strong enough to build its own place of worship, it should meet in a private home or rent a place until sufficient money is collected.

An exception to the above principle may need to be made in the case of large cities. In a big city or a port city, the cost of land, material, and labor can be enormous, and it is often beyond the power of the national church to build its own church building. Without a place of worship, the work suffers. In such cases the mission should seriously consider granting assistance for the construction of a suitable church.

Institutional Work.

The great contribution which mission schools, orphanages, and medical facilities have made is generously acknowledged by Christian and non-Christian, but recently the attitude of some people and some governments has changed. As C. P. Matthew[6] writes: "Christian schools and colleges, hospitals, orphanages are all looked upon with suspicion and even hostility by certain sections of non-Christians." This changed attitude has necessitated a re-thinking of institutional work.

With most national churches hard put to support their pastors and maintain their church buildings, it is premature to ask the church to completely pay the costs of theological schools. To cut foreign support and personnel should be the last-born child of indigenousness, and this should be a gradual process. The church in most places is not yet prepared to take full financial responsibility, and the sudden withdrawal of foreign aid would be disastrous. Therefore, the church should not be unconcerned or irresponsible in this work. The church should be encouraged to observe Bible school Sunday once a quarter, or oftener, as convenient. There should be a challenge to youth, special prayer, and an offering. The church's governing body should make some provision in its annual budget for theological schools. In some cases where a church is too small to maintain its own school, a cooperative education program such as the Union Biblical Seminary at Yeotmal in India might be a solution.

Secular Schools.

Educational work is one of the most expensive forms of mission work. Sometimes the money that would have been used for evangelism is used to perpetuate institutional work. "It isn't education but deep spiritual life that holds young people for the gospel," says Dr. Clyde Taylor.[7]

A careful study needs to be made to see whether church-and mission-related schools and colleges are producing efficient, intellectual Christian leaders in the church and nation. Where essential schools exist, all administrative responsibility should be turned over by the mission to the national church. If the church cannot immediately shoulder the entire financial responsibility, a reduction of subsidy should be carried out over a period of years until the church carries the whole burden. Before administrative responsibility is turned over, all property should be repaired if possible by the mission.

Hospitals, clinics and leprosaria are a boon to the nation. There are other special medical missions also. They are doing effective service. A mission medical institution should be sure it meets not only the physical need of its patients, but their spiritual needs as well.

About one hundred years ago in a large town in India, a mission opened a hospital. It became a well-known landmark. Today that well-established old hospital has been closed by the mission because it did not fulfill the main objective of a spiritual ministry. Physical aid can now be received from more recently-begun government and private hospitals.

Where medical work is still an essential part of evangelism, the national church should be a partner with the supporting mission even though the church is not financially strong enough to take responsibility for the full medical program. Hospitals, clinics, and leprosaria should be administered jointly by mission and church representatives.

The Role and Assignment of Missionaries.

The role of missionaries and their assignments in the indigenous church is one of the most complex problems of modern mission administration. In the early stage of missionary work, the people were considered uncivilized, illiterate and unfit to administer church work, and missionaries adopted a method which could fit in those days. This tendency continued until recently and is still evident in the consideration of procedure by missionary administrators, though the situation has completely changed.

Everywhere people have learned to think. They have been liberated from foreign rule. Nations are rapidly progressing in every respect. If the missionary comes to the field with the old policy in his mind, he hinders the indigenous church. Today missionaries must come with an open mind. It is most essential that missionaries do not initiate projects which will divide workers into mission-paid and church-paid categories. Employment by the mission of national workers should be arranged only after consultation with the national body.

Sometimes missionaries who do not whole-heartedly support the indigenous plan contrive various methods of winning the favor of selected national workers by gifts of money. Such favoritism creates trouble in the national body and the favored individuals tend to become uncontrollable. The work of the indigenous church thus suffers.

Missionaries should not have positions of authority in the church, but they could be invited for consultation if necessary. They should not dictate any policies, but they should help and guide in the implementation of the policy of the national organization. They should be counselors and should guide in teaching, preaching, tithing, and witnessing. Church work should be controlled by the church, not by the missionaries. Although missionaries could be members of the church, they should lovingly withdraw from voting and being elected to administrative positions for the sake of the development of the church.

For better understanding the mission should invite fraternal delegates to the mission conference. Likewise the national body should invite missionary delegates to its conference. The mission should take into consideration the desires of the national body regarding the stationing of missionary personnel.

Most important, missionaries should seek prayerfully to create leaders. Nationals are slow to take responsibility. The preparing of spiritual leadership requires many hours of patient training, many tears, much prayer. Missionaries should not push responsibility on untrained leaders and watch the results, saying, "I am only a counselor or advisor." The glory of the missionary is to prepare great leaders in the church, and to work with them in full cooperation. In this regard the matter of the missionary adapting himself to the way of life of the people among whom he works is essential. For instance, the vital importance of knowing the language of the people can be noted.

Finally, the missionary is not our father or mother, but he should be our friend. He should teach us reliance upon God and not upon the mission. He should always be careful to shun that which will hinder the growth of the church or mar its self-reliance or weaken its witness. Both missionaries and nationals must strive for a progressive viewpoint in relationships, always working toward healthy growth of the church while at the same time allowing no resentment or bitterness to creep in on either side. The philosophy cannot be either that of "I and mine" or "yours alone" but of "we together."

But the nationals should also guard lest they misuse their authority. They also should be Christ-like. In our language there is a saying to the effect that you cannot clap with one hand. Missionaries *and* nationals are needed. Dr. Aggrey of Ghana uses the following illustration: "The piano needs both white and black keys. Leave one set out, and your music is not complete." Together they should prayerfully try to solve the problems, should try to clear away the misunderstanding, should overcome the hindrances, should remove the stumbling blocks. There should be close and mutual cooperation. The attitude of both missionaries and nationals should be one of collaboration and mutual respect. What they do together ultimately counts in the indigenous work. As Paul says, "We are co-laborers together with God." So nationals and missionaries should work hand in hand. This is the key to the growth of the indigenous church.

Thus the Cross of Christ will be lifted high over all.

FOOTNOTES

1. This is the combined program of seven missions and churches in our region.
2. See discussion on page 56 of Report on Asia Conference.
3. President of the National Church of the Christian and Missionary Alliance in Indonesia. See discussion on page 55 of report of Asia Conference.
4. C. A. DeBruin, "The Arcot Mission in a Revolutionary Age," *Revolution in Missions* (Blaise Levai, ed., Madras: The Christian Literary Society, 1957), p. 183.
5. Roland Allen, *The Spontaneous Expansion of the Church* (Grand Rapids: Wm. B. Eerdmans, 1962), p. 141.
6. *Op. cit.*, DeBruin, p. 34.
7. Dr. Clyde W. Taylor's Africa trip report, date unknown.

CHAPTER 15

Mission—And Evangelical Unity

by DR. VERNON MORTENSON

consultants
The Reverend J. Herbert Kane, Dr. Earl Radmacher
Dr. Clyde Taylor, The Reverend I. Ben Wati,
Mr. Charles H. Troutman

The concept of "one world" and the essential unity of mankind has reached a fulfillment in this Twentieth Century that staggers the imagination. Increasingly we think in international terms—and the title "worldwide" appears in the names of several missionary societies. Faster and better communications are largely responsible for this change. In such a world of fermenting restlessness and revolution, problems of cooperation and unity must occupy a large portion of our attention.

Conservative evangelicals are part of this irresistible surge because of the global scope of the Great Commission and universal outreach of the love of God. This involvement, however, does not come from mere pressures of geopolitics, sociology, comparative religion or even from "the rediscovery of the Church."[1] Nor does it come from current institutional patterns such as the United Nations or the Organization of American States. No matter how much we may be influenced by our contemporary world, the nature and form of the unity which we seek is determined otherwise; by revelation.

Long before the Twentieth Century, the oneness and universality of the Church was recognized. The term "catholic" early suggested a universal body, and the term *oikoumene* (originally referring simply to the known, inhabited earth)[2] was applied to church councils to indicate ecclesiastical assemblies in which the entire church of the inhabited world was represented. In time both the Western and Eastern churches began to apply the term to assemblies covering the entire Eastern or the Western church. The Reformation used the term in the same way to apply to all the Reformed churches. Not until the present century did the meaning of the term embrace an interdenominationalism which has as its aim the union of all churches without regard to agreement of confession or polity. An executive officer of the National Council of Churches has written, "They (conservative evangelicals) share with us an intense concern for unity in the body of Christ, but approach that concern from a different perspective." [3]

This difference of perspective is crucial. It is not determined by personalities, by organizational loyalties or by the great trends of our times, but by principles set down by our Lord Himself. This must encompass all believers who are prepared to face the open Scriptures as their sole rule of faith and practice.

I. *Biblical Basis of Unity.*

Our attention is drawn immediately to the great statement on unity expressed in our Lord's high priestly prayer in the Gospel of John, Chapter 17. First, it is essential to place these definitive statements in context. The prayer itself was offered in the Upper Room just before the little band of disciples went across Jerusalem to the Garden of Gethsemane.

Two things stand out in this great prayer. Whether we look at it from the standpoint of the distracted disciples or from the position of the soon-departing Lord, the theme of the prayer can be summed up in the words used by Hudson Taylor, "Union and Communion." [4] The Lord was not praying about the form of His future church nor even about its activities, but about actual, experiential relationships and their effect in public witness to Himself. The Lord's other concern was for the entire body of believers, not merely the group He was facing. He was speaking of a true "communion of the saints," [5] which now includes those who have been glorified, these still in the midst of battle and those even yet to come! Such unity includes both "the dead and the living." [6]

What basic Biblical principles of unity are found in this chapter?

1. The origin of this unity is God.
2. This unity consists of certain people who, whatever else they may or may not be, are separated from the general mass of mankind, which Jesus called "the world."
3. The nature of this unity is comparable to the unity of the three Persons in the holy Trinity, and analogous to that which exists between the Son and those for whom He is praying.
4. The purpose of this unity as expressed by Christ is that the "world might believe." [7]

This 17th chapter of John does not stand alone, but is in harmony with other passages in the New Testament. This is especially true of the 4th chapter of Ephesians understood in context. The essential message of Ephesians 1 is that the "gathering together of all things in Christ" is the result of hearing the word of the Gospel of Jesus Christ and believing it. The second chapter puts the matter even more plainly. What group of people are exhorted to continue in unity? They are those who were dead in trespasses and sins, and, upon believing, they realize that they are members of God's Church, solely because of what Christ has done for them.

In the third chapter, the grand purpose of God is revealed and the "bought ones" are urged to enter more fully into an understanding of God's great design for worldwide witness.

The "therefore" of Ephesians 4:1 indicates once again that the strong doctrinal foundation of the first three chapters is the basis of the appeal to maintain unity. No one questions the place of fellowship in Christian mission or its creative potential, but fellowship as the basis and foundation of unity is completely contrary to the teaching of chapter 4. Christian unity is maintained in fellowship, it is not created therein. In this sense, evangelicals and ecumenicists are going in different directions.

This chapter makes more explicit the fact that the union must be entered by means of faith in the person of Christ as He is revealed in certain truths or propositions concerning His work. For our purposes it is enough to point out that there is a "unity inherent in our faith"[8] and that "unity of the Spirit" cannot be had without agreement as to what that faith consists of—its basic doctrines. And conversely, false doctrine destroys or vitiates the unity of which the New Testament speaks. Evangelicals are profoundly disturbed when ordained teachers in certain denominations continue to teach theological interpretations which seem to acknowledge the uniqueness of Christ but deny vital spiritual truths concerning His virgin birth, atoning death and bodily resurrection.

This study raises the question as to what doctrines must be classed as definitive of New Testament Christianity, without which the faith becomes a different religion. In his paper "Mission and Syncretism" presented to this Congress, Jack Shepherd defines the "core" of the redemptive message:

> What then is that irreducible core that man must believe for his eternal salvation? We affirm this must include the utter lostness of man, "There is none righteous, no, not one," and that the death, burial and bodily resurrection of Christ, God's incarnate Son, has brought full expiation for man's sin and justification before God.

The Apostle Paul does not assume that unity is something that will automatically take care of itself. If in chapter 4, verse 14 he speaks of the negative aspect, in verse 15 he is positive. "Speaking the truth in love, (we) may grow up into Him in all things, which is the head, even Christ." It is clear that part of our development in spiritual maturity lies in our seeking to preserve this unity. The manifestation of biblical unity among the body of believers is one of the great tasks of our time, made especially urgent by the shrinking size of our planet.

To summarize, the nature of Biblical unity is: 1. A unity given by God, to be preserved, and where necessary, to be recovered. 2. A unity of essence, a new regenerate society whose individual members have been given a new nature—life in the Spirit. 3. A unity of belief, centered particularly around the person and work of Jesus Christ and the message of the Gospel. 4. A unity designed for world evangelism, and should be manifested by the effectiveness of its outreach.

II. *Basic Objections to Modern Ecumenism.*

The basic objection of evangelicals to the modern ecumenical movement lies in its deviation from Biblical principles of unity which we have just emphasized. The consequences of such deviation are great, but it is not our purpose here to catalog the results. We are aware of the pressure from ecumenical organizations for organic unity, their neglect of polity and doctrinal issues, the absence of a consistent biblical reference in much of their literature,[9] the lack of alertness to the danger of false teaching and thus of heresy, the growing authority of bureaucratic machinery and the absence of grass-roots enthusiasm—all matters which are sufficiently recognized both within and outside of the World Council of Churches so as not to require further comment.[10] Evangelicals question ecumenical claims of accomplishing the goals to which they are committed. We shall deal with the so-called "sin of division" in a later section. For all the ecumenical claim to inclusiveness evangelicals feel that their own distinctive theological positions are threatened by pressure toward a non-biblical uniformity. However, for consideration at a Congress such as this, two aspects concern us particularly: (1) The mergers and ecumenical commitments which we have observed have not produced a new thrust in Christian outreach, especially in missionary interest, and (2) an ecumenical divisiveness which militates against the effectiveness of existing cooperative efforts.

1. Missionary Interest.

a. The United Church of Canada is the most famous case of church merger in North America, being founded in 1925 by union of Methodist, Congregational and most of the Presbyterian churches.[11] Since one of the arguments for this union was that it would further the witness of the Church, it is legitimate to ask how this has progressed over the intervening years. On the home front in 1925 there was a surplus of ministers; in 1961 the retiring moderator declared a shortage that had reached emergency proportions. On the foreign front, in the face of an overall 250% increase in missionaries from North America, the United Church's force decreased almost 50%.

b. In Asia, the formation of the Church of South India has been observed with keen interest since its establishment in 1947, through the merger of Anglicans, Congregationalists, Methodists, Presbyterians. The negotiations were particularly complicated because there was often more than one missionary society representing a denomination with several different languages involved. Donald McGavran in *How Churches Grow* investigated and assessed the growth of churches around the world and concluded that the Church of South India has not lived up to its expectations because union has made little or no difference in its rate of growth.[12]

c. The proportion of missionary interest in the denominations most deeply involved in the Ecumenical Movement does not nearly approach that of those churches who oppose such union on Biblical principles. For example, if the Methodist and United Presbyterians gave to foreign missions in the same proportion as the Evangelical Free Church, they would together give the staggering sum of 422 million dollars. Or, considering missionary personnel, if these two denominations had the same percentage of their membership in overseas missionary work as the Christian and Missionary Alliance, they would be supporting 187,000 people instead of approximately 3,000. In fact from a time prior to 1914 when the evangelical revival fires stirred the major denominations to worldwide missionary zeal, there has been a decreasing percentage of North American missionaries coming from those groups associated with the National Council of Churches. In 1956, 43.5% of North American missionaries were associated with the Division of Foreign Missions of the National Council of Churches; in 1958, it was 41.2%; in 1960, it was 38%. If the figures for the Seventh-day Adventists were subtracted, the percentage would drop to about 32%.[13]

2. Ecumenical Divisiveness.

In 1891 the first Quadrennial Student Volunteer Movement Convention was held in Cleveland and in the years that followed there was a quickening in tempo and numbers of missionary conventions, culminating in the World Missionary Conference in Edinburgh in 1910. The major denominations as well as the China Inland Mission, the Egypt General Mission, the South Africa General Mission and the Regions Beyond Missionary Union were in attendance. The thrust of these conventions was well within the orthodox theological context. They were truly ecumenical. Subsequent to that time, adoption of liberal theological positions by many of the denominational leaders and their identification with the "social Gospel" divided this worldwide fellowship. Consequently those agencies committed to biblical theology were increasingly separated from this young Ecumenical Movement.[14]

The pressure to conform to a certain type of organic, ecumenical union continues, especially on the mission field. There is a deep-seated conviction among ecumenical leaders not only that the professing church should be united, but that this union should be developed within their particular framework. It is not sufficient for them that a regional or national association of missionaries and local churches already be in existence. We are told there must be an organic union of such associations with the World Council of Churches and a promise to work toward local unification.

In Africa, for example, the activity of ecumenical leaders in pressing for union within the framework of the World Council of Churches has sought to divide a long standing unity. Much of the Christian work in Africa has been thoroughly evangelical. Within the last five years the ecumenical activities in Africa show that the World Council of Churches' goal is to bring the African churches into its own orbit or, failing that, to use indirect means through financial enticements, etc., to win favor for ecumenicity. At the All-Africa Christian Youth Assembly in Nairobi, Kenya (December, 1962, January, 1963) it was understood that the present older leadership of the churches of Africa was not greatly in sympathy with the theology and aims of the Ecumenical Movement. However, the General Secretary of the World Council of Churches in addressing the Assembly stated,

> Youth, you can help to prepare your church for unity. And if you find much resistance, sometimes from older and more influential people, you may have to play the difficult role of being in the opposition.[15]

If the WCC representatives achieve their purpose of setting up some of their agencies in Vietnam, they will succeed in dividing a now unified Christian fellowship of evangelical witness. Evangelicals alone need not be charged with divisiveness. It must not be forgotten that in each of the two outstanding mergers this century in Canada and South India, the union paradoxically divided one of the existing churches.

From the experience of evangelicals it appears that ecumenical unity cannot be defined as cooperation or federation or even negotiation but rather the imposing of a particular form of organizational union. And the exponents of such union often display an insensitivity in recognizing evangelical unity and an intolerance of other points of view.

There is ample evidence that evangelicals do not oppose mergers as such. It must be clear, however, that evangelicals out of deep conviction, do oppose that type of union which syncretizes doctrine and ignores polity and distinctives.

III. *The Place of Diversity.*

"Division," we are told by ecumenical leaders, "is the great sin of our age." Instinctively, evangelicals reject this, emphasizing a rejection of Jesus Christ as far more serious than a mere multiplicity of organizations. As we have seen in Ephesians 4, the *ekklesia,* which God brought into being, is composed of believers who are united organically with Jesus Christ and to one another. They belong to a worldwide and trans-temporal community and only secondarily to a particular congregation, denomination or missionary society. Because of this, a single congregation (or denomination) is related to Christ, not directly, but because its members are members of the larger body of which Christ is the Head. For example, an organization such as The Evangelical Alliance Mission, incorporated under the laws of the State of Illinois, has no direct relationship to Jesus Christ, though its members certainly have. Thus the *ekklesia* should not be described in terms of institutions, but in terms of individuals and interrelated Christians! [16]

Let us repeat the two things of importance to our subject which follow from this Biblical perspective. Paul did not seek to bring the congregations into one institutional set-up; the believers were all *one.* This being the case, the common ecumenical argument that separate organizations, as such tear apart the

Lord's body, is refuted. In fact, the possibility that such separate groups can fragment the *ekklesia* becomes ridiculous as one comes to understand the fundamental significance of this term.[17]

This Biblical understanding of the church also refutes the modern ecumenical position that unity must eventually be demonstrated through a visible institution. In Ephesians 4, the *ekklesia* is united together by the Head—a concept which is not related to polity, but to the nature of God. Unity is not dependent on organizaiton, but on union with Christ.

Evangelicals are not merely tolerating a situation. We believe that there are some things which cannot and ought not to be organizationally united, lest the whole body of Christ be impoverished. However, evangelicals do not glory in diversity. Some of our present fragmentation is acknowledged to be due to the sin of pride, selfishness, and impatience. Other divisions have historical reasons which we are reluctant to forget until such a time as it is clear that situations have changed. For example, evangelicals are very reluctant to forget the issues which produced the divisions of the Reformation, particularly since the Vatican II Council has declared itself continuing its "unchanging" dogma.

There are additional dimensions described by one prominent modern theologian, who is not identified as an evangelical, who states categorically that the union of Protestant churches is impossible because they embody irreconcilable, antithetical formative principles.[18] The Baptist principle of the autonomous congregation stands in irreconcilable conflict with the centralized leadership of the Episcopalian churches. We feel that no amount of ecumenical enthusiasm and discussion will resolve these differences, but rather that if present plans continue, one of the parties will have to capitulate on matters of conscience to the other.

We recognize these principles for what they are, unsolvable as far as we can see, but we do not permit them to interfere with expressions of evangelical unity. Evangelicals understand from this that the various organizations have a common task of evangelism, and that institutional organization is of relative importance only. In other words, the great sin of our age is doctrinal deviation, and institutional diversity is not incompatible with the unity for which Christ prayed.

Paul was no visionary as to the extreme difficulty of manifesting the unity of the body of Christ. Even our Lord realized the roughness of the way as evidenced by His repeated exhortations. Paul urges sacrifice for the sake of unity [19] and places love above freedom in matters of ritual. Once we realize that the manifestation of Christian unity requires the most strenuous effort, then we have begun to grasp something of the anguish of our Lord and His apostle over extra-biblical divisions. Our prayers for this unity will be shallow unless we are prepared for this effort of love—an effort for the sake of those for whom Christ died.

IV. *Present Expressions of Evangelical Unity.*

As we have been considering the principles of Christian unity given in John 17 and Ephesians 4, it will be helpful to call our attention to examples of evangelical unity in missionary areas of the world. We know that there is "yet much land to be possessed," but the illustrations given below show that evangelicals are working out patterns of unity which are in keeping with the Scriptures. This does not represent mere reaction to a host of ecumenical organizations nor should we be surprised to discover that we, too, are producing forms of visible unity in many areas. The type of evangelical unity being developed is an expression of our understanding of the prayer of Christ. The World Evangelical Fellowship, the Evangelical Fellowship of India, the Evangelical Foreign Missions Association, the International Council of Christian Churches, the National Association of Evangelicals, the Interdenominational Foreign Mission Association and similar organizations are sound expressions of Biblical unity.

For example, the whole independent or "faith" mission movement of the past one hundred years has been characterized by interdominational fellowship, and cooperation in its personnel, finances, and governing boards. In addition, there are a number of areas where conservative evangelicals are demonstrating principles of Biblical unity in an increasing manner.

1. Church Unity.

There are many instances of organizational ties which bind evangelical churches together on the foreign field. In Venezuela, as long as 40 years ago, the evangelical churches in the separate areas have met every five years in the United Convention of Evangelical Churches, which includes almost all evangelical churches in Venezuela. The churches established in Vietnam by the Christian and Missionary Alliance and other evangelicals have been linked in the one Evangelical Church of Vietnam.

2. Evangelical Fellowships

Examples of fellowships which have been established are: the Evangelical Fellowship of India, Taiwan Evangelical Fellowship, Evangelical Fellowships in Rhodesia, Malawi, Zambia, Republic of Congo, and Indonesia, and the continent-wide Evangelical Fellowship of Africa and Madagascar, formed in 1966. The linking of many of the regional fellowships in the World Evangelical Fellowship provides a truly worldwide *oikoumene* assocation of believers of like precious faith.

3. Mission Cooperation.

a. Evangelism.

Joint evangelistic campaigns have proved extremely effective. One of the earliest was the Japan Centennial Campaign of 1959. The basis of this cooperation was a strong conservative doctrinal position. Evangelism-in-Depth, originated by the Latin American Mission, has made all-out attempts to mobilize all Christians in countries selected for campaigns, particularly in Latin America. Ministry of special groups have brought evangelicals into close association and cooperation. This has been true of the work of the Pocket Testament League, Youth for Christ International, Gospel Recordings, and Missionary Aviation Fellowship.

b. Literature.

There are numerous examples of inter-mission and inter-church use of literature by evangelicals: e.g. The Christian Witness Press of the Overseas Missionary Fellowship, the Christian Literature Crusade, TEAM's Word of Life ministries, Evangelical Literature Overseas, Moody Literature Mission, Editorial Caribe of the Latin America Mission, Christian and Missionary Alliance publications, the Associated Evangelical publishers of Maracaibo.

c. Radio.

The missionary radio stations, such as ELWA, HCJB, PJA6, HLKX, FEBC, and others, provide time for the broadcasting of programs that will minister to a wide grouping of churches.

d. Training.

One of the oldest of the cooperative training institutes is the Union Bible Institute of the Republic of South Africa, a joint project of six missions. The Union Biblical Seminary of Yeotmal, India, also serves the interest of many evangelical groups. The Japan Christian College in Tokyo, Japan; the Far Eastern Bible Institute and Seminary in Manila; and the Latin America Bible Seminary in San José, Costa Rica, are each the responsibility of one mission, but serve wider church interests.

4. Sending Society Cooperation in the Homeland.

In the United States, there is the Evangelical Foreign Missions Association, the Interdenominational Foreign Mission Association, the Associated Missions of the ICCC. In Canada, a committee on missions of the Canadian Evangelical Fellowship is being formed. In Great Britain, the Evangelical Mission Association serves to unite evangelical groups. In Australia, the various states have Evangelical Mission Fellowships.

In North America, the IFMA and EFMA have joined forces for specific purposes, such as in the Evangelical Committee for Latin America, the Joint Asia Committee, Joint Africa Committee, the Africa Evangelical Office, and the Joint Europe Committee. The CAMEO Committee (Committee to Assist Missionary Education Overseas) has embarked on an ambitious project designed to greatly strengthen missionary training programs overseas. The Evangelical Missions Information Service, which publishes the Evangelical Missions Quarterly, is another example of EFMA-IFMA cooperation. There has also been joint sponsorship of the Summer Institute of Missions at Wheaton College and conferences on business administration.

While this listing of cooperative or joint action is extensive, it represents only a fraction of what could be told if the whole story were presented.

V. *Proposals for Active Evangelical Unity.*

There now exists a great number and variety of groups which

could reap great internal benefits by effective cooperation or amalgamation. This would provide a stronger witness for Christ on the field than is possible at the present time. The following practical steps are suggested for consideration:

1. Amalgamation or Absorption of Missions.

The Interdenominational Foreign Mission Association is facing the problems caused by the large number of small, independent missions. In Japan, for example there are 154 different missions at work, a majority of them with ten or less missionaries. The IFMA has initiated discussions to promote union where doctrinal emphasis and mission practice are compatible.

One plan already proposed would link sixteen missions, forming a society of over 800 missionaries, serving on 22 fields. The executive staff would total one-fourth of the combined staff of the sixteen separate missions. The elimination of waste on the field would be in proportion. The combined effort would certainly strengthen the work, provided, of course, that the same spiritual dedication remains.

2. Unifying Church Establishment.

In the area of church establishment there could be much more of the unifying of church groups which have been brought into being by mission organizations of like doctrine and polity. For example, in Taiwan where many evangelical missions are working without strict comity lines, there are often a number of churches in one town. In the smaller towns it should be possible to channel the fruit of evangelism of several missions into one church and in the larger towns or districts to have only one church name. This has been done to a limited degree in Tokyo and Aomori, Japan.

3. Coordinated Training Programs.

Bible institutes have proliferated to the point of absurdity in certain countries. The whole training program would be tremendously strengthened by coordinated or cooperative action in this field.

4. Adaptability of Correspondence Courses.

Many individual missionaries or missions are preparing correspondence courses where existing courses could easily be used.

5. Unifying Field Ministries.

The outstanding difficulty in the way of efficiency in field ministries is the multiplication of organizations. With more than two hundred sending societies and with many missions having several fields, there are often small groups of missionaries of various societies working in the same areas. Something needs to be done about this.

6. Specialized Functions in Missions.

Much duplication of effort can be avoided by agreements which provide that certain special ministries such as publication offices and schools be operated by one mission with their services being made available to other evangelical groups. There are present examples of successful arrangements of this kind, for example:

> The Word of Life Press in Japan is the responsibility of one mission, but serves many.
>
> Evangelism-in-Depth is administered by the Latin American Mission, but its ministry includes many churches and missions.

This "chosen instrument" approach to unified effort simplifies administration and is usually more successful than simple cooperative efforts.

7. Cooperative Mission Projects.

Certain areas of work which can be cared for only through cooperative action should have much greater attention than at present.

a. The Evangelical Missions Information Service, for example, publishes the *Evangelical Missions Quarterly*, a periodical which has promise of being an instrument to shape mission thinking. EMIS can also serve to coordinate and disseminate vital missionary information. This project now realizes only 25% of its potential because of lack of interest.

b. CAMEO (Committee to Assist Missionary Education Overseas), a joint undertaking by committees of the EFMA and IFMA, can break the bottleneck in missionary education overseas if it gets beyond the committee stage. It needs a full-time director.

c. Evangelical Literature Overseas and Medical Assistance Programs (formerly part of Christian Medical Society) have blazed trails in the fields of missionary literature and missionary medicine to prove what can be done.

8. Coordination.

When cooperation procedures are not possible, it is still important to coordinate various types of mission activity; and committees for this purpose serve a useful purpose. An example of such coordination is the setting up of joint literature committees to confer on publication plans.

9. Church Fellowships.

While the establishment of independent, autonomous churches is the goal of many missions, it is belatedly evident that local Christians need and want fellowship. The forming of larger church fellowships within a district or a country will surely strengthen the witness of the churches. Such fellowships can include churches of varying origins having common adherence to evangelical doctrine and common or similar polity.

10. Inter-Association Coordination.

Continued cooperation by the IFMA and the EFMA in defined areas while maintaining their distinct organizations is recommended. The success of the Africa Evangelical office in furthering evangelical fellowship and in helping to safeguard the Gospel testimony from ecumenical inroads gives indication of possibilities for the future.

Conclusion.

The world of rapid mass communications, of revolution and an exploding population, cries out for the knowledge of Jesus Christ in a thousand ways. Our Lord prays that this world may see the unity which binds us to Himself and to one another. Our world cannot see the mystical bond that unites us, but it can understand love and fellowship and cooperation. Such a witness demands wise, resolute and Spirit-directed action by delegates to this Congress who have responsible positions in their own societies.

FOOTNOTES

1. John A. Mackay, Ecumenics, *The Science of the Church Universal* (New York: Prentice Hall, 1960), pp. 3-6.
2. Luke 2:1.
3. Eugene L. Smith, "The Conservative Evangelicals and the World Council of Churches," *Ecumenical Review* (January, 1963), p. 183.

4. J. Hudson Taylor, *Union and Communion* (The China Inland Mission, 1937).
5. The Apostles' Creed.
6. Romans 14:9.
7. Martin Lloyd-Jones, *The Basis of Christian Unity* (Grand Rapids: Wm. B. Eerdmans, 1965). The exposition of both John 17 and Ephesians 4 is more thoroughly developed in this book.
8. Ephesians 4:13, New English Bible.
9. Emile Gailliet, "An Ecumenical Self-Indictment," *Christianity Today* (July 5, 1963), p. 965.
10. *Unity in Mid-Career, An Ecumenical Critique* (K. R. Bridstow and W. D. Wagoner, eds., 1963).
11. Harold Lindsell, "Ecumenical Merger and Mission," *Christianity Today* (March 30, 1962). This article provided most of the analysis in this section.
12. *Ibid.*, quoted by Harold Lindsell.
13. Quoted by Robert Smith from *IFMA Missionary News* (March-April, 1965), data received for the year 1963.
14. *Op. cit.*, quoted by Harold Lindsell.
15. Quoted from a report of the Assembly by Kenneth L. Downing, circulated by the Africa Evangelical Office, Nairobi (1963).
16. Ernest Best, *One Body in Christ* (London: Society for the Propagation of Christian Knowledge, 1955), p. 8.
17. J. M. Kik, *Ecumenism and the Evangelical* (Philadelphia: Presbyterian and Reformed Publishing Company, 1958), pp. 100, 101.
18. Emil Brunner, *The Christian Doctrine of the Church, Faith and the Consummation* (Philadelphia: The Westminster Press, 1962), pp. 127, 128.
19. Romans 14:20.

CHAPTER 16

Mission—And Evaluating Methods

by Dr. H. Wilbert Norton

consultants:
The Reverend Linwood Barney, The Reverend Ralph Christensen, Dr. Harold Cook, The Reverend Sidney Langford, Mr. Lorne Sanny

This Congress, having worldwide representation and studying contemporary issues, should ask itself two questions: (1) Should evangelical missions continue to use present methods in the missionary witness of the Church, and (2) should a concerted effort be made to evaluate the procedures and methods currently used throughout the world?

In the early 1930's one such evaluation was made through the Layman's Foreign Missions Inquiry, as seen in its report, *Rethinking Missions*.[1] At that time interest in world missions was falling off. The younger post-war leadership emphasized the social gospel and advocated student representation at the Geneva Peace Conference. The result was doubt, lack of confidence, and distrust in the validity of the Great Commission.

The authors of *Rethinking Missions* further clouded the basic issue. In the words of Henry P. Van Dusen:

> It appears to have conveyed the impression that there were a few, probably a very few, individual instances of Christian work abroad which merited continuance; but that missions by and large were of dubious value and validity, hardly justifying well-considered support. . . .[2]

Our present concern, however, is neither to duplicate the Layman's Inquiry nor to evaluate contemporary missions with a view to vindicating the existence of the evangelical, worldwide witness to Christ. Currently a great host of volunteers have demonstrated their interest in overseas service. The great Urbana missionary conventions, sponsored by the Inter-Varsity Christian Fellowship and the Student Foreign Missions Fellowship, together with thousands of evangelical churches throughout the United States and other parts of the world, continue to provide hundreds of volunteers for evangelical missions. The 1964 Urbana convention numbered more than 7,000 students and missionaries collectively studying the Bible, reviewing world needs, and dedicating themselves to the call of God to a worldwide service with Christ.

Our concern is to be seen, rather, in the questions, Are the methods used producing maximum results consonant with the continuing Biblical basis of mission and in proper proportion to the numbers sent and to the efforts expended? To answer this question, we must consider what we are trying to do and how we are attempting to realize our basic goal.

I. *The Basics of Mission.*

The Biblical view, foundational to the objective of this Congress, insists that each man must confess Jesus Christ and receive the forgiveness of sins and the new life of righteousness by faith.

1. *The New Evangelism.*

The man-to-man presentation of Christ to seekers and non-seekers alike is not the Christian mission as conceived by Canon Max Warren, former secretary of the Church Missionary Society. To him, salvation is the general salvation of mankind, a universalism.

> . . . The great end to which creation is moved by the will of God is ". . . the redeeming of all the myriad relationships of existence into a new heaven and a new earth, the city of God, the Body of Christ." The Biblical view of salvation is nothing if it is not the salvation of mankind and it is even that only within the restoration of all things.[3]

Canon Warren has clearly departed from the historic New Testament view of the Christian mission. Missionary methods for Warren are not established on statements of Scripture that men individually are lost, that justification is an act whereby

God accounts a believing sinner to be righteous and that a man thus becomes a new creature in Christ.[4]

The focus on the two antithetical conceptions of world evangelism is sharpened by Norman Goodall:

> One view of evangelism is reflected in the statement of the East Asia Christian Conference concerning the redemption "of the whole created world" and of evangelism which includes "an attempt of faith to discern Him in the social change of our nations." The other regards evangelism as exclusively concerned with Christ's redeeming work in the soul of the individual, with redemption *from* this world rather than *within* a social and temporal order which is itself an object of Christ's reconciling work.[5]

Goodall's reference to the East Asia Conference confirms clearly the official attitudes aligned with the "new look" of world missions and evangelism in its neo-universalism and social concern. The "new evangelism" of contemporary liberal ecumenism, geared to a secular world in the post World War II period, is universalistic. The ecumenist missionaries (nonprofessional lay workers)

> . . . will stand in the midst of all the vicissitudes of life and steadily do what is necessary to further the civilizing process. This is the new evangelism for a secular world and is utterly necessary if the church is to be the self-conscious people of God in this present age.[6]

In a happy inclusivism in the ecumenical awakening we are told that

> . . . the church has been forging a brand new functional image of itself as mission to the world . . . the image of the people of God as perpetual revolutionaries in the human drama of civilization, those who give their lives wherever human need is present to forge new structures for human existence on behalf of all mankind.[7]

The larger American denominations within contemporary ecumenism have embraced this notable change in the mission of the church while the smaller conservative missionary societies hold to Goodall's second concept of individualistic soul-redemption.

Franklin H. Littell contrasts the waning willingness in Christian mission of the larger denominations with the vibrant missionary spirit of the "smaller, fundamentalistic and pentecostal groups" which he calls "a third type" alongside Roman Catholic and classical Protestant churches.[8] But he admits that progress in worldwide missions stems from the groups literally obedient to the Great Commission,

> Thus the expanding edge of Christianity is not only staked out by the Free Churches rather than the state churches, but—to a remarkable degree—by small restitutionist groups which count the gift of the Spirit and/or the process of sanctification conclusive evidences of the existence of the True Church. They attempt to recapitulate the mission and style of the Early Church, with literal obedience to the Great Commission one of the prime points.[9]

2. *Jesus Christ the Redemptive Message and Method.*

But what is our view? Simply that the success or failure of any missionary method—technical device, linguistic development, or innovation in evangelism—must be measured against the timeless standard of Jesus Christ. The effectiveness of a method is in direct proportion to its relationship to Jesus Christ. God's method is uniquely Jesus Christ (I Timothy 2:5; John 3:16) who surrendered Himself in obedience "unto death" (Philippians 2:8) in identification with man in his need. The triumph of God's unique method is attested by Christ's resurrection and exaltation,

> Wherefore God also hath highly exalted Him, and given Him a name which is above every name. . . . Jesus Christ is Lord, to the glory of God the Father (Philippians 2:9, 11b).

Christ alone by His death, His resurrection, and His ascension has unique and ultimate authority in establishing missionary methods. He constitutes the basic principle and criterion of all missionary methodology.

3. *Christ and the Authority of the Old Testament.*

Christ pointed to the fulfillment of the authoritative Word of God, the Old Testament. It provided Him with His Messianic goal and integrated His earthly life with God's purpose (John

17). At the moment of Peter's confession, Jesus quickly interpreted to the disciples His Messianic goal:

> how that He must go unto Jerusalem and suffer many things of the elders and chief priests and scribes, and be killed and be raised again the third day (Matthew 16:21).

Immediately before His death Christ gave an accounting of His stewardship of time and energies expended in His ministry, declaring openly to His Father, "I have given unto them the words which Thou gavest Me" (John 17:8). His conscious union with the Father made it imperative that He communicate fully the Father's words, the written Word, interpreted in the light of His Messianic *diaconate* (service).

Again, the totality of the meaning of the Old Testament for Him motivated Jesus as He approached the threshold of Gethsemane.

> For I say unto you, that this that is written must yet be accomplished in Me, and He was reckoned among the transgressors: for the things concerning me have an end (Luke 22:37).

Christ declared the ultimate significance of the written Word of God after His resurrection.

> All things must be fulfilled, which were written in the law of Moses, and in the prophets, and in the psalms, concerning me. Then opened He their understanding that they might understand the Scriptures, and said unto them, Thus it is written, and thus it behooved Christ to suffer, and to rise from the dead the third day, and that repentance and remission of sins should be preached in His name among all nations, beginning at Jerusalem. And ye are witnesses of these things (Luke 24:44-48).

Jesus' post-resurrection overview of the Old Testament emphasizes the centrality of the written revelation. The Holy Spirit at Pentecost empowered the disciples whose collective mind (reason and understanding) had been "opened" only a short time earlier by the resurrected Lord through His interpretation of the Old Testament Scriptures—the objective revelation! A sense of destiny, an eschatological drive, motivated them with the urgency of men involved in the climax of all history.

4. *The Apostolic Witness.*

God and the apostles witnessed concurrently at Pentecost: the Holy Spirit in the sound and the fire; the apostles in the languages of the nations. Thereby they announced the historic fact of "Jesus of Nazareth, a man approved of God among you" (Acts 2:22) who "hath poured forth this, which ye see and hear." Joel the prophet had declared Pentecost would occur. David had announced the resurrection of Christ. The phenomenon of Pentecost was derived from the phenomenon of Calvary. Both phenomena emerged from the written Word of God.

The witness of the early Church succeeded because it was the witness to the redeeming Lord documented by the written Word. The written Word, the changeless Word in the living Christ (Hebrews 13:8), and the eternally divine Spirit of God lead us to understand that the available supernatural dynamic of the believing church today is continuous with that of the early Church. Dr. Eugene Nida speaks of the supernaturalism of Christian witness:

> The revelation of God in Jesus Christ and as recorded in the Scriptures is uniquely supernatural, for its source is none other than God Himself. . . . Only by the supernatural activity of the Spirit can men possibly experience for themselves the transforming grace of God. . . . The encounter men have is not merely with an idea, but with God Himself. Hence the communication in which we are involved is not only supernatural in content (in that it is derived from God); it is also supernatural in process, for the Spirit of God alone makes this message to live within the hearts of men.[10]

The unity of the church is the unity of living submission to the headship of Jesus Christ, communicating life through believers. Dr. Nida continues,

> This communication of life by life is primarily through the life of the Son, given that man might be reconciled to God. But in a secondary sense this life is communicated by the life of the Church, which is "to complete that which is lacking in the afflictions of Christ" (Colossians 1:24), as epistles "read of all men" (II Corinthians 5:18), called of God to be identified with men in order that "at the name of Jesus

every knee should bow in heaven and on earth and under the earth, and every tongue should confess that Jesus Christ is Lord, to the glory of God the Father" (Philippians 2:10, 11).[11]

5. *Christ, the Head.*

Essentially the basic of Christian mission is grateful recognition of the working of the living Lord as Head of His Body, the Church, in fulfillment of His promise, "I will build my Church" (Matthew 16:18).

6. *The Unity of the Body, the Church.*

The primitive unity of the church was based on Scriptures, individually accepted as authoritative, and on a personal relationship to the living Lord in corporate fellowship with the Head of the Body directing the building of His Church. In the context of the "fellowship *(koinonia)* of the Gospel" (Philippians 1:5) the exhortation of the apostle Paul in Philippians 2 is to likemindedness (2:2) and Christ-mindedness (2:5). Only Christ-minded (Christo-phrenic) witnessing results in the universal exaltation of Christ as Lord. The controlling mind of Christ, as Head of the Body (Ephesians 4:15), directs the collective service of the members of the Body in conscious submission to Him, united with Him by faith in His death and resurrection (Romans 6; Galatians 2:20; Colossians 3:1,3).

Collectively the apostolic, Christ-minded Body, composed of multi-gifted members, was a redemptive unit under God and in the Spirit, coordinated by the Head, Jesus Christ (Romans 12:3-8; I Corinthians 12:1-31; Galatians 3:28; Ephesians 4:1-16; Colossians 1:18). The compelling continuity of Christ, the same yesterday, today, and forever (Hebrews 13:8) carries particular meaning for the contemporary evangelical church.

The supernaturalism of the Christ-minded witness of Peter in Acts 1 and 2 was a characteristic of all the apostolic witness of the first century. Stephen preached Christ's post-resurrection interpretation of the Old Testament as recorded in Acts 7. Paul's dramatic conversion to Christ occurred in the wake of Stephen's "new" interpretation of the Old Testament.

Paul's clear understanding of the Old Testament from the

viewpoint of Christ (Luke 24) re-oriented his thinking, his values, and his goals into a total Christ-minded life of commitment and sacrifice. In Acts 13 he initiated his Gentile ministry at Antioch of Pisidia by calling Moses, the psalms, and the prophets to witness both to the suffering and the death of Christ and to His resurrection. Meanwhile, he identified himself with the fulfillment of the third prophetic element of the interpretation, "that repentance and remission of sins should be preached in his name among all the nations" (Luke 24:47). He wrote his epistles to churches of believing Christians, and Christians in Jerusalem, Antioch, Asia, Galatia, Macedonia, Achaia, and Rome shared the evangel with Greeks and Romans, barbarians and Jews during the first century of Christian witness.

John speaks clearly of the same meaning of Christ's interpretation to witness in his Gospel when Philip finds Nathaniel and declares, "we have found him, of whom Moses in the law, and the prophets, wrote, Jesus of Nazareth" (John 1:45).

We can conclude that the missionary thrust of the early church received its *dunamis* from the Christ-minded interpretation of the Old Testament Word. The Spirit-given Word witnesses in total commitment through individual identification with Christ in His death and motivating resurrection. *The inspired Scriptures became the inspiring Scriptures* identifying believers with the living Lord and motivating them to bring unbelievers into an identifying relationship with Him also.

II. *The Basics of Evaluation.*

1. *The Church, a Social Organism.*

The church is composed of redeemed men socially related to one another. Wherever human beings gather, relationships are established. These relationships must be understood. Leadership develops. Goals, aims, and objectives become defined. Organization evolves. Methods are formulated. So also in the church.[12]

Our present concern is with methods in the missionary outreach. Are missionary methods keeping up with the times— world need, technological developments, restricted finances and inflation, and developing national churches? Ordway Tead, long a specialist in the management of philanthropic, humanitarian, and religious organizations, suggests periodic evaluation and examination. He says:

> Hardening of the arteries is a danger of the middle years which can only be withstood as organization leaders give special thought to the problems which age brings. Over centralized authority, confused responsibilities, a sense of vested rights in jobs, lessened clarity and certainty about the central aims . . . the dwindling interest of financial supporters . . . bedevil the executives of organizations . . . which no amount of sheer good will and moral fervor can of themselves solve.[13]

It seems reasonable that evaluation and appraisal is the valid function of church and missionary societies in their worldwide outreach.

2. *Church Objectives.*

First, the aims of the missionary organization must be clearly defined and understood. Primary Biblical objectives of evangelism, church planting, Bible translating, and teaching should be stated. Secondary aims relate to educational, medical, agricultural, and vocational programs.

Each field council also needs to state its local objectives to assure the active missionary staff of its aims, thus creating the kind of *esprit de corps* necessary for harmonious prayer fellowship and corporate achievement.

Tead reminds us that objectives need to be evaluated periodically.

> . . . the need for revaluation is perennial . . . the danger always is . . . to get so immersed in carrying on the secondary efforts that they have not the means nor the time nor even the inclination for the main drive. The means thus become the end.[14]

Overwhelming changes are occurring in many mission lands after national independence—political unrest, realignment of church leadership from mission to national personnel, urgent appeals from governments for help in secondary education, social and economic trials and developments and their significance to the church. These changes are some of the reasons objectives and aims must be evaluated in this period of expansion of the church. Primary aims may need to be redefined. Secondary aims may need to be eliminated or adjusted. The danger always exists of "majoring in the minors." Donald A. McGavran warns of substituting secondary objectives for the primary goal of church planting and growth.

Specialized activities of modern missions can readily appear to be sufficient ends. . . . They thus lead churchmen astray. . . . Are these activities, then, a mistake? Let us be clear at this crucial point. The establishment of an organization solely to help the hungry grow more food in a given district may be good. What is bad is the leap of theory arising out of this separate organization which affirms that growing more food for the population is in itself as important as discipling. From right activities men leap to wrong theories.[15]

3. *Leadership.*

Leadership determines objectives. Leadership is the activity of getting people to work together to achieve a common goal. The Apostle Paul recognized the meaning of true leadership: "And the things which thou hast heard of me among many witnesses the same commit thou to faithful men, who shall be able to teach others also (II Timothy 2:2).

Three guiding principles undergird the basics of evaluation: (1) The service of redeemed men is essential to the spread of the Gospel universally. (2) The resources—human energies and availability of finances—are severely limited. (3) The restrictions of time demand the most expeditious use of the hours and moments to share Christ with the world of men for whom He died.

Questions must be raised and answers faced realistically by all. Some of the questions are: What planning is currently underway with a view to achieving our global goal—in our individual mission societies, field churches and mission councils, and through collective efforts in the IFMA and EFMA? Have we organizational structures in our societies and churches which lend themselves to the greatest economies in the use of human and financial resources while freeing the greatest amount of spiritual energies in the direction of our primary goal? Have we learned to define the roles and delegate authority trustingly and confidently in the development of the national churches (I Corinthians 4:17; Exodus 18:13-26; II Timothy 1:11; 2:13)? Are we teaching our colleagues how to complement one another in achieving our objectives? Are the processes of decision-making and problem analysis adequately outlined for implementation by those involved? What do we understand by communication and what kind of communication exists between us and the various groups and personalities, organizations, and governments involved in our fields of service? Are we providing the motivation needed by the members of the Body of Christ among whom and with whom we work? (II Timothy 2:10). Does the selectivity and development of our missionary personnel reflect the demands of our times (II Timothy 3:10-14)? Is there adequate evaluation and control of activities, encouraging self-criticism and self-improvement with the ultimate goal in view (II Timothy 4:5-8)?

4. *Cooperative Efforts.*

Our redemptive experience of Jesus Christ constrains us to seek the highest level of joint efforts in proclaiming the Gospel. Worldwide recognition is being given to the unity of evangelical effort in New Testament evangelism. Cooperative efforts in literature, pastoral training and teacher education, hospital and medical work have increased greatly in the years since World War II. Nevertheless, there are many areas where cooperation can supersede duplication of work, especially in leadership training with the younger churches.

Business procedures, accounting practices and mechanized office activities are areas where groups of mission boards should evaluate the economics of their current administrative operations. It is reasonable to think that many boards could establish coordinated programming to handle their gift accounts and their mailings. We have not yet begun to ask the basic questions regarding methods of improving our business procedures in the light of the technological developments available to us.

Complaints are commonly heard about the paucity of missionary candidates. The question might be asked, "Have mission boards seriously evaluated their recruiting methods?" If so, what criteria have been employed? There are dedicated Christian students who would respond to the "call" if the basic information were communicated to them. No missionary physician would be expected to volunteer for missionary medical service if there were no opportunity for a medical doctor to serve in a specific area. Christian teachers likewise need basic information regarding opportunities to teach in the various church and mission schools. Qualified missionary pastors could be secured also if told of the opportunities.

Are methods of recruiting candidates commensurate with the pressures of other opportunities for service which also demand a hearing? Would area workshops for pastors, Sunday school superintendents and local church youth workers, conducted by groups of missionary societies, aid in recruitment? How do Sunday school materials and national Christian youth and student organizations lend themselves to recruitment education? In what age-groups can the most effective recruitment take place? How can any of these programs be used most effectively by the younger churches?

Another area in missionary relations which needs some clarification is the place of the mission board in rehabilitating missionaries who cannot return to the field. The Reverend Ian M. Hay, Home Director of the Sudan Interior Mission, undescores the seriousness of the casualty problem:

> Missions must look inwardly and seek to determine their own failures in such cases. . . . Mission organizations which have been raised up to help Christians fulfill their God-given commission must be very certain that they adequately select, prepare and utilize the talents of these consecrated young people. . . . This pinpoints the need for close scrutiny of all orientation procedures both for candidates and newly appointed missionaries. A missionary organization with slipshod procedures and no field orientation may be held responsible by God for casualties. It is no light thing to blunt the usefulness of one of God's tools through improper handling.[16]

Field methods center around the birth, growth and development of the church. But the demands for philanthropy are overwhelming. Donald McGavran states the issue succinctly,

> There are so many good things to do. . . . A decision to undertake one enterprise means leaving others crying for

action. Hence, intelligent decision requires both a clear-cut theory of missions which states the priorities; and constant measurement of achievements so that the theory believed to be God's will—and not some other which creeps in the back door—may be implemented.[17]

Are the evangelistic methods used in any one area effective? Can they be improved? Have church growth studies been made? Would an adapted form of Evangelism-in-Depth spark a new thrust in church planting? What anthropological factors in the culture lend themselves to evangelism and church growth? Are the resources of national leadership used to the maximum of their capabilities? Answers to these questions might set off a chain reaction in evangelism and church growth in many areas of the world.

Do the associated services of medicine, education, and specialized vocational and skill training on the various mission fields contribute to the growth of the church and its evangelistic outreach? Serious questions should be raised and studies made regarding the value and place of radio, TV, literature, and correspondence courses in their relationship to the churches of the areas where they are used.

Is the supernatural power of the risen Lord of the harvest claimed by faith on behalf of the efforts of His sent ones storming Satanic strongholds with the Gospel? Have we willfully neglected the fact that mission is a spiritual warfare? Have we forgotten II Corinthians 2:14, "Now thanks be unto God, which always causeth us to triumph in Christ, and maketh manifest through us the savor of His knowledge by us in every place"?

III. *Summary.*

Mission is the continuing flow of the life of Christ through His believing disciples in total identification with Him through the reconciling act of His atonement. Missions is reaching out to draw all men who will believe to faith in Christ as Saviour and into fellowship with the Lord as the Head of all believers in the Body of Christ.

The Church is a supernatural organism, created supernaturally of individuals supernaturally re-born of the Holy Spirit with a supernatural message transmitted by a supernatural revelation accepted as the authority of, and fulfilled by, the supernatural personality, Jesus Christ, who presently is the Head of the supernatural Body, the Church. Nevertheless, the church is also a social organism with earthly ties and relationships which must be developed and strengthened in the Spirit to fulfill its ministry.

Sanctified creativity under the guidance of the Holy Spirit will provide the balance needed in reconciling methods with objectives. Intensive and extensive reading must be carried out and the results communicated to the persons involved to assure effective trans-cultural communication of the Gospel. Language programs must be given serious professional evaluation to determine the effectiveness of present language learning techniques.

To some it would seem sacrilegious to suggest that time studies be made of some of the phases of missionary work, especially when missionaries are so greatly understaffed and overworked. In a day of short-term missionary involvement it is reasonable to believe that much more might be accomplished in evangelism and church planting by those qualified to do so if actual studies indicated the areas where short-term aid would materially assist in achieving primary goals.

Never has the urgency been greater. Never has the moment been more opportune. Never could failure be more catastrophic and calamitous for the Church and the nations.

Thus we are stirred to renewed surrender and commitment together in identification with the Lord and Head of the Body.[18] The apostle to the *ethnoi* stated it clearly, "It is God who worketh in you" (Philippians 2:13) echoing the Old Testament prophet, "by *my Spirit,* saith the Lord of hosts" (Zechariah 4:6).

FOOTNOTES

1. *Rethinking Missions: A Layman's Inquiry after One Hhundred Years* (W. E. Hocking, ed., New York: Harper Brothers, 1932).
2. Henry P. Van Dusen, *For the Healing of Nations,* p. 5.
3. Max Warren, *The Christian Mission, Challenge and Response* (New York: Morehouse Barlow Company, 1959), p. 115. Cf. J. A. T. Robinson, *In The End, God,* p. 89.
4. Romans 3:23; 5:12; 4:4, 16; 12:1,2; Ephesians 1:7; John 1:12; 3:36; II Corinthians 5:17-19; *et al.*
5. *New Frontiers of Christianity* (Norman Goodall and Ralph C. Raughley, Jr., eds., New York: Association Press), p. 151.

6. "International Evangelism," *Ecumenical Institute,* II:9.
7. *Ibid.,* p. 2.
8. Franklin Hamlin Littell, *From State Church to Pluralism* (Chicago: Aldine Publishing Company, 1962), p. 130.
9. *Ibid.*
10. Eugene Nida, *Message and Mission* (New York: Harper Brothers, 1960), pp. 228, 229.
11. *Ibid.,* p. 229.
12. David O. Moberg, *The Church as a Social Institution* (Englewood Cliffs, N. J.: Prentice-Hall, 1962), chapter 9: "The Church as a Missionary Institution at Home and Abroad." A well-documented study including the social influences and effects of missions.
13. Ordway Tead, *Democratic Administration* (New York: Harper Brothers, 1959), p. 7.
14. *Ibid.,* p. 40.
15. Donald A. McGavran, *How the Churches Grow* (New York: Friendship, 1959), pp. 74-76. The author defines "parallelism" in terms of methodological equalitarianism, all activities in general missionary work having an equal value in the work, "results in church establishment becoming merely one among many good tasks."
16. Ian M. Hay, "Orientation: Casualty Preventive," *Africa Now,* No. 23.
17. *Op cit.,* Donald A. McGavran, p. 148.
18. Stephen Neill, *The Unfinished Task* (London: Edinburgh House Press, 1958), p. 223. "The Gospel we bring to the world is the Gospel of hope because it is the Gosepl of the resurrection. But that Gospel has power only because the resurrection is the resurrection of the Crucified."

CHAPTER 17

Mission—And Social Concern

by Dr. Horace L. Fenton, Jr.

consultants:
The Reverend Art Johnston, Dr. Rufus Jones,
The Reverend William A. Mahlow, Dr. Merrill C. Tenney

The shortest word in the title of this paper has unusual significance. Here there is no attempt to equate mission and social concern, or to debate their relative importance, or to define their relationship. But at least the conjunction "and" indicates that such a relationship does exist.

On occasion, we evangelicals have treated the elements of mission and social concern as though they were inevitably in tension and inherently antithetic. There is nothing new about this, of course. Kathleen Heasman tells us that in the Victorian era there was a feeling among many evangelicals that a choice had to be made between evangelism and social concern.[1]

Timothy Smith finds many examples of this same kind of tension in mid-nineteenth century America. In those days, the American Tract Society faced the problem of how far to go in this realm. For years, its executive committee banned all mention of slavery in its publications because of the rule that the Society's tracts must be "calculated to receive the approbation of all evangelical Christians." A special committee appointed to investigate this policy decided "that the Society had every right and duty to publish against the *evils* of slavery, as distinct from the institution itself, or the mode of its abolition, or the question of communion with slaveholders. But the publishing committee professed themselves unable to find a manuscript which even on this point would meet the approval of all Christians!"[2]

Given these tensions in other periods of church history, it is doubly significant that in our day we are not necessarily faced with an 'either-or" choice here. Yet many in our circles persist in seeing an irreconcilable antithesis here. Almost twenty years ago, as Moberg points out, "Carl F. H. Henry noted that the redemptive gospel was once a world-changing message, but that it had been narrowed to a world-resisting message by an embarrassing divorce between individual salvation and community responsibility."[3]

While some see a real swing in our own day from such an isolationist viewpoint, there is still plenty of evidence that the basic issue remains unresolved among us. And there is equally strong evidence that few of us are adequately implementing what we claim to believe about the close relationship between mission and social concern. Our topic should therefore be one of lively concern to us.

I. *Reasons for Neglect of Social Concern by Evangelicals.*

We may well begin by noting some of the basic causes of the tendency to underemphasize social concern in evangelical circles. Undoubtedly, the strongest fear has been that of allowing some new emphasis to divert us from our primary mission of presenting salvation through Christ to those who are lost apart from Him. There is much evidence that such a deviation from the heart of the Gospel message *has* frequently taken place. The good too often becomes the enemy of the best, and anything which hinders or supersedes our preaching of redemption through Christ's atonement may well be part of Satan's strategy. The result of such departure from the central message has always been spiritual sterility.

It is not surprising that, seeing the weakness and sterility of the social emphasis and its seemingly inevitable tendency to usurp the place of a gospel of redemption, "evangelical Christianity reacted against the liberal Protestant concentration of effort in this area of concern by non-involvement."[4] We evangelicals need to be warned, as a recent article reminds us, by the experience of "that large segment (of the church) which has leaped ahead to social involvement but without a spiritual dynamic."[5]

Moreover, many fear that a strong emphasis on social concern tends to give undue emphasis to those very things which Scripture teaches are of secondary importance, thereby contradicting Christ's insistence that "a man's life consisteth not in the abundance of the things which he possesseth."[6] A leader in the ecumenical movement confesses that he sees more of a tension in the Scripture between the Christian and the world than most enthusiasts for social concern have dared to admit: "A simple positive affirmation of the world as good, or a simple injunction for the Church to become 'involved' in the world, is nowhere seen in the New Testament."[7]

Then, too, our reluctance to get involved in social concern may be due to our fear of wasting our time and energies on problems which have no solution. Also, we can all point out examples of individuals and groups who give strong emphasis to individual salvation, and little or no stress to the Christian's social responsibility—and who seem to enjoy an unusual measure of God's blessing on their ministry. By contrast, a like degree of fruitfulness seems conspicuously absent from the endeavors of some who major on social concern.

Perhaps, we tell ourselves, these people who are so insistent that we couple social concern with mission have failed to realize that the Gospel, faithfully presented, will inevitably produce the social results they are so concerned about. But note that the word "inevitably" as used here needs careful examination.

II. *The Pragmatic Results of our Suspicion of Social Concern.*

Many evangelicals seem to have concluded that while compassion and charity are certainly an important part of our message, this does not imply a deep sense of social responsibility on the part of the church. There are a few books which recount the social efforts of evangelicals in other ages, and a few more prophetic voices challenging us to involvement in our day, but not much else. The preaching from our evangelical pulpits is often almost exclusively of an other-worldly nature. As one evangelical observer notes, "Some evangelical pastors have, indeed, publicly preached and taught the dignity of the human race on the basis of creation and redemption, and have deplored cutting off any segment of the body of humanity. But in the matter of expounding the biblical principles of social justice . . . the evangelical churches ought to have been *in the vanguard*. . . . So Christianity suffered this defeat: many liberal and neo-orthodox spokesmen neglected biblical principles and transgressed community laws but responded existentially to the needs and rights of persons, while many conservative churches neglected principles and persons and pleaded only for legal proprieties and for the peace of the community church."[8]

And Moberg points out: "Christians who attempt to be neutral toward . . . social issues . . . are . . . saying . . . that their spiritual message is totally irrelevant to practical problems . . . [and] the attempt to be neutral through a policy of inaction also conveys, implicitly, an endorsement of the *status quo*."[9]

These are serious charges and they are not to be lightly dismissed. But fortunately, they do not tell the whole story. Many evangelicals today show a changed attitude toward these matters and recognize the importance of social concern as a manifestation of their obedience to Christ. For them, it is clearly mission *and* social concern, not mission *or* social concern.

III. *The Bases of a Revived Interest in our Social Responsibility.*

A careful re-examination of the scriptural teaching on the subject has led many evangelicals to feel that they have been unconsciously overlooking certain biblical emphases. We have come to realize anew that "the heritage of evangelical Christianity includes both Jesus' Sermon on the Mount and His delineation of the Good Samaritan, and Paul's account of civil government as an agent of justice."[10]

Our Lord's earthly life clearly teaches us that, He never minimized or ignored the physical needs of men. Our Lord gives us a new understanding of the nature of our witness. There is a deep sense in which "as Christ entered into human flesh, so the Christian must be at home in the world, not in some hidden way, not in a raid to 'take scalps,' but going 'native in all things save faith and morals,' in Auden's fine phrase."[11]

Then, too, we have been confronted afresh with the facts of church history, and have seen that there has not always been a divorce between these two elements, even among evangelicals. Miller reminds us that a concern for society's needs may be traced to the Reformation itself, and particularly to the work of Calvin and Luther.[12] He points out that in the antislavery struggle in our own country, many of those most concerned about slavery's evils were "orthodox revivalists in the more evangelical denominations."[13]

Heasman testifies that in the Victorian era, Evangelicals did far more social work than High Church, Roman Catholic, or Jewish groups.[14] These socially minded Evangelicals, she says, "were all agreed upon salvation by faith and the infallibility and overriding importance of the Scriptures."[15] They saw a real connection between salvation and social work, and both Finney and Moody stressed this connection.

F. B. Meyer, beloved Bible teacher, seems to have had a social dimension to his ministry that too many of us evangelicals have forgotten. Strongly influenced by Moody's emphasis on meeting men's social needs as part of a Gospel witness, Meyer opened an interdenominational chapel in Leicester as a center for social work (1874-1888), and "started a prison-gate mission, a home for friendless boys, a wood-chopping yard, and a window-cleaning brigade for the unemployed. It was a common sight in Leicester at that time to see carts with 'F. B. Meyer, firewood merchant' inscribed on the side, or to meet men engaged in window cleaning with 'F. B. Meyer' on their hats."[16]

We are also learning that, while the faithful preaching of the Gospel has social effects, these results do not necessarily follow as an inevitable, automatic consequence. The insistence of Scripture is that the new life in Christ must be nurtured and disciplined. There are instances which can be cited of helpful social consequences which have been manifested upon the acceptance of the Gospel.[17, 18] But without discounting these instances, we need to remember that most new Christians need clear teaching by the Holy Spirit, through the church, of the far-reaching implications of their new-found faith.

We do not minimize the work of the Holy Spirit or the reality of regeneration when we insist that a Christian often needs to be *taught* what his attitudes and actions are to be in the new life, and how to express his love for God and men. It is all too possible for an individual believer to fail to see the connection between his love for God and his responsibility to his fellow men, unless it is pointed out to him—not just once, but many times.

There is an increasing awareness on the part of evangelicals that the relationship of mission and social concern is made doubly important by the revolutionary nature of the times in which we live. Nor can we long hope for a sympathetic hearing for the Gospel if men have reason to believe that we have no concern for their physical needs. In Latin America today a whole generation is turning away from religion and the church, because religion as they have known it has for four centuries been sublimely indifferent to many of the basic needs of the people. If, by our lack of social concern, we bring the same opprobrium upon the evangelical message, we shall have only ourselves to blame for the fact that we cannot get an audience. And we shall answer to God for the inadequate and inaccurate way in which we have represented Him.

Ruben Lores sounds a clarion call: "The social order is transitory, but we as individuals and the churches as institutions form an essential part of this order. Our destiny is inseparably linked to the here and now of our time and place. . . . The worldly order is transitory. But this is no excuse for not acting creatively."[19] Any evangelism which ignores social concern is by its nature an incomplete and unscriptural evangelism, and it will likely end up by being an unheeded evangelism.

IV. *Some Guidelines for Mission and Social Concern.*

In the first place, any program of social action must point men to—not away from—the central message of redemption through the blood of Christ. It is no favor to feed a man, without seeking an opportunity to point him to the Bread of Life, or to meet all his physical needs without facing him with the fact that his spiritual needs are infinitely more real and more significant—and that Jesus Christ alone can meet them.

George Webber has an arresting word for us here: "Jesus fed the hungry with food, but He reminded them of their deeper hunger that bread alone could not fill. Thus compassion for those in need is supplemented with the kind of comprehension that is concerned with more than the immediate problem. . . . Christ, not all the human schemes put together, is finally sufficient. To Christ, not to their program to help drug addicts, men must point. It is His healing and love they mediate."[20]

In the second place, therefore, our expression of social concern must provide, wherever possible, for a spoken witness to Christ, recognizing the incompleteness and consequent inadequacy of nonverbal witness.

Webber writes: "I would suggest that the congregation as such should enter primarily into tasks of service and obedience that give some opportunity of witnessing to the Lord who directs them there."[21] The whole point is that, because we desire the best for the one to whom we minister, we long that our expression of social concern shall be an introduction to Jesus Christ, who can meet their needs in a way and to an extent never possible to us.

Thirdly, we must make sure that our efforts do not arouse idealistic and unscriptural expectations. What we do must be an expression, not only of the love of God, but of the biblical revelation concerning the nature of man, and of the continuing consequences of sin in the world. We identify ourselves gladly, as servants of Christ, with the struggles for a just social order, at the same time remembering—and pointing out—the fact that man's highest hopes in this realm will be realized, not through any man-made institution, but only by Christ at His coming.

Fourthly, our desire to do good in the name of Christ should not lead us into wasteful competition with secular agencies. Berkhof's word is timely: "The unique task (of the church) is to be the help of the helpless. . . . When others do it as well or even better her service has lost its significance as a symbol of God's restoration. . . . The first task of the church is to keep her eyes open and . . . to have the courage, not only to take up new tasks but also (which is perhaps more difficult) to give up forms of help which have lost their witness character."[22]

V. *Three Practical Demonstrations of the Relationship between Mission and Social Concern.*

In a number of countries of Latin America, evangelical missions have expressed their social concern in recent years through the sending out of "Good Will Caravans" to needy areas. These caravans have been composed of teams of specialists—doctors, nurses, dentists, literacy experts, agricultural engineers, children's workers, and evangelists. The work of these caravans has been praised by government officials and by the needy themselves, who have rejoiced in the thoroughgoing interest displayed by evangelicals in *all* their needs—both physical and spiritual.

The saving power of Christ has been amply seen in these efforts. The caravans could be called a real Christian witness, even if evangelistic results were limited, but the fact of the matter is that scores of souls have been won to Christ through this medium. The Holy Spirit has been able to move hearts made tender by the love shown to them. And it is safe to assume that many of these people would have been reached *in no other way.*

Here, too, is visible evidence of the unity of the Body of Christ. The caravans are a cooperative enterprise, carried on by Christians of many different denominations, who by the love of Christ are constrained to work together. This fact is not lost upon the needy ones. This is not compromise; it is putting the Gospel of Christ and human need before secondary distinctives; it is proclaiming the Gospel, by word and deed, *together.*

Another form of social ministry which has been greatly blessed in Latin America has been the promotion, by evangelical forces, of literacy campaigns. These campaigns bear a similar witness to that of the caravans. In addition, they testify to our recognition that the economic level of a people is directly related to the literacy factor, and to the readiness of evangelicals to do something more than just hope and pray that the wretched lot of the poor may be improved. The ability to read the Word of God is a priceless thing, and literacy campaigns are a practical expression of this conviction.

Evangelicals are also beginning to enter more fully into relief programs. These, carefully organized and controlled, are not only a legitimate but also an essential demonstration of Christian social concern. Admittedly, this is a most difficult area of missionary service, replete with built-in problems. But we dare not allow ourselves to be paralyzed into inactivity. For one thing, we say that any legitimate concern of a needy person is a concern of ours, because the love of Christ constrains us—and that we reject unscriptural distinctions as to what is spiritual and what is physical. Moreover, we testify that the gifts God has bestowed on us in such abundance are gifts of His grace, meant to be shared, not hoarded or selfishly enjoyed. Then, too, we are telling men that their secondary needs are not unimportant.

We say, too, that while we fear—and will do anything to avoid—the making of "rice Christians," there are some things we fear even more: chief among them, the danger of shutting our hearts to those whose need is heavy on the heart of Christ. We fear the danger of cutting ourselves off, in an unscriptural way, from the very world Christ came to save. As one author has pointed out, there is a danger of talking too freely and too lightly about "rice Christians." He reminds us that only Christians who have never been hungry can so speak."[23]

This whole area of social concern, and its relationship to mission, is a very sensitive one. There is always the danger of going to extremes. But the scriptural alternative to these extremes is *not* to do nothing. We dare not allow our fears to paralyze us into inactivity.

Lesslie Newbigin points out that, "The preaching of the Gospel and the service of men's need are equally authentic and essential parts of the Church's responsibility. But neither is a substitute for the other. No amount of service, however expert and however generous, is a substitute for the explicit testimony to Jesus Christ. . . . There is no equivalent to the Name of Jesus. But equally, the preaching of that Name will be empty, if he who speaks it is not willing to deal honestly and realistically with the issues that his hearers have to face."[24]

We have, as evangelicals, something unique to bring to the realm of mission and social concern. There are, to be sure, many unanswered questions, many unsolved problems. But there are great rewards, too, here and hereafter. And the price of failure, brought about by presenting an incomplete, irrelevant Gospel, is *very* high.

FOOTNOTES

1. Kathleen Heasman, *Evangelicals in Action: An Appraisal of Their Social Work in the Victorian Era,* Geoffrey Bles, 1962, pp. 19, 20.
2. *Ibid.,* pp. 193, 194.
3. David O. Moberg, *Inasmuch* (Grand Rapids: Wm. B. Eerdmans, 1965), p. 5, referring to Carl F. H. Henry, *The Uneasy Conscience of Modern Fundamentalism* (Grand Rapids: Wm. B. Eerdmans, 1947).
4. Carl F. H. Henry, "Evangelicals in the Social Struggle," *Christianity Today* (October 8, 1965), p. 4.
5. "The Church Involved in a World in Crisis," unsigned article in leaflet, *The Evangelical Imperative* (National Association of Evangelicals, 1965).
6. Luke 12:15.
7. Father Paul Verghese, *Consultation Digest* (Denmark: World Council of Churches, Division of Inter-Church Aid, Refugee and World Service, World Consultation, 1962), pp. 19, 21.
8. Carl F. H. Henry, *Aspects of Christian Social Ethics* (Grand Rapids: Wm. B. Eerdmans, 1964), pp. 122, 123.
9. Moberg, *op. cit.,* p. 14.
10. Henry, "Evangelicals in the Social Struggle," p. 3.
11. George W. Webber, *The Congregation in Mission* (New York: Abingdon Press, 1964), p. 138.
12. Robert Moats Miller, *American Protestantism and Social Issues, 1919-1939* (Chapel Hill: University of North Carolina Press, 1958), p. 3.
13. *Ibid.,* p. 11.
14. Heasman, *op. cit.,* p. 13.
15. *Ibid.,* p. 16.
16. *Ibid.,* pp. 57, 58.
17. In a letter to the author of this paper, Dr. Merrill C. Tenney, Dean of Wheaton College Graduate School, cites the fact that "in Viet Nam, in some of the tribes' villages in which the majority became Christians, . . . sanitary control and hygienic care followed almost automatically without instruction from the missionaries."
18. In a letter to the author of this paper, Rev. Arthur Johnston, the Evangelical Alliance Mission's field chairman in France, reports that "within twenty or thirty years thousands of gypsies in France have been transformed by the Gospel from a stealing, dirty, illiterate people to clean respectable, honest, working (and evangelizing) citizens." And this has been accomplished through the ministry of Pentecostal groups who have *not* laid formal stress on social concern. He also points out that in TEAM's work, "after only ten years in Orly, the social progress among these Christians in a poorer communistic suburb is appreciable. The influence is beginning to be felt in the community—where the mayor had all but given up in despair. Yet our ministry is primarily 'church-planting.'"
19. From a syllabus of a course on "Church and World," taught by Ruben Lores in the Seminario Biblico Latinoamericano, San José, Costa Rica.
20. Webber, *op. cit.,* pp. 154, 155.

21. *Ibid.*, pp. 175, 176.
22. *Ibid.*, pp. 175, 176, quoted from H. Berkhof, *op. cit.*, pp. 29-31.
23. Eugene Carson Blake, quoting D. T. Niles, in *Consultation Digest*, p. 56.
24. "From the Editor," *International Review of Missions* Vol. LIV, No. 216, (October, 1965), p. 422.

CHAPTER 18

Mission—And a Hostile World

by The Reverend Alfred Larson

consultants:
The Reverend W. Elwyn Davies, Dr. Wesley Duewel,
The Reverend Douglas Percy, The Reverend Kermit Zopfi,
Dr. Arthur F. Glasser

Introduction: The Church Today.

The Christian Church faces graver threats today than in any previous generation in its total history. Never have so many hostile forces been arrayed against it.

At this moment, in various parts of the world, the Church's very right to exist and propagate its message is being hotly challenged. More Christians have been put to death in the last three decades than in any comparable period since Pentecost. Church history witnesses to dark periods in the past when whole sections of the Church were obliterated by persecution. It also records how churches destroyed themselves through tolerating unbelief, syncretistic tendencies, and worldliness within their ranks. In the worldwide Church today, there is much evidence pointing to the possibility of history repeating itself.

Almost 40% of the world's population is under Communist control (up from 8% in 1940). The new nationalism of Africa and Asia is uniformly hostile to the supra-national loyalty which Christ expects His people to hold toward one another. Ancient paganism in 20th century resurgence, as indicated by the increasing growth and militancy of the ethnic religions, is likewise exclusivistic. Neo-Romanism stirs and makes plans for a vast increase in its missionary outreach, especially in Latin America. Secularism with its "God is dead" theology and "new morality" ethic is contemptuously permeating Protestantism.

Within evangelical Protestantism there is also a strange hostility toward Biblical discipleship. Pastors seem reluctant to press upon their congregations the claims of sacrificial stewardship, earnest intercession, and full time service. Christian parents tend to discourage their children from missionary service. More oppressive than Communism and more stifling than secularism and materialism, however, is the spiritual deadness that seems to smother the Church. It seems to have lost its differentness, its buoyancy, its outgoing concern for men. It is harassed by its enemies, within and without. It is surrounded by a hostile world.

I. *Hostility: The Spiritual Dimension.*

Why the tension of these times? Whence the menacing challenges to the very life and existence of the Church? How to triumph in mission in the midst of these enemies?

1. *The "World".*

When man sinned in the Garden of Eden, he deliberately forfeited any further right to the divine image and likeness. He responsibly chose an existence separate from God. In so doing, he lost his freedom and came under the control of the Tempter.

After the Fall the human race—now children of wrath and of the devil—entered upon an existence of ceaseless, restless searching for something to fill the void created when God was displaced from their hearts and lives. They became absorbed in creating a world system that would bring meaning to life. Energized by Satan they created what the Bible calls *kosmos*, "the world." Admittedly, the world is imposing and powerful. It is cultured and elegant. But it is also filled with selfishness, greed, violence, tensions and rivalries. It only is held together in any real crisis by either the display or exercise of armed force.

Arndt and Gingrich have summarized the meaning and usage of *kosmos* as it appears in the New Testament and in early Christian literature:

> The world and everything that belongs to it is at enmity with God, . . . The *kosmos* stands in opposition to God and hence is incapable of knowing God and is excluded from

> Christ's intercession. Neither Christ nor His own belong in any way to the world. Rather Christ has chosen them out of the world, even though for the present they must still live in the world. All the trouble that they must undergo because of this means nothing compared with the victorious conviction that Christ and the believers with Him have overcome the world and that it is doomed to pass away.

It is in the context of this world the Church is called on to carry out its worldwide mission.

2. *The "Prince of This World".*

There is a "mystery of lawlessness" (II Thessalonians 2:7) behind all the wicked rulers who think they dominate the human scene. The Apostle Paul spoke of "principalities . . . the powers . . . the world rulers of this present darkness . . . the spiritual hosts of wickedness in the heavenly places" (Ephesians 6:12, RSV) as real and active, though working behind the scenes. Satan is the directing head (Matthew 4:8,9; John 12:31). His over-riding concern is that mankind not respond to God's gracious offer of salvation in Christ.

Satanic hostility to the worldwide mission of the Church, therefore, is going to manifest itself in many ways. He will manipulate even good human rulers as pawns on his international chessboard (Romans 13:1). Satan can more easily use wicked rulers to make war against God's people (Revelation 13:1-8). Within the Church itself Satan plants his tares. Indeed, Scripture traces all perversion of truth and godliness to the activity of Satan and his demonic host (I Timothy 4:1).

The subtle allurement of idolatry, found even within the Church, can be explained in terms of Satanic activity. Again and again the thrust of Scripture is that the Christians' only sure protection against all this despoiling of truth, is the Bible rightly understood and implicitly obeyed (Matthew 4:1-11; II Timothy 3:13; 4:4). It is in the presence of Satan and his hosts that the Church is called upon to carry out its worldwide mission.

3. *Christ's Call to War.*

When Christ called His disciples to Him, He "bid them come and die." He called them to lives of self-repudiation, self-denial.

This meant servanthood, bearing the yoke, and "learning obedience" by suffering (Matthew 11:29; Hebrews 5:8).

Apostolic service in the New Testament involved "suffering in passion for the perfection of the Church and the accomplishment of its mission." On the one hand the apostles labored in service and travailed in prayer for the growth and maturation of their fellow Christians (Galatians 4:19; I Corinthians 12:26,27). They became a spectacle to men. The Cross they proclaimed they willingly bore. The flame in their hearts set other hearts aglow.

Some of the most profound passages in the New Testament reflect this intimate association between conflict and mission, suffering and mission (e.g., Colossians 1:24; 2:1). Apparently it is impossible to be spiritually fruitful without embracing this truth. This means that the hostility of the world is but the necessary context in which these spiritual principles can be implemented, to the glory of God and the blessing of mankind. The Apostle Paul admonished young Timothy as follows: "Take your share of hardship, like a good soldier of Christ Jesus. A soldier on active duty will not let himself be involved in civilian affairs; he must be wholly at his commanding officer's disposal" (II Timothy 2:3,4, NEB). The responsible Christian today can only conclude that serving Christ will inescapably involve him in a ceaseless spiritual struggle. He should be ashamed of neither Christ nor His calling to mission. He should glorify God. He is following in the steps of Jesus Christ.

II. *Hostility: Some Representative Problems.*

1. *Mission—and Nationalism.*

Since World War II approximately one billion people have gained their political independence. Almost 60 new nations have been formed, and 50 colonial territories still await attaining nationhood (31 within the dismantled empire of Great Britain).[1] Woodrow Wilson's call for the self-determination of all peoples has certainly not gone unheeded. In the tensions and conflicts of today's world the nationalist can easily lose his sense of logic and proportion. Racial pride and a warped sense of cultural superiority can transform his patriotism into something fiercely self-assertive, what Toynbee calls "the worship of collective human power within local limits." As such it easily becomes the mortal enemy of the supra-national loyalty of the Christian Church.

Obviously the Church needs to beware of the dangers lurking within this loyalty. Its leadership, particularly, needs the grace of discernment to realize that Caesar is never the friend of Jesus Christ. To illustrate: Many Congolese Christians joined Patrice Lumumba's political party. When his M.N.C. party became dominant some Christians began equating membership in the M.N.C. with God's will for all Congolese Christians. Then the communist-led rebel movement absorbed the M.N.C. A Christian, a local political leader of the M.N.C., told national church leaders and missionaries that all things would work out very well. But when he tried to stop these rebels from sacking his church buildings they turned against him. Today he is somewhere in the forest, hiding from the national army which wants to prosecute him as a traitor and from the rebels who want him executed for the same reason.

God is calling His Church, in today's world, to beware of holding too tightly its loyalty to its nation, its flag, and its Caesar. True, all Christians should stand with their fellow-citizens in their national aspirations for political integrity, social justice and economic vitality. But they should guard against being so captured by the State that they are not able freely to witness to God and His salvation.

2. *Mission—and the Ethnic Religions.*

Concurrent with the worldwide emergence of nationalism has been the resurgence of ancient religious systems. No less an expert than Holter states:

> How do we account for the resurgence of the old religions, and especially the three great religions—Hinduism, Buddhism, and Islam? There are several contributing factors. One is the missionary activity of the Christian church with its many influences. Another is the impact of the modern Western world. But for the most recent drive, however, these might have led to a destruction of the old religions. It is to nationalism, more than any other impulse, that the traditional religions owe their new life and a place of new respect.[2]

This resurgence has not been uniform. Some are "reform" movements in which unscientific and outmoded elements are replaced by insights and practices unabashedly borrowed from the West. Buddhists now have their version of the Sunday School, and their young scholars sing, 'Buddha loves me this I know, for the Dharma tells me so. . . ." Other religious systems are "revived" by merely clothing the old principles and practice with modern dress. Still other religions are in "renaissance" due to the fusion of the ancient with the modern. Finally, there are those religions whose resurgence is nothing short of a "revolt" against their ancient forms. Old fundamentals are replaced by contemporary dogmas. Today Mohammed would not recognize the Ahmadiyya movement currently spearheading the penetration of Islam into the nations of the West.[3]

There are those who affirm the Christian Church is on the threshold of a new era of contact and dialogue with the representatives of these other religions.

For instance, consider the Buddhist. He knows of the growth of secularism in the West. When he proclaims his faith he can appeal to elements in Western thought far more congenial to his message than to the Christian's. It is preoccupied with the problem of suffering. Western literature is filled with this theme. Buddhist salvation is primarily salvation 'from oneself.' This fits in with the contemporary interest in psychological analysis. Buddhists hold that every man is self-perfectible. This appeals to man's penchant for self-sufficiency. Buddhism denies the existence of a personal God and belittles ejaculatory prayer. This is consonant with modern skepticism. Buddhism has no dogma. Secularism has no place for dogma either.[4]

An Austrian Jew, first looked at Christianity and, finding it wanting, turned to Islam. He said of its contemporaneity:

> . . . for the first time I had come across a community in which kinship between man and man was not due to accidents of common racial or economic interest, but to something far deeper and far more stable: a kinship of a common outlook which lifted all the barriers of loneliness between man and man.[5]

What can the Christian response be to this phenomenon?

At the first it must be affirmed that the Christian gospel is God's response to the religious quest of man. It is His answer to the needs of all men everywhere. The religious encounter facing the Church in our day must be conducted on a positive basis. It is pointless and profitless to debate religion vs. religion, insight vs. insight. Better to start with the individual man in his personal need. What solution does he find for the problem of his sin? What has he done with the one true God? In this connection James Packer suggests:

> We shall measure them (non-Christian religions) exclusively by what they say, or omit to say, about God and this man's relation to Him. We shall labor to show the real problem of religion to which the Gospel gives the answer, namely, how a sinner may get right with his Maker. We shall diligently look for the hints and fragments of truth which these religions contain, and appeal to them (set in their proper theological perspective) as pointers to the true knowledge of God. And we shall do all this under a sense of compulsion (for Christ has sent us), in love (for non-Christians are our fellow-creatures, and without Christ they cannot be saved), and with all humility (for we are sinners ourselves, and there is nothing, no part of our message, not even our faith, which we have not received). So with help from on high, we shall both honor God and bear testimony of Him before men.[6]

Obviously, this type of confrontation calls for a far better grasp of the basic elements of these religious systems and their practices than was previously regarded as the essential equipment of the pastor, the evangelist, the missionary, and the lay witness. Forever gone is the day when one could confine his preparation for the religious encounter to mastering a few Bible texts, to be quoted to all and sundry with a "that-settles-it" finality.

3. *Mission—and Communism.*

Communism exceeds all other modern ideologies in its all-out assault on the Christian faith and the Christian Church. By "Communism" we mean all that is embraced in its separate components—a philosophical system, an economic theory and practice, a political system, and a revolutionary movement—in short, a complex system of ideas, loyalties and programs challenging the Church and its worldwide mission. It is "the most coherent philosophy, and the greatest single emotional drive with which this generation has to deal" (Miller). No use fulminating against its bad manners and aggressive stance. The issue is far more than power politics. Communism claims to provide the only truly scientific explanation of the world. It alone claims to be able to give meaning to life. It is a formidable opponent to all that Jesus Christ is and stands for.

There are three major "communisms" in today's world. The virulent Chinese "orthodox" communism with its determination to penetrate the non-white world and start "wars of national liberation." The mutated Russian "reformed" communism with its hopes for winning the world to Marxism through the pressure of its example of rapidly attaining vast military and economic power by drastically changing the basic social structure of a nation. The indifferent-to-world-revolution "nationalist" communism of the Red States of Eastern Europe with their relaxed utilization of Marxist dogma and method, and their neutralist approach to the cold war. ("The central event of this decade is the disintegration of the Soviet Empire. Soviet hegemony in Eastern Europe is fragmenting, and this process is bound to continue. Here is where the dream of Communist internationalism lies buried." [7])

The Communist bloc has its inner contradictions and divisions. This does not necessarily mean, however, that it is any less a menace to the peace of the world. Communism, whatever its political form, still manages to give Western nations a guilty conscience because of their lethargy in coping with such acute issues as social inequality, racial bigotry, and economic exploitation. The churches in the West, however, are made particularly uncertain by the communists. Christians have never adequately mobilized their forces to check evils in society. Throughout the nineteenth century, and deep into the present century, the working man has all too frequently concluded that the Church possesses a remarkable capacity for invariably being on the selfish side of social and political issues. It clings to its privileges within their societies. Marx's jibe often hits home: "When you Christians believe yourselves to be standing up for the truth of God, are you not in fact really defending your own interests and the interests of your own class in concealed form?"

Wherever the Communists gain civil control, they implement a deliberate strategy against the Church embracing repressive legislation, indirect discrimination, and everything but outright religious persecution. Their objective set forth by Lenin is remorselessly pursued: "Eradicate the idea of God from the mind of man." Wherever the structured church still exists in totalitarian Communist states today, one can be sure that its place in society is precarious at best. The sequence of this strategy of penetration is as follows:

1. Isolate the church from all connections with the West.
2. Penetrate the church through exploiting national loyalty. Those who do not cooperate are regarded as disloyal, unpatriotic, reactionary.
3. Destroy the inner cohesion of congregations.
4. Distort the Christian witness.
5. Discriminate against the faithful.

Communism like Islam is doubtless going to prove a long term problem for the world and for the Christian Church. There may be long periods of peaceful coexistence between Communist and non-Communist nations. It is conceivably possible that Marxism might achieve worldwide victory. Scripture seems to indicate that this Age may end with totalitarianism dominant.

If Christianity is to survive it must combine the material and spiritual as they are combined in Scripture. It cannot be content with a mere mastering of "Christian answers" to Communist dogma. Christians must seek out personal face-to-face dialogue with Communists, "getting inside their skins" down to where they disclose that they too are people with anxieties, doubts, and uncertainties—sinners in need of the grace of God.

What needs to be kept in mind is that Marxist ideology is in great flux. Deterioration, erosion, and fatigue will increasingly characterize its orthodoxy. This apostasy will produce restlessness and uncertainty. This means that Christians and churches already within Communist states are the key to all strategy for the evangelization of the Communist world. Self-denying, importunate prayer should be made for them:

- that they will preserve inviolate their deposit of "the faith once delivered unto the saints."
- that they will proclaim the Gospel to unbelievers in every way and by whatever means available to them, and
- that they will conduct themselves as befits the children of God, as responsible citizens in Caesar's world.

III. *Response: The Crucial Issues.*

Is it true that truth never proves its victory in a hostile world until it is crucified? The truth that is unconquerable is the truth that "stedfastly sets its face to go to Jerusalem." "We wrestle not against flesh and blood. . . ." "The weapons of our warfare are not carnal, but mighty through God." "Pray for us that the word of the Lord may have free course and be glorified." "Pray for us that we may be delivered from unreasonable and wicked men." "Pray for us, that God would open unto us a door of utterance." "Strive together with me in your prayers to God for me."

This is the missing factor in so much of the debate on the strategy of mission in a hostile world. "Prayer for the church in action demands striving, continuing, watching, employing all prayer and supplication, perseverance and conflict" (Kerr). Luther in his "Sermon on Good Works" said, "The devil fears a roof of thatch beneath which the church is at prayer more than he does a splendid church in which many masses are celebrated. . . . The Christian Church on earth has not any greater strength than its common prayer against all that might strike against it. Prayer is invincible."

God has called us to mission in a hostile world. What better way can we respond to this calling and this hostility than to reaffirm and embrace anew our Lord's formula of response? Why not love our enemies, bless those who curse us, do good to those that hate us, and pray for those who despitefully use us and persecute us (Matthew 5:44)? Why not persist in aggressive evangelism, all the while reaffirming and trusting in the sovereignty of God? Why not alert one another to the evils latent in all racial, cultural, social and national loyalties, rendering only to Caesar that which is rightfully his? Why not encourage all missionaries to give themselves to self-criticism that all unnecessary sources of tension between themselves and national Christians shall be removed? Why not bring all paternalism, all social indifference, all racial pride, all political loyalties under the judgment of the Cross?

FOOTNOTES

1. *Time Magazine* (March 1, 1966).
2. D. W. Holter, *The Christian Mission Today* (New York: Abingdon Press), p. 192.
3. These various movements are detailed by R. B. Manikam, *Christianity and the Asian Revolution* (New York: Friendship), pp. 118f.
4. For an interesting development of this type of presentation, consult Douglas Webster, *Into All the World* (London: S. P. C. K., 1959), chapter 5.
5. Mohammad Asad, *The Road to Mecca,* quoted by Webster, p. 60.
6. James Packer, "Christianity and the Non-Christian Religions," *Christianity Today* (December 21, 1959), p. 5.
7. *Time Magazine* (March 18, 1966).
8. Ephesians 6:12; II Corinthians 10:4; II Thessalonians 3:1; Colossians 4:4; Romans 15:30.
9. William N. Kerr, "Suffering as an Element in the Strategy of Missions," *Gordon Theological Seminary Bulletin.*

PART 3

THE WHEATON DECLARATION

Introduction

The Wheaton Declaration was unanimously adopted by the delegates to the Congress on the Church's Worldwide Mission, an eight day convocation of evangelicals from around the world. It must be understood in the light of the background, the purposes, the expectations and the accomplishments of the Congress.

Co-chairman Louis L. King, addressed the delegates prior to the presentation of the Declaration. He said the Congress registered 938 accredited delegates from 71 countries. One hundred boards affiliated with the Interdenominational Foreign Mission Association and the Evangelical Foreign Missions Association were represented. Fifty additional agencies not affiliated with either convening association sent representatives. In addition 39 special mission interest groups, 14 non-North American agencies and 55 schools participated. The Congress was ecumenical and irenic, determined to articulate its viewpoint within the context of historic orthodoxy.

Mr. King made it clear that the Declaration was drawn by fallible, finite men who made no claim to omniscience. It is only a beginning and is subject to correction and change as God gives new insights and evangelicals reflect on the implications of what they have said. The Declaration is conditioned by the problems peculiar to our age and it addresses itself to those issues. Changing circumstances in the future will undoubtedly call for more congresses and additional declarations.

It was not anticipated that all of the delegates would agree with everything in the Declaration, nor was it intended that they should. In its final form it was a consensus, a collective opinion, of the Congress. The conclusions reflect the opinions of the delegates after they had discussed the position papers, and their judgments were passed on to those responsible for drawing up the final draft.

The Congress, due to inherent limitations, was unable to discuss some important subjects of current interest, but their omission is no indication of unconcern. Nothing was said about the Jews. War and peace were not discussed. Communism as such was not on the agenda. The role of the United Nations and China's relation to it and to the world were excluded. The Congress deliberately limited its discussions and its Declaration to the ten subjects agreed upon in advance.

The Declaration does not bind those agencies whose delegates adopted it unanimously. It is passed on to them and to others to whom it is addressed as an expression of the deepest convictions of the Congress. Every agency is called upon to study it, to test its statements and to accept and act upon them as they are convinced of the truths contained therein.

Following the adoption of the Declaration the delegates solemnly repeated in unison the Covenant which binds them to finish the Church's God-given task of evangelizing the world in this generation. They sang A Mighty Fortress, *the hymn composed by Martin Luther, conscious of the abiding presence of the Holy Spirit and confident that He had spoken through the Congress to them and to the world.*

CHAPTER 

Wheaton Declaration

Subscribed by the Delegates to
THE CONGRESS ON THE
CHURCH'S WORLDWIDE MISSION
Convened at Wheaton, Illinois
April 9-16, 1966

What urgency has prompted one thousand representatives and servants of the Church of our Lord Jesus Christ to convene this Congress on the Church's Worldwide Mission? What contemporary situation has compelled us to meet together to engage in serious study and consultation? What warrants the audacity that directs a comprehensive Declaration from ourselves to our constituencies, to fellow believers beyond our boundaries, and to a non-believing world? What challenges, what issues confronting Christians everywhere necessitate this kind of reaction and response?

In answer to these questions we make earnest and detailed reply. We are constrained to speak out of a love for Christ, a jealous regard for His glory in the Church, and a deep concern for man's eternal welfare. Indeed, our response to God's calling leaves no alternative. WE MUST SPEAK.

CERTAINTY IS NEEDED . . .

Many evangelical Christians are anxious and uneasy. Some are uncertain about the validity of biblical affirmations in this age of change. Why should we put heart, strength, and resources into the proclamation of Christ to every tribe, tongue, and nation of this burgeoning generation? This uncertainty demands that we make a Declaration to bring the biblical mission of the Church back into focus. WE MUST REITERATE OUR CERTAINTY.

COMMITMENT IS NEEDED . . .

Disturbing secular forces are at work in the hearts of Christians, eroding their commitment to Christ and His missionary purpose. We increasingly shrink from a "tough world growing tougher," turn deaf ears to appeals for costly advance, and rationalize: "Why not be content with past gains? After all, the Church is now worldwide. Let the younger churches finish the job." We need honest self-criticism and ruthless exposure of our heart attitudes in the light of Holy Scripture. Self-examination must be followed by application of the correctives. The situation demands deep renewal of our commitment to Christ's Lordship and willingness to pay any price and suffer, if need be, that this may be accomplished by the Holy Spirit in us and in His Church. WE MUST ISSUE AND HEED THIS CALL.

DISCERNMENT IS NEEDED . . .

Protestantism is afflicted with doctrinal uncertainty, theological novelties, and outright apostasy. Satan is active, sowing tares among the wheat, energizing false witnesses to propagate doubt and destroying true faith. Christians need the will and ability to "discern the spirits whether they be of God." The Church needs the courage to implement the New Testament disciplinary process to guard its purity, its peace, and its unity. God's people need the prophetic voice, calling for a separation from sin and error. WE MUST LIFT THAT VOICE.

HOPE IS NEEDED . . .

The world is in upheaval. Forces inimical to the Christian faith are growing stronger and more aggressive. Political movements, especially communism, call for the worship of collective man. They boast that man, unaided by any "god," will perfect society. They often lock step with ancient ethnic religions, resurgent and militant in outreach. Pseudo-Christian cults multiply and grow, feeding on man's innate desire for spiritual authority. A new challenge faces the Church loyal to biblical Christianity. What of the abiding sufficiency of Jesus Christ in this context of struggle and mounting hostility to His people? A declaration of hope is urgently needed. WE MUST PROCLAIM THAT HOPE.

CONFIDENCE IS NEEDED . . .

God is sovereign in our times. We believe in Him, in the progress of His gospel, and in His triumph in history. We see abundant evidence of His gracious working in the Church and among the nations. We rejoice that we can speak of the Church's universality. We believe there are witnesses to Christ and His gospel in every nation, pointing to the certainty of God's ultimate triumph. "This gospel of the kingdom shall be preached in all the world for a witness unto all nations; and then shall the end come. (Matthew 24:14). The Scriptures emphatically declare that Christ will return when the gathering out of His true Church is completed. All human history shall be consummated in Him (Ephesians 1:10, Phillips). WE MUST AFFIRM THIS CONFIDENCE.

CONFESSION IS NEEDED . . .

Acknowledging our unworthiness, we address the worldwide household of faith, our brothers and sisters in Christ throughout the nations. Although we, like them, are the objects of God's grace, having been "washed . . . sanctified . . . justified in the name of the Lord Jesus, and by the Spirit of our God," we nonetheless feel the shortcomings of our service in the Church.

We have sinned grievously. We are guilty of an unscriptural isolation from the world that too often keeps us from honestly facing and coping with its concerns. In our Christian service we depend too much on promotion and publicity, too little on importunate prayer and the Holy Spirit. We frequently fail to communicate the gospel in a relevant, winsome fashion. We do not consistently develop Christians of outgoing evangelistic witness and high ethical concern. We ask our God and our brethren to forgive us.

But our confession must be more specific. When we make an honest, objective appraisal of our past ministry in the light of the Scriptures, we find that we have often failed:

To stress sufficiently the blessed hope of our Lord's return as an incentive to personal holiness and missionary passion.

To discern in any adequate fashion the strategic significance of the task of multiplying churches in receptive populations.

To trust fully the Holy Spirit's leadership in newly planted congregations, thereby perpetuating paternalism and provoking unnecessary tensions between national churches and missionary societies.

To apply Scriptural principles to such problems as racism, war, population explosion, poverty, family disintegration, social revolution, and communism.

To encourage that form of cooperation that would eliminate costly, inefficient duplication of administrative structures and increase the extent of our outreach.

These failures, which we recognize with contrition, require of us this objective appraisal, and an obedient response to the corrective authority of Scripture. WE MAKE THIS CONFESSION.

EVANGELICAL CONSENSUS IS NEEDED . . .

In addition to examining and rectifying our failures, we have an obligation to examine religious movements that challenge the uniqueness and finality of biblical Christianity. This Congress has been convened because of our concern for deeper insight and more balanced thinking about the peculiar threat they pose to our biblical faith.

The Roman Catholic Church, its outward stance and internal organization altered by Vatican II and its previous intolerance tempered by an apparent desire for open dialogue, requires our careful assessment and response.

Contemporary Protestant movements that boldly contend for the non-existence of the Gospel revealed by God, that propagate a neo-universalism denying eternal condemnation, that substitute inter-church reconciling service for aggressive evangelism, that blur the biblical distinction between "Church" and "Mission" between Romanism and Protestantism, and that create ecclesiastical organizations moving in the direction of a worldwide religious monopoly, likewise demand a careful assessment and response.

Pseudo-Christian cults that feed on man's innate desire for spiritual authority, in their intensive efforts to subvert the faith of untaught Christians and in their deceitful parading of themselves as the true followers of Christ, likewise demand a careful assessment and response.

Non-Christian religious systems, such as Islam, Hinduism and Buddhism in their new missionary vigor, pose an oppressive threat to the growth of the Church and likewise demand careful assessment and response. WE MUST DEFINE THIS CONSENSUS.

OUR AUTHORITY . . .

In line with apostolic precedent, we appeal in the many issues that confront us to the Bible, the inspired, the only authoritative, inerrant Word of God. The Scriptures constitute our final rule of faith and practice. With the Apostle Paul, "we also believe, and therefore speak" (II Corinthians 4:13). Furthermore, the New Testament gives us the apostolic norm for balance between proclamation (*kerygma*) and service (*diakonia*). We ask only that those of like faith ponder our words in the light of Scripture, and thereby ascertain their truthfulness.

THE GOSPEL . . .

We regard as crucial the "evangelistic mandate." The gospel must be preached in our generation to the peoples of every tribe, tongue and nation. This is the supreme task of the Church. We accept the New Testament description of "the gospel." By it we have entered into spiritual life. The gospel concerns the God-man, Jesus of Nazareth, who appeared in time and through whom God acted in a unique fashion. Though crucified and put to death, He was resurrected bodily by God's power. Christ died for us, shedding His blood as an atonement for our sins. In and through Him all men can be reconciled to God, made fit for His presence and His fellowship.

In Him has been made possible a new type of life, a Christ-centered, Christ-controlled life. Through the crucified and risen Lord Jesus Christ, we call every man, wherever he may be, to a change of heart toward God (repentance), personal faith in Jesus Christ as Savior, and surrender to His Lordship. The proclamation of this "good news" has at its heart the explicit imperative, "Ye must be born again," (John 3:7). God says He will judge the world by His crucified, risen Son. We believe that if men are not born again they will be subject to eternal separation from a righteous, holy God. "Except ye repent, ye shall all likewise perish" (Luke 13:3).

WE NOW ADDRESS OURSELVES TO THOSE CRUCIAL ISSUES PARTICULARLY RELATED TO THE CHURCH'S WORLDWIDE MISSION IN OUR DAY . . .

MISSION–AND SYNCRETISM

The Underlying Issues.

On this shrinking planet, with all human affairs moving toward an age of universality never previously witnessed, many voices call for a religion that has universal validity. The gospel of Jesus Christ is the message that has this validity. Syncretism, for our purposes, is the attempt to unite or reconcile biblically revealed Christian truth with the diverse or opposing tenets and practices of non-Christian religions or other systems of thought that deny it. Alarming are the deviant and heretical views within Christendom advocating a depersonalized theism acceptable to religions of East and West. Such syncretism denies the uniqueness and finality of Christian truth.

Since syncretism readily develops where the gospel is least understood and experienced, great clarity must be sought in presenting the uniqueness of Jesus Christ and the precise message of His saving work as revealed in the Bible. For effective, relevant communication of the gospel across cultural and religious barriers, we must first divest our presentation of those cultural accretions which are not pertinent to essential gospel truth. The truth should then be communicated in the context of the meaningful and pertinent linguistic and cultural terms of people that they may also come to a decisive understanding of the gospel.

We must resist syncretism in spite of any opposition we may encounter, and we must bear our testimony with humility and dignity.

The Witness of the Scriptures.

The Old Testament prophets were unrelenting in their witness against the syncretistic practices of Israel. The New Testament apostles likewise combatted the syncretistic tendencies of their age, such as Gnosticism, in their defense of the gospel. Our dominant thrust is that the one and only true God has disclosed Himself in Jesus Christ, the incarnate Word, and in the Scriptures, the written Word. Biblical faith is unique because it is revealed. To add to it or to change it is to pervert it. "God, who . . . spake in time past unto the fathers by the prophets, hath in these last days spoken unto us by his Son . . ." (Hebrews 1:1,2).

WE THEREFORE DECLARE

That, while seeking greater effectiveness in the communication of the Christian faith and acknowledging the uniqueness and finality of Jesus Christ, we will expose the dangers of syncretism.

That, in the communication of our faith we must avoid unbiblical cultural accretions and emphases that may tend to obscure Christian truth.

That, we will acquaint our total leadership more carefully with the religious beliefs and thought-forms of the peoples among whom they live and serve, relative to syncretistic tendencies.

MISSION—AND NEO-UNIVERSALISM

The Underlying Issues.

During the first nineteen centuries of the history of the Church, any teaching suggesting that all men ultimately would be redeemed was vigorously rejected as heretical. In our day, universalism is rapidly coming into the mainstream of teaching acceptable to some leading Protestant and Roman Catholic theologians. Many prominent church leaders increasingly champion this viewpoint. The new universalism is based upon a fragmented usage of Scripture, not on an exposition of the Scriptures in total wholeness and context.

The teaching of universalism, which we reject, states that, because Christ died for all, He will sovereignly and out of love bring all men to salvation. It proclaims the essential and final unity of the human race, which will never be broken—now or in the future—by God or by man. All mankind is "reconciled"; those who have met Christ have an advantage above those who have not, but it is a difference in degree, not in principle. If men do not believe the gospel in this life—even if they reject it—their guilt and punishment will ultimately be removed. They are simply not conscious of the riches they possess.

The issue with universalism is not simply one of elevating human reason above the clear witness of the Scriptures and biblical Christianity. The whole mission of the Church is affected. The universalist merely proclaims a universal Lordship of Christ and summons men to acknowledge it in their lives. This can readily lead to syncretism and the eventual abandonment by the Church of its missionary calling. Christ is being betrayed by those calling themselves His friends.

The Witness of the Scriptures.

We fervently accept the universal character of the claims of Scripture: God loves the world (John 3:16); Christ is the propitiation for the sins of the whole world (I John 2:2); all things have been reconciled to God through Christ (Colossians 1:20). God desires all men to be saved (I Timothy 2:4), and to unite all things in Christ (Ephesians 1:9, 10) so that every knee should bow and every tongue confess His Lordship (Philippians 2:10, 11), "that God may be all in all" (I Corinthians 15:28). Scripture, however, must explain Scripture. Christ taught eternal punishment as well as eternal life. He spoke of the cursed as well as the blessed (Matthew 25:34, 41, 46). Paul taught eternal destruction and exclusion from the presence of the Lord of all who obey not the gospel of our Lord Jesus (II Thessalonians 1:8, 9). Although God's claims are universal and His triumph will be universal, yet His saving grace is effective only in those who believe on Christ (John 1:12). There is a heaven and a hell; there are the saved and the lost. Scriptures gives us no other alternative; we must take seriously all it says of the wrath and judgments of the God and Father of our Lord Jesus Christ.

WE THEREFORE DECLARE

That, we will, ourselves, be more forthright and thorough in our preaching and teaching of the testimony of the Bible on the awful reality of eternal loss through sin and unbelief.

That, we shall encourage all evangelical theologians to intensify their exegetical study of the Scriptures relating to eternal punishment and the call to redemption and reconciliation.

That, since the mission of the Church inescapably commits us to proclaim the gospel which offers men the forgiveness of sins only through faith in Jesus Christ, our verbal witness to Him should accompany our service to the poor, the sick, the needy, and the oppressed.

That, the repudiation of universalism obliges all evangelicals to preach the gospel to all men before they die in their sins. To fail to do this is to accept in practice what we deny in principle.

MISSION–AND PROSELYTISM

The Underlying Issues.

The word "proselytism" means "the making of a convert, especially to some religious sect, or to some opinion, system, or party." Recently the word has also been used as a charge against evangelistic effort, especially among those who are members of any denomination or other ecclesiastical body. In reaction to the dynamic witness of evangelicals, some religious groups and nationalistic forces have demanded that "proselytism can and should be controlled."

The proselytism that includes forced conversions or the use of unethical means (material and/or social) is contrary to the gospel of Christ and should be distinguished from that which is biblical and genuine.

The Witness of the Scriptures.

Throughout the New Testament the apostles and other Christians ceaselessly proclaimed Christ and persuaded men to accept Him, renouncing their old religious allegiances and joining the Christian church (Acts 5:29; 8:4; 13:15-41; 18:4-11; 19:8). The Jews through whom the revelation of God was transmitted and the idol-worshipping Gentiles alike were exhorted to repent, believe, and be baptized; they then became members of a church.

WE THEREFORE DECLARE

That, all followers of Christ must disciple their fellowmen. From this obligation there can be neither retreat nor compromise.

That, we shall urge church and government leaders throughout the world to work for the inalienable right of full religious liberty everywhere. This means freedom to propagate and to change one's faith or church affiliation, as well as the freedom to worship God.

That, we shall obey God rather than men in resisting the monopolistic tendencies both within and without Christendom that seek to stifle evangelical witness to Jesus Christ.

That, we shall not use unbiblical, unethical methods of persuading people to change their religious allegiance. However, when we seek the conversion of unregenerate men, even though they may be attached to some church or other religion, we are fulfilling our biblical mandate.

MISSION—AND NEO-ROMANISM

The Underlying Issues.

Some remarkable changes have taken place within the Roman Catholic Church that have introduced a new climate in its relations with Protestantism, Orthodoxy, Judaism, and the secular world. Differences that were once clearly etched have now become blurred. In this revolutionary age, churchmen increasingly call for Catholic and Protestant renewal in order to solve cooperatively the human problems of our era.

Vatican II has accelerated this desire for renewal. New emphases on biblical research have created formidable problems for Roman Catholic leaders.

Catholic Church authorities have never been so vocal in calling for an intensification of worldwide missionary activity. Many of their theologians display great interest in speculative universalism and existentialism. They also consider Protestants as "separated brethren" and desire friendly relations with them. And yet, whereas Roman Catholic practices may change, they say their dogmas are unchangeable. According to the Roman Catholic view, reunion of the churches must be on papal terms.

Though the Roman Catholic Church has a high view of Scripture, tradition continues to have a determinative authority. Its reform of the Mass is only a reform of the liturgy of the Mass.

It has not abandoned any of its unbiblical dogmas concerning Mary, papal infallibility, etc.

The Witness of the Scriptures.

The Word of God pronounces its own judgment upon the sacerdotalism and sacramentalism of the Roman Catholic Church. The Scriptures teach:

- The Bible as the infallible revelation from God (*sola scriptura*) (II Timothy 4:15-17).
- There is "one mediator between God and men, the man Christ Jesus" (I Timothy 2:5).
- The finished work of Christ with no re-presentation of that sacrifice (Hebrews 10:14).
- Justification by faith alone, apart from works (*sola fide*) (Romans 1:17; 3:20-26).
- The universal priesthood of all believers (I Peter 2:5, 9; Hebrews 10:19-22).
- Mary herself needed a Savior (Luke 1:46-48).
- In the celebration of the Lord's Supper the elements remain, in form and essence, bread and wine (I Corinthians 11:25-26 with I Corinthians 10:17).
- Jesus Christ is the only Head of the Body which is His Church (Ephesians 1:20-23).

WE THEREFORE DECLARE

That, we rejoice in the wider use of the Scriptures among Roman Catholics.

That, we shall pray that all those who study the Scriptures may be led by the Holy Spirit to saving faith in Christ.

That, we shall urge evangelicals to seize today's unique opportunities for witness among Roman Catholics.

That, we recognize the danger of regarding the Roman Catholic Church as "our great sister Church," even as we reaffirm the abiding validity of the Scriptural principles of the Reformers, that salvation is through faith in Christ alone and that the Bible is the only rule of faith and practice.

MISSION—AND CHURCH GROWTH

The Underlying Issues.

The Church's work is to preach the gospel and plant congregations in every community. The implementation of this mission is being retarded by:

- Too little sensitiviity to the authority and strategy of the Holy Spirit.
- Too much missionary control.
- Too much dependence on paid workers.
- Too little training and use of the great body of laymen.
- Complacency with small results long after a larger response could have been the norm.
- Failure to take full advantage of the response of receptive peoples.
- Overemphasis on institutionalism at the expense of multiplying churches.

In today's world vast untouched areas are still to be found near existing churches. Huge sections of cities containing but a few congregations are increasingly responsive to the gospel. It is God's will that churches be multipled. Thus the missionary still has an essential place in the dynamism of church growth even as he continues to exercise a spiritual ministry in the churches already established. But his particular ministry will be in the vanguard of planting new congregations.

The Witness of the Scriptures.

In the Acts of the Apostles local congregations were God's primary agents for the widespread dissemination of the gospel. The total mobilization of the people and resources of the churches in effective, continuous evangelistic outreach is indispensable to the evangelization of the world (Acts 17:1-4 with I Thessalonians 1:8, 9; Ephesians 4:16). Church planting has the priority among all other missionary activities, necessary and helpful though they may be.

Apostolic procedures point to a confidence in the local church under the control of the Holy Spirit (Acts 14:23, Romans 15:14). True, on occasion, local churches experienced spiritual failure, but despite such setbacks the church moved on and outward. From the beginning the churches governed, supported, and reproduced themselves (Acts 19:10, 20).

WE THEREFORE DECLARE

That, we reaffirm our confidence in and dependence on the Holy Spirit and call on the church to pray for that revival which is indispensable for its growth and outreach.

That, we call upon all churches, mission societies and training institutions to study diligently the nature, ministry and growth of the church as set forth in the Scriptures.

That, we urge that research be carried on by nationals and missionaries in all parts of the world to learn why churches are or are not growing and make such knowledge available.

That, we urge the missionary enterprise to evaluate church growth opportunities now overlooked and to review the role, methods, and expenditures of our agencies in the light of their significance to evangelism and church growth.

That, we should devote special attention to those people who are unusually responsive to the gospel and will reinforce those fields with many laborers.

That, we must pray earnestly that the Holy Spirit will bring the less responsive fields to early harvest. We will not leave them untended.

MISSION–AND FOREIGN MISSIONS

The Underlying Issues.

In this day of unprecedented missionary activity, urgent questions are being asked. What is the role of the missionary? What is his relation to the national church? Is his allegiance primarily to the church that sent him or to the newly established national church with which he serves? Who is to administer funds coming from the sending churches? How should such funds be used? Should the churches be fully self-supporting? Should church and mission organizations remain separate and distinct, or should the latter lose their identity? The issue is whether missionary service as presently conducted is in accord with Scripture.

Currently many claim it is impossible to maintain on biblical grounds the concept of the missionary society as a sending agency distinct from any national organization of churches on the field. Such thinking tends to obliterate the distinctive ministry of "foreign missionary." This kind of emphasis may diminish interest in missionary vocation on the part of Christian youth.

The Witness of the Scriptures.

In obedience to the Great Commission, the Church has the continuing responsibility to send missionaries into all the world (Matthew 28:18-20; Acts 13:1-4).

The New Testament says many went forth according to our Lord's command. As a result believers were added to the Body of Christ. (Acts 8:12; 11:21, 24). New converts were gathered into congregations where they found fellowship and grew in grace (Acts 2:42; 9:31).

God gave to the churches apostles, prophets, evangelists, and teaching pastors (Ephesians 4:11). The apostles founded churches; they taught and functioned as advisors in the selection of local leadership (Titus 1:5); they strengthened and exhorted the churches (Acts 14:22; 15:41); they charged leaders with specific responsibilities of office (I Timothy 1:18; 3:1-14); they also gave guidance in matters of discipline and doctrine (I Corinthians; Acts 15). The Holy Spirit works similarly through missionaries today.

In the New Testament no clearly defined structure for church-mission relationships can be adduced.

WE THEREFORE DECLARE

That, we encourage church and mission leaders to define the role and to enlarge the vision of those called to pastoral or missionary service.

That, the proper relationship between churches and missions can only be realized in a cooperative partnership in order to fulfill the mission of the Church to evangelize the world in this generation.

That, the mission society exists to evangelize, to multiply churches, and to strengthen the existing churches. Therefore we recognize a continuing distinction between the church established on the field and the missionary agency.

MISSION—AND EVANGELICAL UNITY

The Underlying Issues.

The unity of the Church of Jesus Christ is directly and significantly related to her worldwide mission. Our Lord's earnest petition to the Father on behalf of His Church (John 17) was for her essential spiritual unity and its visible expression in the world. His concern "that they all may be one" was in order "that the world may know that thou hast sent me."

Today many voices call for organizational church union at the expense of doctrine and practice (faith and order). Denominational divisions are seen as the great "scandal" of our day. Union becomes a major objective. However, organizational church union of itself has seldom released a fresh missionary dynamism or an upsurge of missionary recruitment.

Christians having been regenerated by the Holy Spirit and who agree on the basic evangelical doctrines can experience a genuine biblical oneness, even if they belong to different denominations. Such biblical oneness cannot exist among those who have not been regenerated or among those who disagree on the basic evangelical doctrines, even if they belong to the same denomination. Evangelicals, however, have not fully manifested this biblical oneness because of carnal differences and personal grievances; and thus missionary advance and the fulfillment of the Great Commission have been hindered.

The Witness of the Scriptures.

Concerning the nature of the unity of the Church we learn from Scripture:

- It is a unity given by God, to be preserved (John 17:21; Ephesians 4:3-6).
- It is a unity of essence, a new regenerate society whose individual members have been given a new nature—life in the Spirit (John 3:6; I Corinthians 12:13; II Corinthians 5:17; II Peter 1:4).
- It is a unity of belief, centered in the Person and work of Jesus Christ (I Corinthians 15:1-4 with Galatians 1:8; Ephesians 4:12-16; Colossians 1:27-29).
- It is a unity intrinsic to the fulfillment of God's missionary purpose for the world (John 17:20, 21, 23; Ephesians 4:16; Philippians 1:27).

WE THEREFORE DECLARE

That, we are one in Christ Jesus, members of His Body, born again of His Holy Spirit, although we may be diverse in our structured relationships.

That, we will endeavor to keep the unity of the Spirit in the bond of peace so that the world may believe.

That, we will encourage and assist in the organization of evangelical fellowships among churches and missionary societies at national, regional, and international levels.

That, we will encourage evangelical mission mergers when such will eliminate duplication of administration, produce more efficient stewardship of personnel and resources, and strengthen their ministries.

That, we caution evangelicals to avoid establishing new churches or organizations where existing groups of like precious faith satisfactorily fill the role.

MISSION—AND EVALUATING METHODS

The Underlying Issues.

A new age of intellectual advance has brought with it radical changes that require a new appraisal of missionary methodology. We are faced with new masses of humanity, we have developed new means of mass communication, we have been caught up in the maelstrom of new learning in the social sciences, and we sense man's frightening estrangement from God, himself, and society.

Churches and missions have been influenced by this ferment. Some have profited greatly from the insights of psychology, anthropology, sociology, and business management. Others regard the use of such insights as a wrong invasion of the religious by the secular. They question evaluating personal and organizational activity in the light of such procedures.

The best results come when, under the Holy Spirit, good principles of communication are combined with clear understanding of cultural and social patterns and applied to the proclamation of the Gospel. The great danger arises when there is an overdependence on techniques and learning that minimizes or leaves out the Holy Spirit.

Missionary methodology cannot be evaluated only in terms of anthropological and sociological relevance. Two realms are involved: the Church, as it reflects the holiness and redemptive purpose of God; and culture, as it reflects finite and sinful man. Hence, while the social sciences afford considerable insights for missionary methods, yet these must be subjected to the corrective judgment of Scripture.

The Witness of the Scriptures.

Christ left us His example of evaluating one's life and service (John 17). His disciples knew themselves to be God's men, doing God's work in God's way; and they called on Christians to follow their example (I Corinthians 4:17; 11:1; Philippians 3: 17; II Timothy 1:8, 13; 2:2, 7; 3:10-15). Their communication of the gospel was culturally relevant among Jews, barbarians, and intellectual Greeks (Acts 13:14-43; 14:8-18; 17:22-31; I Corinthians 9:19-23).

The Scriptures approve organization and the delegation of authority (Acts 6:2-4). They do not detail methods of organization and ministry, but they emphasize our dependence upon the Holy Spirit to produce spiritual results in the lives of people (I Corinthians 2:1-5).

Christ thoroughly instructed and trained His disciples in personal conduct and in methods of evangelism. He also taught them their need of the Holy Spirit's ministry (Luke 24:49; John 15:5, 26, 27; 16:7-15).

WE THEREFORE DECLARE

That, we acknowledge our utter dependence upon the Holy Spirit in every aspect of our missionary calling.

That, God's primary method for evangelism and church planting is the ministry of Spirit-gifted and empowered men and women preaching and teaching the Word of God.

That, we will engage in periodic self-criticism in the light of the Scriptures and contemporary insights and seek more effective ways to attain our objectives.

That, we urge extensive reading and research in the field of cross-cultural communication in order to propagate the gospel better.

That, we will make the best use of all means for communicating the gospel, carefully guarding ourselves against overdependence upon mass media at the expense of personal witness.

That, we encourage all missionaries and candidates to study in such areas as mass communication, anthropology, and sociology, while recognizing the priority of Bible knowledge and spiritual preparation.

That, we will seek more effective means to evangelize and bring to spiritual maturity the masses of youth in the world today.

That, we need to improve our missionary recruiting techniques, upgrade missionary educational preparation and reduce our drop-out rates.

MISSION—AND SOCIAL CONCERN

The Underlying Issues.

Whereas evangelicals in the Eighteenth and Nineteenth Centuries led in social concern, in the Twentieth Century many have lost the biblical perspective and limited themselves only to preaching a gospel of individual salvation without sufficient involvement in their social and community responsibilities.

When theological liberalism and humanism invaded historic Protestant churches and proclaimed a "social gospel," the conviction grew among evangelicals that an antithesis existed between social involvement and gospel witness.

Today, however, evangelicals are increasingly convinced that they must involve themselves in the great social problems men are facing. They are concerned for the needs of the whole man, because of their Lord's example, His constraining love, their identity with the human race, and the challenge of their evangelical heritage.

Evangelicals look to the Scriptures for guidance as to what they should do and how far they should go in expressing this social concern, without minimizing the priority of preaching the gospel of individual salvation.

The Witness of the Scriptures.

The Old Testament manifests God's concern for social justice (Micah 6:8). Our Lord, by precept and example, stressed the importance of ministering to the physical and social, as well as spiritual needs of men (Matthew 5-9). His dealings with the Samaritans involved Him in racial and social issues (Luke 9:51-56; John 4:1-30; Luke 10:25-37).

His disciples followed His example (Galatians 2:10; Colossians 3:11; James 1:27; 2:9-11). They taught and respected the role of government in promoting civil justice (Romans 13 and I Peter 2). The two great commandments are: "Love the Lord thy God . . . and thy neighbor as thyself" (Mark 12:29-31).

WE THEREFORE DECLARE

That, we reaffirm unreservedly the primacy of preaching the gospel to every creature, and we will demonstrate anew God's concern for social justice and human welfare.

That, evangelical social action will include, wherever possible, a verbal witness to Jesus Christ.

That, evangelical social action must avoid wasteful and unnecessary competition.

That, when Christian institutions no longer fulfill their distinctively evangelical functions they should be relinquished.

That, we urge all evangelicals to stand openly and firmly for racial equality, human freedom, and all forms of social justice throughout the world.

MISSION–AND A HOSTILE WORLD

The Underlying Issues.

The world is hostile to the Church because it is hostile to God. His Church is at war, not at rest. True to the prophecy of the Lord, the faithful Church has always experienced hostility.

In our age, however, this hostility has been intensified by the rise of atheistic communism, extreme nationalism, resurgent ethnic religions, secularism, and corrupted forms of Christianity. The ultimate source of hostility is the "Prince of this World." He has even infiltrated some churches, whose apathy, indifference, selfishness, and failure to fulfill their mission disclose only too well Satan's opposition.

The Church is often rent asunder. Suffering defeat, crowded and buffeted, it seeks to understand the paradox of the promise of the Lord that the gates of hell shall not prevail against it.

However, we need not despair of the Church for we believe in its final triumph.

The Witness of the Scriptures.

Christ witnessed to the personality, purpose and power of Satan (Matthew 4:1-11; Luke 8:12; 11:14-26). The apostles recognized Satan's ceaseless opposition to the propagation of the gospel and the growth of the Church (Ephesians 6:10-18; II Corinthians 4:4; I Thessalonians 2:18).

Satan's strategy is varied (II Corinthians 2:11), subtle (II Corinthians 11:3, 4), and relentless (I Peter, 5:8). He inspires false christs (Matthew 24:5), false preachers (II Corinthians 11:13-15), false prophets and teachers (II Peter 2:1-3), and false doctrines (I Timothy 4:1-3).

Christians are called to follow Christ, to believe and to suffer, to witness and to bear the cross (John 20:21; Philippians 1:29; Luke 9:23-26). In love for God and man, they suffer to effect the calling out and perfection of the Church (Colossians 1:24). Faithful Christians strive together in persevering prayer (Acts 4:24-31).

WE THEREFORE DECLARE

That, we reaffirm our trust in the sovereign God, His triumph in history and the victory of His Church.

That, we will seek to recognize Satan's devices in the light of Scripture and resist him in the power of the Holy Spirit and on the basis of the finished work of Christ.

That, we should meet persecution by obeying the Lord's command to love our enemies, bless those who curse us, do good to those who hate us, and pray for those who despitefully use us.

That, our supreme loyalty is to Jesus Christ and all of our racial, cultural, social, and national loyalties are to be in subjection to Him. We will particularly encourage all Christian workers in churches and missions to discern and remove the tension among themselves.

That, we are deeply moved by the courageous witness of suffering Christians in many lands; that we will sustain them more faithfully by prayer; and that we will trust God for grace, should we be called upon to suffer for His sake.

That, we call all believers to persistent prayer in the Spirit, believing that prayer and the proclamation of the gospel are the weapons of our warfare.

IN THE SUPPORT OF THIS DECLARATION
WE
the delegates here assembled
in adoration of the Triune God,
with full confidence in Holy Scripture,
in submission to the Lord Jesus Christ,
and looking for His coming again,
DO COVENANT TOGETHER
for God's eternal glory,
and in response to the Holy Spirit,
with renewed dedication,
and in our oneness in Christ as the people of God,
TO SEEK
under the leadership of our Head,
with full assurance of His power and presence,
THE MOBILIZATION OF THE CHURCH
its people, its prayers, and resources,
FOR THE EVANGELIZATION OF THE WORLD IN THIS GENERATION
so, help us God!
AMEN.

Wheaton, Illinois
April 16, 1966

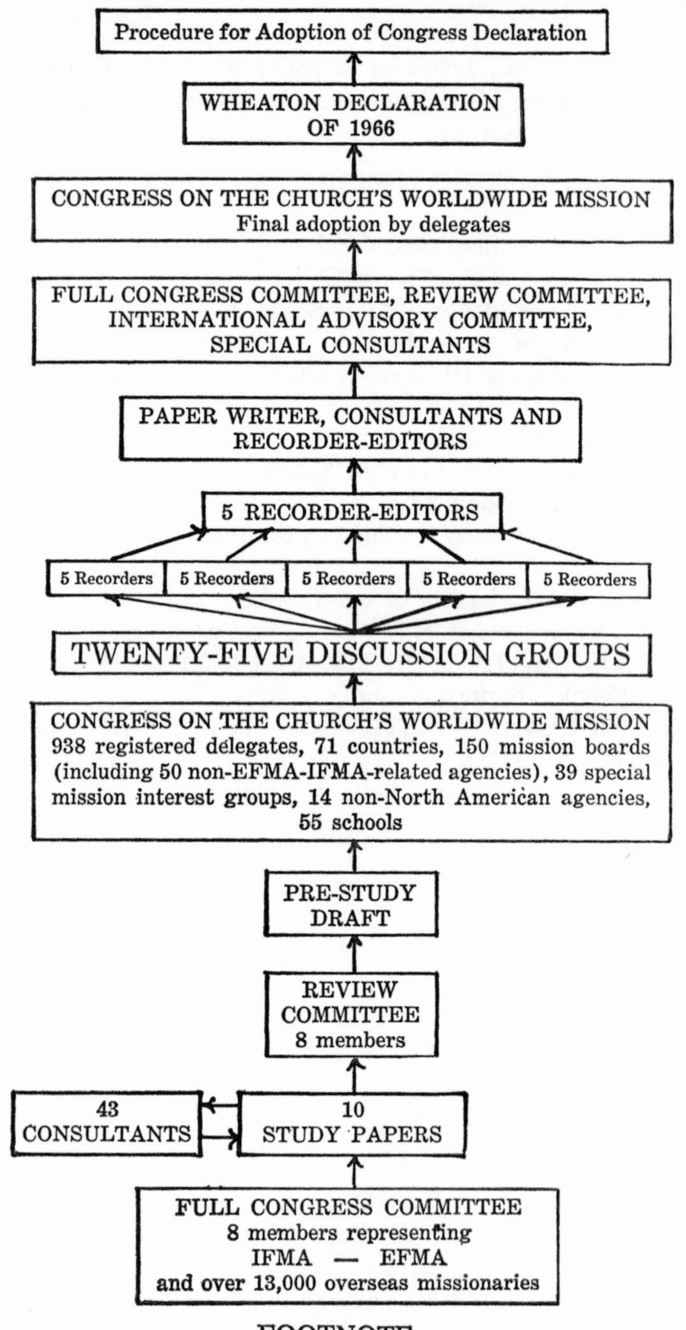

FOOTNOTE

The Wheaton Declaration reprinted by permission of Evangelical Missions Information Service, Washington, D.C.

PART 4

AREA REPORTS

CHAPTER 20

Africa

by The Reverend James Kayode Bolarin

More than ever before the Church in Africa faces perilous times. The Devil has multiplied his strategies to pull down the work church leaders and pioneers sacrificed their lives to build. One of his subtle attacks is neo-colonialism and being tied to the mission apron strings. He also attacks today by throwing darts at those who faithfully cling to the teachings of the Holy Scriptures.

National awakening, false prophets and doctrines, modernism, and secret cults are found in almost every country in this great continent. Islam continues its march south; Muslims claim that the whole of Africa north of the Equator is more than 50 per cent Muslim, and deep inroads are being made into African countries south of the Equator.

Persecutions, violence, threats, and even death—as in the southern Sudan, for instance—are sometimes directed against the adherents of Christianity. This has had its good result; for while the masses are falling away, the faithful few are standing firm by their confession. As the winds of persecution blow they separate the chaff from the grain!

Now for a quick summary of some of the significant things happening in Africa today. It is impossible to mention every one of Africa's 38 countries, but we shall divide the continent into four areas—South, Central, East and West.

SOUTH AFRICA

The African state everyone is talking about is Rhodesia. What is the church situation there?

The churches in Rhodesia have never experienced the flame

of revival which has burned in some other African countries. Nevertheless, Christians are very busy generating conditions which make it easy for God to have a grip upon His own people. There is heated persecution which one may not pray for God to remove, but rather that He should use it to accomplish His redemptive purpose.

The main strategy of Satan in Rhodesia is raising up false prophets. Through their activities, many who once belonged to the churches have now forsaken them. Further, Satan has wrought havoc among many of the churches through the influence of modernism.

On the other hand, we thank God for a new emphasis on cooperation among evangelicals. Real efforts are being made to remove inter-church and inter-mission rivalries.

South Africa has had the Gospel since the end of the 18th century. The results have been very encouraging; progress has been made, and many churches have attained autonomous status. Most are self-supporting.

The greatest problem in South Africa, of course, is racism. It is summed up in the words of a young Zulu: "They told us of God and the Bible and how all men were equal before God, but they do not treat us as equals. What can we believe?" While some churches dismiss this problem as merely political, others have taken their stand.

CENTRAL AFRICA

The political crisis in Congo-Leopoldville since independence in 1960 has nearly paralyzed church work. Some areas are still in rebel hands. The Evangelical Church of Upper Congo reports nine of its stations still blocked by rebels. However, things are gradually returning to normal; missionaries are returning, elementary schools have been re-opened and the gospel is being preached among rebels and soldiers.

Apart from political disruption, evangelicals in Congo see the Protestant Council of Congo as a great threat to freedom. This body, which belongs to the ecumenical movement, is seeking to control religious teaching in schools, have all church property placed under its authority, and represent all Protestant churches before the government.

To offset this, an Evangelical Alliance of Congo has been formed, with the objective of providing opportunities for Bible teaching and spiritual fellowship, and to awaken Christians to the dangers of ecumenism, modernism and false cults. Truly the churches in Congo need our fervent and unceasing prayers.

EAST AFRICA

Ethiopia is the oldest independent country in Africa. About 60 per cent of the people belong to the ancient Coptic Church, which follows elaborate ritual. Emperor Haile Selassie has tried to institute various reforms in the church, but little has changed. Evangelical missions from Europe and America are working mainly in the pagan areas of the West and South. The chief problem of the Church in Ethiopia is lack of trained Christian workers. Missionary advisers are urgently required.

The situation in Sudan gives much cause for concern. Since the Muslim government expelled all missionaries from the southern provinces, reports have been received of terrible persecutions among the Christians. The future of Christianity in Sudan is at stake unless the Lord Himself works through persecution to establish His work there.

Tanzania finds herself in a strategic position, bounded by eight other African states. The door to the gospel there is wide open. Two interesting items—Roman Catholic priests are buying hundreds of Bibles to distribute among their own people; and Jehovah's Witnesses are banned from the country.

WEST AFRICA

West Africa has 5 English-speaking states, and 9 French-speaking states. Nigeria is the largest of the English-speaking states, and with a population of 55 million, is the most populous country in Africa. Christianity there is faced with the force of Islam in the North. Muslim missionaries and money are pouring into the country. Evangelistic campaigns and religious broadcasts are undertaken by Muslim preachers to refute the God-sonship of Christ. Islamic schools are increasing in number.

However, some evangelical churches are alert to their responsibilities. A gospel campaign called "New Life For All" (Based on South America's Evangelism-in-Depth) has been operating in Northern Nigeria with great success. Many Muslims and pagans have been converted, and churches revived. It is planned to extend the campaign to the whole of Nigeria very soon.

In the South missions have been working for over 120 years, and churches are firmly established. Materialism and liberalism have sapped much of the spiritual life, but there is evidence of a hunger for something real among the people. It is possible that God will do a new and wonderful thing in Nigeria sooner than we think. Perhaps I may be allowed to mention also the work of the magazine *African Challenge,* which over the years has been used to win many for Christ.

Roman Catholicism is strong in the former French colonies. The first West African Cardinal recently appointed by the Pope comes from Upper Volta. In the same country Catholics invited Protestants to prayers for unity—further evidence of Rome's new, friendly approach.

We have seen, briefly, some of the problems hindering the work of God in Africa. Because of the growth of ecumenism, and out of a desire for greater cooperation, many evangelical churches felt the need for forming an evangelical fellowship. That fellowship, called the Association of Evangelicals of Africa and Madagascar, was formed at Nairobi, Kenya, earlier this year. This is a real step forward.

The faithful few have to be on the alert, eager in their efforts to serve and save the witness of the churches. Christ asked a painful question when He was about to leave here: "Shall I meet faith on earth when I come back again?"

In order that He may meet faith when He comes back, there is a great need for revival in the churches now. Men need to know that Christ alone saves and salvation does not come by the merit of our own good work. We must be willing to surrender our own wills to the Lord Jesus Christ.

The Gospel of Christ must be preached to all men, because we are made the keepers of our brothers whose souls are very precious to God and for them Christ came to lay down His life.

Many have asserted that Christianity is failing in Africa. But it is not Christianity that has failed—it is the Christians who are failing in their task. The Lord is coming soon. May we not be put to shame when He comes!

CHAPTER 

Report on Europe

by Dr. Robert P. Evans

As Europe nears the final quarter of this century she stands on the highest pinnacle of her long and complex history. Never before have Europeans been so prosperous and progressive. But in contrast to her material success, Europe grows more bankrupt every year in the spiritual realm. Even the ecumenists agree on this finding. In the words of Bishop Stephen Neill, professor of missions and ecumenics at the University of Hamburg,

> "Church attendance in Europe is everywhere declining; the lack of ordained ministers is grave in every country, whether Roman Catholic or Protestant. The secularization of life proceeds apace. We seem to be watching a steady diminution of the spiritual capital of Europe, the disappearance of the old European synthesis of religion and culture, and a desiccation of the human spirit, as a result of which men not merely are not religious, but can see no reason why they should concern themselves beyond the world of the senses."

It might be well to open our discussion on the work of evangelical missions in Europe by noting the number of missionaries at work there. Of 1200 foreign Christian workers, some 810 are from the IFMA-EFMA societies. These represent about 4.8% of the total personnel of the societies. But is that ratio sufficient for a continent which has 16% of the world's population? Since Europe is the homeland of western civilization, surely she should have a much larger share in missionary investment. We pay for this neglect on mission fields in other parts of the world where European religious and cultural influences are often inimical to the Word of God.

As to the influence of foreign missions in Europe, a realistic critique must include both a debit and credit side. Let us start with the debit column. First, missions in Europe are, as a whole, too vague and undecided about their long-range goals. Many missions seemingly do not follow any clear plan to evangelize a given area. Other societies which have outlined a strategy sometimes fail to indoctrinate their workers in it. In any case, a strategy for Europe needs constant review in the light of changing conditions. This is true within each mission, and on a broader level, among associations of missions.

There are many sides to the question of strategy. For instance, should not a plan for Europe include the capture of leadership for Christ? Yet few workers make any real attempt to influence the leadership classes, the student world, or the shapers of national destiny. We seldom evaluate demographic or sociological data like the problems of population movement and urbanization. As a result most of us concentrate on the lower middle class, the clerks, peasants and shopkeepers. Consequently the social and intellectual elite, the upper middle class, and the lower working class are almost completely ignored—perhaps because the missionary himself was not born into these classes and does not feel at home in them. Another aspect of poor planning is the apparently haphazard entry of missions into new countries. Often it appears badly-timed, without enough forethought, and determined more by the appearance of a volunteer for that country than by any other consideration. Nor is there any logic to the heavier concentration of missionaries in northern or Protestant Europe, to the expense of southern Roman Catholic Europe. Survey, that *sina qua non* of missions, is sometimes so superficial that the path toward maximum response to the gospel remains uncharted.

A second negative point is the absence of creative contact between the field leaders of different evangelical missions. While stimulating inter-mission conferences do take place in a few countries, upper-level consultation between field leaders of our missions in Europe are not the practice. Though home executives of IFMA-EFMA missions often meet, and consider the travel expense well spent, their field counterparts in Europe do not follow suit. Confusion and waste sometimes result. For example, two leaders approach the same governments to ask a license for a powerful Europe-wide radio transmitter, putting officials there in a quandry. Two societies translate and publish some of the same books. Two missions unknowingly enter the same city, settle their workers within blocks of each other, but leave other pagan cities in the same country without witness. Again, through lack of communication one mission repeats mistakes made by another in its relation to the local government. Then, because our differing postures toward European church life remain undiscussed and unreconciled we see an ugly spectacle like the members of one IFMA-EFMA mission calling the members of another one liberal. To avoid such incidents we are not advocating uniformity in strategy, nor control and approval by any group. We only believe that prayerful fellowship would transform our fragmented missionary "presence" into a militant unity. In the words of T. Stanley Soltau, "In any situation, if a minority is to make any real impact on a majority, its members must act in perfect oneness." This would seem especially important in view of the growing integration of forces in Europe, both Protestant and otherwise, opposed to the true gospel.

A third failure concerns the misuse of money. Some organizations have seemingly felt that the greatest contribution they can make to Europe is to give generously. It is certainly the easiest. But unless a prayerful scrutiny of motive and much biblical teaching on stewardship accompany such giving the results can be disastrous. Even though freehanded subsidy is not as flagrant as just after World War II, some foreign organizations still subsidize denominations, churches, and nationals. Several times we have observed evangelical leaders emerge one day from their transatlantic planes, sign on an English-speaking national as their representative, and fly away the next day—all without investigation or indoctrination beyond the peremptory order, "Be sure to send me a monthly report about your work for our magazine."

A fourth weakness lies in our failure to formulate and implement a "philosophy of the church" which makes an impact on European culture. Should the foreign missionary disown and castigate the old denominations of Europe, with their shaky theology and questionable ties? If he does, will he also renounce the sometimes large elements within these old churches who love Christ, seek fellowship, and traditionally remain inside the larger body? Or on the other hand should the missionary seek a biblically faithful denomination and add his converts to it? Or should he strike out on his own and form a new denomination? Whatever degree of separationism or inclusivism they may espouse, foreign missions in Europe have yet to find solutions to this problem which have vitally affected the masses or their culture to any extent.

When we turn to the credit side of the ledger, we find much in European missions to praise. In spite of obstacles, the great advances of the last five years suggest that the Lord of missions is about to bring in a harvest of souls. Specifically, what signs point in this direction?

Probably the outstanding evidence of the work of the Holy Spirit in Europe today is the current literature offensive. In an apparently unrelated fashion, and without prior consultation with each other, a number of literature organizations decided, over a period of about five years, to concentrate on Europe. Some of us who have prayed for a long while for a massive sowing of the Word of God as a preliminary to wider evangelism could scarcely believe the answers to our prayers, when we saw them. Movements like Evangelical Literature Overseas, World Literature Crusade, the Pocket Testament League, the Scripture Gift Mission, Operation Mobilization and the various Bible societies have all been heavily committed to this program. For example, we have seen over a thousand European young people undergoing special training in a tent city on the 18-acre campus of the European Bible Institute near Paris. While 70 trucks were prepared to bear 250 tons of literature to the villagers of Latin Europe, these young people engaged in long sessions of orientation and intercession. That particular campaign was only the opening one by Operation Mobilization, a movement notable for its daring, its emphasis on prayer and its wide outreach.

Then there is the bold planning of the Worldwide Literature Crusade. After setting a goal to reach 154 million Europeans of 12 countries with literature, this organization is well on its way to completion of distribution to 40 million homes. In response to 44 million gospel portions distributed they have received 74,065 responses from the recipients. Operation Mobilization estimates that it has distributed 34 million tracts and about 4 million booklets and gospels. The sale of complete books like Billy Graham's *Peace with God* and others have exceeded 300,000 copies. Bibles and testaments given out by Operation Mobilization exceed 60,000. Now if we add the distribution by World Literature Crusade to that by Operation Mobilization, we get a total of over 80 million pieces of literature. Then if we further add the huge distributions of the Pocket Testament League and the Scripture Gift Mission of London, plus the sales of the Bible societies, we find that the circulation of literature containing evangelical truth has exceeded 90 million units in the past five years. This averages 18 million pieces of literature a year. While these figures are immense to us, we must remember that a much higher saturation program must be reached if most Europeans are really to read the gospel.

It is easier to grasp the present distribution if we think in terms of countries rather than the whole continent. For instance, the World Literature Crusade has distributed 8 million scripture portions in Belgium, or almost one for each of the country's 9,650,000 population. In France Operation Mobilization and World Literature Crusader together have put in the hands of the people almost 20 million pieces of literature, which approaches one piece for every two French people. Together the two movements have given 50 million people of Italy almost 30 million pieces.

Correspondence course follow-up is used with much blessing. The Spanish pastor in charge of this ministry for Operation Mobilization reported that he picked up over 10,000 correspondence students after one summer's distribution in Spain. World Literature Crusade also has an extensive correspondence course work, with a world-wide enrollment of over a million, and 165,000 graduates. The latter has a specialized literature outreach to European students.

The second asset of European missions naturally flows from the first: The Holy Spirit is bringing to Christ a swiftly-increasing number of Europeans from all walks of life. It would of course be impossible to state accurately how many Europeans are accepting the Saviour through missionaries and the nationals they influence. But after a recent study of mission reports we would estimate that the total efforts of our European missions, with their various outreaches like radio and literature, produce over 10,000 converts a year. That figure is probably conservative. It is partially reflected in growing enrollments in institutions for Christian training, in the creation of more such institutions, and in the founding of churches.

We are thankful to God for the emphasis on many forms of evangelism by the missions. Almost every method is used, and many of them work. The very uniqueness of the foreign missionary is that he sees Europe as a mission field. He is not affected by the often limited perspective of many European evangelicals, who fail to see their own country in missionary terms, let alone other countries of the continent.

In recent years converts have been especially numerous in Portugal and Germany. While we can explain why a half-Protestant Germany, with its roots deep in the Bible and the Reformation, should be responsive, we have more difficulty understanding Portugal's reaction. Missionaries sowed the Word there for over one hundred years without noticeable result. Now a harvest is coming in. It is safe to say that, in proportion to Protestant ratio of its population, Portugal has one of the largest concentrations of new converts, especially among young people.

Our third point is that the number of missionaries to Europe is rising sharply. A few years ago many evangelical schools and societies in North America did not classify Europe as a mission field. That has changed. Now the spiritual need of the Old World is widely accepted among us. Some of the larger societies in our midst are entering Europe, and missionaries from closing countries in Africa and Asia are arriving on a continent which poses few problems confronted in the new and developing lands. The number of North American missionaries to Europe has risen by more than a third in the last four years. The dramatic rise in personnel and funds for Europe is visible in several missions which have doubled their missionary manpower within the last few years. One mission plans to double its number again within two or three years, basing its hopes on present inquiries and the climbing recruitment rate. This growth trend is strong and we hope it will continue.

Surely it implies, along with the other assets we have mentioned, a divine purpose. This seems to be Europe's hour! Compared with the rest of the world, this continent is relatively stable in politics. No rabid racism or particularly virulent nationalism plagues the foreign worker. Communism is quiescent and a climate of growing religious tolerance in southern Europe makes witness for Christ there much easier today. With rich and flexible languages at his disposal, the missionary in Europe can proclaim the gospel freely to an intelligent, largely literate people. In other words, Europe is in many respects the ideal mission field, yet one in which ideal results for the gospel have yet to be obtained. Perhaps the period just ahead will see our hopes realized of a total evangelization, out of which our Lord shall draw His body and bride, the Church for which He died.

CHAPTER 22

Latin America

by THE REVEREND JUAN M. ISAIS

The other day someone told me he had seen a sign on a wall in Buenos Aires saying "Yankees go home" but underneath someone had scribbled "By Pan American." In Santo Domingo there is a similar sign of "Yankees go home" but at the end it says "And take me with you!!"

The concepts expressed here are the result of a survey of 53 leaders from 19 different Latin American countries. I am nothing more than the mouthpiece for their opinions.

A few years ago the ex-president of Mexico, Adolfo Lopez Mateos, said in his election campaign: "There is only one path: Mexico." Today, along Conde Street in Santo Domingo, you read: "There is only one path: the Popular Revolution." Whatever these phrases may mean to the common people, they are genuine expressions of a continent which is awakening, politically, economically, culturally and religiously. Latin America today has all the characteristics of the adolescent, and sometimes her actions seem to indicate a total lack of common sense. But we must remember that she yearns to be perfectly independent, to make her own decisions in accord with her legitimate interests, and to express herself freely.

Politically, Latin America is in the center of a battlefield where two philosophies fight to give concrete expression to their ideals. Revolution, social justice, liberty, and such concepts are the dreams of our young people, but each phrase takes on different dimensions depending on who is in power at the moment. In this regard I quote a poem written in Spanish by a lawyer in the Dominican Republic, Alfonso Lockward:

"Upon the green carpet of your fields of sugar cane,
Play the two passions of the world's Goliaths,
And I feel myself, my country, to be no more than a chip
That moves back and forth on the table . . . a point in
the game.

In essence, you and I are of no importance,
The important ones are those who rival,
One method against another method,
Code against code, to see which one wins!

What are we? Nothing, simply nothing,
Elements of the game between two Cyclops
Who have but one point of view."

The common Latin American is confused, and perhaps for that reason he allies himself easily with anything which produces benefits in a short time. On the other hand, his highly developed individualism keeps him from tolerating the permanence of any ideology that annuls his personality. Precisely for this very reason, I firmly believe that international Communism cannot put down roots in Latin America: we are socialists, yes, but never Communists.

Educationally, we are going upwards, not only in theory, but in practice. Thirty years ago my parents were excommunicated from the Catholic Church for sending me to public school. In those days, going to school in Mexico was synonymous with being a Communist. Today, our governments, private institutions and churches are attaching great importance to education, and they are taking the necessary steps toward solving the serious problem of illiteracy. Let me note here, by the way, that in all of our Latin American countries, the evangelicals are more literate than the population in general. The well-known ex-president of Costa Rica, Jose Figueres, said in 1962, "If we don't redouble our efforts in the field of education, within 20 years we will have more illiteracy than we have now."[1]

For the Catholic Church, this preoccupation has taken concrete form. According to *Time* magazine, it has at least 46 universities, and many primary and secondary schools, generally serving the privileged class. These Catholic institutions are increasing steadily, while we evangelicals cut back our efforts or simply do not advance in line with the rhythm of opportunity.

From the religious point of view, Latin America is seeing drastic changes. The Catholic Church, with her gestures of friendship, represents an enigma for the evangelicals who have lived with her in the past. Conscious of his previous experience, the Latin American asks: Is the Catholic Church changing because it wants to recover its political power? Dr. Alfonso Lloreda[2] says: "With the visit of the Pope to the United Nations, Paul the Sixth turned the Vatican Council completely around. It was expected that a less powerful Pope would be the result, but exactly the opposite has happened."

Furthermore, is this new ecumenical policy simply an effort to get ahead of an evangelical church which is growing in greater proportion than the population, and thus avoid losing the little spiritual power which still remains with the Catholics? The Jesuit priest Pedro Rivera says regarding Protestant growth in Mexico: "Supposing that the growth of the last 11 years does not follow a rising trend but just remains stable, even so the panorama presents itself with extraordinary seriousness (for the Catholics). In fact, taking into account the constant increase of the population and the 150% increase of the Protestant community, we can reach the following data for the future: in 1970 the population of Mexico will be some 35 million. Of these, 7.5% as a minimum will be Protestant; for 1980, the total population will be 40 million inhabitants. Of these, approximately a minimum of 16.5% will be Protestant. As a result, even taking the conservative position that we have taken, the perspective for the future, based on statistics, cannot do less than impress us."[3] What he says about Mexico could also be said of other countries.

It cannot be denied that the peace offensive which the Vatican has initiated is of such breadth that it is difficult to ignore, although the cordiality, real or imagined, is felt mostly on the leadership level. Of course, we must recognize that there are various types of reactions within the evangelical church. On the one hand there are those who refuse to see the new open door with its opportunity to evangelize: there is still some opposition, yes, but less violent than previously. On the extreme right there are those who ignore the evangelical realities of Latin America and proclaim every wind of doctrine that comes from the continent or elsewhere. And in a third position are those who evaluate each situation objectively and separately, in the light of our own culture.

In spite of the above, we find a magnificent spirit of cooperation among the various groups and denominations, especially in evangelism. But in many cases, the poor education of the pastors makes this evangelism all too similar. In ten countries, the formal training of many leaders does not reach even the high school level. Fortunately, in Brazil, Mexico, Puerto Rico, and Uruguay the cultural level of the pastors is superior. At present, our existing seminaries do not yet have enough Latin American faculty members with sufficient education. It should be kept in mind that the future of the church lies in strategic investment. The Bible Institutes should continue, but should be producing lay leaders, not pastors in the present sense. In educating our pastors we are still doing a mediocre and irresponsible job, especially because we have gone to extremes, moved by a spirit of generalization, opening one door while closing another.

The leadership of evangelical work, thanks to the vision of some missionary statesmen like the late Dr. Kenneth Strachan, is falling more and more into the hands of nationals. This foreshadows a permanent stability for our message. It must be kept in mind that in circumstances like these, the progress of the work should not depend on currents of publicity but on the reality of a world that yearns to hear the Gospel. Latin America is predominantly conservative in doctrine because that way of thinking is more consonant with our culture. Dr. Manuel Sanchez, Ambassador of Chile in Israel, speaking in the Hebrew University of Jerusalem in homage to the Chilean poet Gabriela Mistral, said recently: "Gabriela had drunk her divine inspiration from the Bible, which we Latin Americans have made our own . . . whose message has introduced us to the mysteries of the chosen people." The Latin American evangelical church now has its own personality, and because of it, the scientific development of that personality will determine the power, the initiative and the stability of the church of tomorrow. Nevertheless, we must recognize that we do not live in the era of contrasts, but of reconsideration.

By the grace of God, Latin American governments sympathize with the gospel. There are a few countries which report some difficulties, but in general we are enjoying a freedom that many do not take full advantage of. Preaching by radio and television is legally within our reach, even though in practice it is not always so. Nevertheless, at present even in Mexico the gospel can be preached through these media. In other countries Bible classes can be given in the schools, although not without a struggle. Programs such as Evangelism-in-Depth help a great deal to create a favorable atmosphere toward evangelicals on the part of the governments, to the degree that they list them as positive values for the nation, in spite of the accusations of some Catholic priests who continue saying that Protestantism "is almost always disposed to making pacts with Communism".[4] Fortunately, the moral authority which evangelicals enjoy in the majority of countries makes such accusations fall on deaf ears.

The need to step up evangelical work is indisputable. The door of opportunity is before us, and we should enter it, accompanied by an unprecedented spirit of evangelism, flexible enough to take the fullest possible advantage of this new situation which the future apparently offers us at the cost of simple friendship.

In general, the evangelical churches are awakening to this new era. Much is still to be desired, but this is mostly due to the fact that the church has not learned to analyze itself nor to chart its own course independently. Our institutions should not base their criteria for growth on the flow of propaganda, but rather in the light of reality. Today there are still 190 million people in Latin America who do not know our form of Christianity, whose essence is the personal experience of having Christ as our only and all-sufficient Saviour.

The partial interpretation of the indigenous church principle ought to disappear. It should have a new interpretation, but this time a complete one. A self-propagating church does not mean fewer workers in the untouched fields, and much less does it mean that we should relate our national or foreign workers solely with the existing church. This is only a tiny edge of the coin. Those who limit these principles to the visible church alone are perhaps doing something wonderful in the eyes of a world which responds to trends of publicity, but they are failing in their true apostolic responsibility. In order for indigenous principles to have their full value, they should be practiced both inside and out of the present church. They should not signify a slackening of forces, but rather an increase; not retirement of funds, but reallocation of them; not reduction of projects, but an ever greater number of them. Today more than ever we need men from every nation who are moved, not by the flow of publicity, but by the cosmic passion of the Great Commission.

Our watchword should be for men of every race, every tongue, every calibre, every age, every gift: "Go ye into all the world and preach the Gospel to every creature"—in every place, using every method, but above all, with everyone working together at the same time to fulfill our obligation as disciples of Jesus Christ in the twentieth century.

FOOTNOTES

1. From a discourse in the Hotel Costa Rica, November 1962.
2. Prominent Colombian leader of the Presbyterians, now in Mexico.
3. Translated for *Protestantismo Mexicano* (1961), p. 105. Father Rivera is Professor of Comparative Religions in the Institute of Historical Investigations of the Ibero-American University, Mexico.
4. Pedro Rivera, *Institutiones Protestantes en Mexico* (1962), p. 163.

CHAPTER 23

South and Southeast Asia

by THE REVEREND PHU HOANG LE

The term *South Asia* designates the area encompased by Afghanistan, Bhutan, Ceylon, India, Nepal, and Pakistan. *Southeast Asia* is employed to denote the area of Burma, Thailand, Cambodia, Laos, Viet Nam, Malaysia, and Singapore.

The stark and stirring truth is that South and Southeast Asia are experiencing gigantic upheavals in population growth as well as in politics and religion.

In most of South and Southeast Asia, mortality is declining with unprecedented speed. This with an unusually high birth rate has caused a "vicious circle of poverty and disease." The sharply reduced death rate and the high birth rate are producing a population explosion unparalleled in world history. The annual population increase in India alone is more than the total population of Australia and New Zealand combined.

South and Southeast Asia have seven times the number of people in North America. More than half of them are under twenty years of age, and the proportion of children and youth to the total population continually increases. Saigon, Viet Nam, is a city of two million people. One-half of them are under twenty years of age. One-third are children under ten. Of Singapore's population, 60 per cent are now under twenty years of age.

Communism's glittering promises of social and economic justice, of racial equality and of victory over supposed western imperialism have been enormously appealing in a region where glaring wealth exists side by side with unbelievable poverty and degradation. Since World War II, Communism has speedily gained the favorable attention of so many people in so many countries that its growth and power are probably without parallel in any other political movement. Ceylon, Burma, Cambodia, Viet Nam, and India are vitally affected by it. Communism is reaching for total victory.

In South and Southeast Asia non-Christian forces have never been so formidable as they are today. Until recently, Hinduism and Buddhism were passive in their resistance to the Christian gospel. Today that situation is profoundly changed. Hinduism and Buddhism now are militant missionary faiths, confronting both Protestant and Catholic witness with strengthened opposition.

The result has been a religious revival for the people of South and Southeast Asia. They are turning to their ancestral religions with new hope and a new sense of pride. They are engaging in open conflict with Christianity. As never before, they question Christianity's claim to be the final and absolute truth for all time. There is also a strong tendency to equate adherence to the ancient religion with loyal citizenship.

Hinduism is the religion of one-fifth of the world's population. But it is a new Hinduism with a modern set of ideas and practices superimposed on the old inherited pattern of life. The result is a formidable defense for Christianity to penetrate.

Buddhism, the faith of one-third of the world's population, openly challenges Christianity as a rival option for a troubled world. It teaches that Christianity has miserably failed, as evidenced by two world wars and the Korean and Viet Nam conflicts. Buddhists believe—and teach—that before Christian nations blow up the world, Buddhism must intervene and restore peace. By presenting Buddhism as a force for world peace, Buddhists possess a most effective propaganda weapon.

The modern Buddhist missionary movement is one of the most powerfully dynamic forces in Asia. Buddhist scriptures have been translated into a number of languages. The Missionary Training College, Rangoon, Burma, has a five-year course for preparing foreign missionaries. There is a similar school in Colombo, Ceylon. In Ceylon, advertisements invite contributions for a missionary society "for the spread of the gospel of Buddhism among the heathen of Europe."

In its missionary efforts, Buddhism can count on the sympathy of most Asian governments. Some governments actively support it, in particular Bhutan, Ceylon, Burma, Thailand, Cambodia, and Laos. The Buddhist state of Bhutan prohibits all Christian gospel witness. Burma has asked all Christian missionaries who entered after 1948 to leave by the end of 1966. Buddhism urgently seeks to block the progress of Christianity.

Islam is strong in Afghanistan. No representatives of Christ travel the seven important trade routes across the country. The Muslims forbid missionaries to enter. Profession of faith in Christ is punishable by death. Pakistan is also an Islamic state. Although religious tolerance is practiced, relatively few Pakistanis are Christians.

Against this ominously dark background, the Christian Church is living and working. From a human viewpoint, it occupies a precarious position. To date the Protestant community—a term designating baptized and non-baptized adherents—is a mere 1 percent of the population. But God can save by few as well as by many. In accordance with His Word, one shall chase a thousand, for the Lord God battles for us.

For years, Nepal was tightly closed to gospel messengers. Then fifteen years ago God used the visit of a Christian ornithologist, hunting for rare birds, to open the country to the missionary. Today there are more than one hundred Christian doctors, nurses, and technicians ministering in crowded hospitals and dispensaries. Despite restrictions the Christian Church is beginning to take firm root.

Evangelicals in India have vastly increased their witness through bookstores, reading rooms, Bible correspondence courses, and radio programs. Evangelism-in-Depth and other programs for total mobilization of the Church are significantly strengthening the spiritual life of the Church. They are also bringing many into the fold of Christ.

The Union Biblical Seminary, Yeotmal, truly evangelical and fully accredited, continues to produce graduates who are proving to be well-trained leaders for the Indian Church. Some have gone forth as foreign missionaries.

The well-organized Evangelical Fellowship of India seeks to heighten the spiritual life of the churches through spiritual life conferences, the publication of evangelical literature, and prayer retreats. It is an organization that could well be emulated in other countries. One of its projects was the All-India Bible Commentary, a monumental work which has taken ten years to produce. Written in India for publication in seven languages, it covers the whole Bible and is slanted toward Christian leaders and teachers who normally do not read English *(World Vision,* November, 1965, page 12).

Although the Protestant community in Burma is but 2 percent of the total population, 40 percent of the Karen tribe is Protestant. Theirs is one of the strongest churches of Southeast Asia. It is self-reliant and vigorously evangelistic and missionary minded. It is also in tension with the prevailing communistic government of Burma.

The Protestant community of Thailand, after 130 years of effort, totals approximately one-tenth of 1 percent of Thailand's twenty-eight million people. The efforts of six hundred missionaries in every type of missionary service have not brought forth a large or aggressively evangelistic church.

As in Thailand, so in Cambodia. Buddhism is the state religion; to embrace Christianity is to be a traitor. After centuries of rigid exclusion, Protestant missionaries gained entrance in 1923, but because of stringent government restrictions only nine of the sixteen provinces of Cambodia were permitted to have missionaries in residence. In 42 years, there is a church of only 750 baptized Christians. Now the anti-American position of the government has forced out all American missionaries. Meetings on church premises have been forbidden, although Christians may meet in private homes.

In war-torn Laos, there are eleven thousand tribal Christians. Many of these have made a determined stand to oppose Communism. Several thousand have settled in "free" centers inside the communist-held territory. Uprooted from their homesteads and surrounded by rebel forces, these believers have shown tremendous growth and stability. Not a few who left the Communist territory have spread the gospel into areas hitherto unreached by Christians. The war in Laos has turned out for the furtherance of the gospel.

Incredible as it may seem, the work of the gospel in South Viet

Nam continues with unparalleled success. Three missionaries, several pastors, and many Christians have been killed. Three missionaries are being held by the Viet Cong. Still the work goes on from strength to strength. The church reported that 1965 was a record year for baptism. In March a spiritual life conference, attended by 380 missionaries and pastors, was epochal in its spiritual impact. From April 2-10—last week—the Saigon churches banded together for a city Crusade for Christ in a 20,000-seat stadium. A five-year program of accelerated evangelism has been adopted by church and mission. They expect a great ingathering of souls.

Several truly significant facts emerge from the current situation in South and Southeast Asia. There are whole areas where from five to fifteen million people have never heard of Jesus. More countries are either closed to missionary work or restrict missionary work than anywhere else in the world. On the other hand, in Ceylon and to some extent in Viet Nam the Christian community is middle class, which argues well for the Church's future. From the eastern 15 provinces of Thailand all the way east to the China Sea, only evangelical churches and missions are at work. Liberal Christianity is not yet a serious threat. Tribal groups in all of these countries are amazingly responsive to the gospel of Christ.

The situation in South and Southeast Asia may not be entirely bright, but neither is it altogether dark. Guarded optimism and optimistic realism ought to characterize the Church's continued advance in these two areas.

CHAPTER 

Far East/Pacific

by Gadiel T. Isidro

Once the largest mission field in the world, China is today a closed country. The mass evacuation of all missionaries in the early 1950's was tragic but not catastrophic. The churches, though under constant surveillance and subject to terrific pressure from the government, gallantly carried on a modified form of Christian witness until 1958, when the introduction of the People's Communes dealt a body blow to organized religion.

Since that time the picture has become increasingly confused. Nothing authentic is known about the rural churches. It is safe to assume that few continue to exist. We do know that the number of urban churches has been drastically reduced. Cities such as Shanghai, Nanking, and Tientsin, which once boasted of a hundred or more churches, now have only three or four, and they are a pale imitation of their former selves. All Protestant churches are under the control of the Three-Self-Movement, of which Dr. Wu Yao-Tsung is still the national chairman. Nanking Theological Seminary is the only seminary now permitted to function; it has about 100 students in residence. The fate of the Yenching Union Seminary is uncertain owing to conflicting reports.

On three previous occasions Christianity was planted in China, but each time it died out. Will it survive the fourth planting? Humanly speaking, the future is not hopeful. Protestant Christians, once a million strong, do not now number more than 700,000. They represent one-tenth of one per cent of the population—certainly a "little flock." The suffering church in China is a rebuke to our complacency and a challenge to our intercession. From every point of view Taiwan represents one of the bright spots in the Far East. Church growth in Taiwan has been extremely rapid in this post war period. During the past decade the Presbyterian Church of Taiwan has organized 453 new churches, bringing the total to 800 churches with a total membership of 180,000. The Protestant Centenary in 1965, celebrated by 22 denominations, attracted 300 delegates from overseas.

Two post war developments are worthy of mention: the large influx of new missions; and a massive breakthrough among the mountain tribes, referred to as "Pentecost in the Hills."

With the evacuation of China in the early 1950's many societies naturally turned their attention to Taiwan, resulting in a vast proliferation of foreign missionary societies. Where formerly there had been but two missions, today there are well over seventy, most of them from the United States.

As a result of a genuine mass movement among the 200,000 tribal peoples, 80 per cent of them are now Christian. They are about equally divided between Roman Catholics and Protestants. Bible translation is proceeding in most of the ten tribal dialects. With a well equipped studio in Taichung, The Evangelical Alliance Mission is releasing Christian broadcasts over commercial stations in ten cities of the island. Of the two million mainlanders, perhaps 100,000 are Protestant Christians.

The church in Japan is predominantly urban; 90 per cent of the congregations are located in the cities. The Christians, on the whole, are fairly well-to-do and highly literate. In spite of a cultural barrier and a strong feeling of nationalism among the people, Protestant church membership doubled between 1945 and 1963. Today all Protestant churches combined have about half a million members. The Roman Catholics number about 300,000. Together they represent less than one per cent of the population—after one hundred years of missionary activity.

The MacArthur era witnessed a sudden influx of new missions which brought the number of missionaries to an all-time high of 2,000. The 1965 edition of the *Japan Christian Year Book* lists 155 foreign mission societies and 37 Christian agencies. In 1964 the Bible Society reported a distribution of more than four million copies of the Scriptures—an increase of 30 per cent over 1963.

Fifty million radios and 18 million television sets afford a unique opportunity for mass communication which Christian missions have been quick to exploit. Thirty-eight missions sponsor 72 weekly broadcasts over commercial stations. The Lutheran Hour drama, "Behold the Christ", heard over 105 stations, has received the greatest listener response.

Along with the unprecedented opportunities there are adversaries. The many "new religions," with their evangelistic atmosphere, testimony meetings, faith healings and group therapy, confront Christianity with a new form of competition. Most aggressive and fastest growing is Soka Gakkai, a fanatical sect which preaches prayer and politics. Once a religious organization, recently it has entered politics; already it is the third largest party in the House of Councillors. Membership has grown from 5,000 families in 1951 to 5 million families today. The most ominous aspect of Soka Gakkai is its coercive conversion methods, its intolerance of all other faiths, and its ambition to become a global religion. Already it has sent missionaries to Korea, Taiwan and the USA.

Christianity has registered greater gains in Korea than any other country of the Far East. Ever since 1919 the Church has spearheaded the drive for freedom and democracy, first against the Japanese, later against the Communists in the North, and more recently against military rule in the South.

The widespread adoption of the Nevius Method of missionary work and the great revival of 1907 have been contributing factors in the success of the Christian cause in Korea.

Four Presbyterian denominations with 5,000 churches, the Methodist Church with 1200 churches, and the Holiness Church (OMS) with 500 churches represent 90 per cent of the Protestant community of a million and a half. Nothing is known of the fate of the churches in North Korea. There is reason to believe that the Communists there have been even more repressive than in North Vietnam or China, perhaps because of the strong anti-communist stand taken by the church leaders.

Until the widespread devastation of the Korean War all the churches were self-supporting. It has taken them some years to get back into financial shape. The missions have done an excellent job in higher education. Christian universities have had a tremendous influence on the life of the nation. Some of the largest and finest theological schools in the world are in Korea. In 1964 there were 302 Christian chaplains in the armed forces.

In recent years Christian broadcasting has played an increasingly important role. Five strategically located stations, sponsored by the Presbyterians, afford fairly adequate coverage of South Korea. TEAM's station, HLKX at Inchon, besides serving South Korea beams the Gospel into North Korea, Siberia, and Communist China with gratifying results.

Unfortunately divisions have plagued the churches in Korea. The four-year rift in the Holiness Church was healed in 1965. The schism in the Presbyterian ranks still remains.

After four centuries of Catholic missions, 26 million Filipinos (84 per cent of the population) are claimed by the Roman Catholic Church. This makes the Philippines the only Christian country in Asia. The next largest group, with one and a half million adherents, is the Philippine Independent Church which, in the revolt led by Father Gregorio Aglipay, broke with Rome in 1902. The largest Protestant Church is the United Church of Christ; in the 1960 census it reported a constituency of 300,000. Other large churches include the Methodists, Baptists, Lutherans, and others. Two non-Christian groups are the pagans (800,000) and the Muslims (1,500,000).

An estimated 95 per cent of the 950 Protestant missionaries are from the USA, with the result that the Filipino Church, like the country, has been greatly "Americanized." As elsewhere, fragmentation plagues the Protestant scene. A recent publication listed 113 denominations and 65 seminaries and Bible schools in the Philippines.

Bible translation, always a reliable barometer of evangelical progress, has been promoted consistently, with the result that the Scriptures are now available in 34 of the 89 dialects of the Islands.

The American penchant for higher education is reflected in the presence of two full-fledged Christian universities and nine theological seminaries, a good record for any country where Protestants are a small minority.

The post war period has witnessed a large influx of new

missions, most of them belonging to the "conservative evangelical" wing of the Church. Honorable mention should be made of the radio station, the *Voice of the Orient,* in Manila, whose 17 transmitters are broadcasting the Gospel to all parts of Asia and the Far East in some 36 languages with amazing results.

In closing it might be helpful to make certain general observations regarding the Far East. First, American missions have dominated the situation from the beginning, about one hundred years ago. Consequently the national churches there have tended to be "Americanized" to an unhealthy degree. Secondly, the national churches, though constantly spoken of as being independent, are in many instances still receiving large subsidies from America which means that they are not truly independent. Thirdly, most of the missionary work has been done by the historic denominations. It is only in this post war period that IFMA-EFMA missions in any numbers have entered this region. Fourthly, the national churches in this area are much stronger in leadership than their counterparts in other areas of the world. Fifthly, the national churches in three countries (Japan, Korea and the Philippines) have a commendable program of home and foreign missions. Hundreds of missionaries have been sent abroad, not only to other parts of Asia but also to North and South America. The "new instrument" of the Overseas Missionary Fellowship, by which Oriental missionaries are accepted into the Fellowship, represents a breakthrough in mission strategy and augurs well for the future of missionary work in the Far East.

APPENDIX

CHAPTER 25

The EFMA and the IFMA: Descriptive Background and Doctrinal Commitment

A Brief Sketch of the Evangelical Foreign Missions Association
1405 G Street, N.W., Washington, D.C. 20005
Executive Secretary: Dr. Clyde W. Taylor

The Evangelical Foreign Missions Association, since its establishment in 1945, has operated as a voluntary association of denominational and non-denominational foreign mission agencies. Fifty-nine agencies comprise the membership of EFMA, with 6,452 missionaries who serve in 120 mission fields on all continents outside the United States. One of every four Protestant foreign missionaries from the United States is serving under an EFMA-member organization. The association is affiliated with the National Association of Evangelicals.

PURPOSE

EFMA desires to develop wider fellowship and a greater spiritual unity among evangelical missions. It encourages consultation and cooperation among evangelicals in national and international projects.

OFFICES

Maintaining a headquarters and service office under the direction of Dr. Clyde W. Taylor, the Association provides united representation before governments, information on government regulations and international affairs which affect foreign missions, assistance in securing passports, visas and other legal documents, booklets on current missionary topics, and a semi-monthly

Missionary News Service. The Headquarters Office is in Washington, D.C.

The EFMA Purchasing Office, under the direction of Mr. G. Allan Small, at 120 Liberty Street, New York, New York 10006, assists in purchasing at wholesale prices equipment and supplies for missionaries and other Christian workers. In 1964 the Office purchased over $1 million worth of equipment.

A travel agency, under the direction of Mr. A. S. Bowker, Universal Travel Service, 100 West Monroe Street, Chicago, Illinois 60603, serves the general public but specializes in travel arrangements for missionaries and other Christian workers.

COOPERATION

The Congress on the Church's Worldwide Mission is but one project in which EFMA is cooperating with the IFMA (Interdenominational Foreign Mission Association). The Africa Evangelical Office in Nairobi, Kenya, is the outgrowth of the Joint Africa Committee of EFMA and IFMA. *The Evangelical Missions Quarterly,* a scholarly journal of missions, is a joint effort of EFMA and IFMA.

The EFMA believes—

a. The Bible to be the inspired, the only infallible, authoritative Word of God.
b. That there is one God, eternally existent in three Persons: Father, Son, and Holy Spirit.
c. In the deity of our Lord Jesus Christ, in His virgin birth, in His sinless life, in His miracles, in His vicarious and atoning death through His shed blood, in His bodily resurrection, in His ascension to the right hand of the Father, and in His personal return in power and glory.
d. That for the salvation of lost and sinful man regeneration by the Holy Spirit is absolutely essential.
e. In the present ministry of the Holy Spirit by whose indwelling the Christian is enabled to live a godly life.
f. In the resurrection of both the saved and the lost; they that are saved unto the resurrection of life and they that are lost unto the resurrection of damnation.
g. In the spiritual unity of believers in our Lord Jesus Christ.

A Brief Sketch of the
Interdenominational Foreign Mission Association
54 Bergen Avenue, Ridgefield Park, New Jersey 07660
Executive Secretary: Mr. Edward L. Frizen, Jr.

The IFMA was organized on March 31, 1917, by leaders of several well-known faith missions (missions without denominational affiliation) for purposes of spiritual fellowship and co-operation. Although not superimposing administrative authority over member missions, IFMA functions in behalf of its members in accrediting them to the Christian public as societies worthy of support. Standards of membership and evangelical doctrinal convictions have had a large part in establishing public confidence in IFMA missions.

Applicants for full membership in the IFMA must:

- be governed by a properly constituted board of directors, with foreign mission work its major responsibility.
- be a society with at least 10 North American missionaries supported by North American funds, or be a service organization which by its services contributes to the effectiveness of other member missions.
- evangelize and engage in the formation and/or furtherance of the indigenous church.
- present evidence satisfactory to the Association as to the necessity and purpose of its existence.
- issue a properly audited annual financial report.
- through prayer and faith, rely upon God for the provision of the needs of His work committed unto it.
- be approved by the member missions as to its policies and practices at home and on the field.

IFMA acts as an information center on missionary societies and activities around the world. IFMA assists pastors and churches in establishing a church-missionary program. IFMA experience is available to member missions and others desiring help and advice in mission administration, Internal Revenue Service matters, and other areas of government affairs.

The Association maintains an office at 54 Bergen Avenue, Ridgefield Park, New Jersey 07660. Mr. Edwin L. Frizen, Jr., is

Executive Secretary. To promote the cause of missions at home IFMA publishes bi-monthly (except July-August) the *IFMA News* with information and prayer requests on missionary work around the world. Other literature includes booklets and pamphlets on a variety of missionary concerns.

From its original membership of four societies, IFMA in less than fifty years, has grown to a membership of 46 societies representing 8,400 missionaries.

In recent years, because of its sound and spiritual leadership, its sane principles and policies of missionary work, its solid achievements on the mission field, its continued emphasis on evangelism and the indigenous church, and its strong evangelical position, IFMA has been looked to as an accrediting association in the field of inter-denominational missions.

Officers of the Association, elected each year, include the president (J. Morris Rockness, Overseas Missionary Fellowship), two vice-presidents (Sidney Langford, Africa Inland Mission; J. Hubert Cook, Evangelical Union of South America), and secretary (Arthur H. Salter, Bible Christian Union). There are ten additional members of the Official Board. There are twelve specialized IFMA committees, and IFMA is represented on eight joint committees with the Evangelical Foreign Missions Association.

The IFMA believes—

a. The Bible, which is verbally inspired by the Holy Spirit in the original manuscripts and is the infallible and authoritative Word of God.

b. The Triune Godhead in Three Persons—Father, Son and Holy Spirit.

c. The personality of Satan, called the Devil, and his present control over unregenerate mankind.

d. The fall and lost estate of man, whose total depravity makes necessary the new birth.

e. The deity of Jesus Christ, His virgin birth, death, bodily resurrection, present exaltation at God's right hand, and personal and imminent return.

f. The atonement by the substitutionary death and shed blood of Jesus Christ our Lord and Saviour.

g. The resurrection of the saved unto everlasting life and

blessedness in heaven, and the resurrection of the unsaved unto everlasting punishment in hell.

h. The Church, the Body or Bride of Christ, consisting only of those who are born again, for whom He now makes intercession in heaven and for whom He shall come again.
i. Christ's great commission to the Church to go into all the world and preach the gospel to every creature, baptizing and teaching those who believe.

CHAPTER 

Congress Committees

Full Congress Committee
IFMA-EFMA

Dr. Vernon Mortenson	Dr. Louis L. King

Co-chairmen

Rev. Edwin L. Frizen, Jr.	Dr. Clyde W. Taylor
Dr. Raymond J. Davis	Dr. Milton Baker
Rev. J. Morris Rockness	Rev. Norman L. Cummings

International Advisory Committee

Rev. Timothy Kamau ....Kenya
Rev. Akira Hatori ....Japan
Dr. Jacques Blocher ....France
Rev. Doan Van Mieng ....Viet Nam
Rev. Ruben Lores ....Costa Rica

Sub-Committees

Accreditation ....Cummings, Mortenson, Frizen, Taylor
Arrangements ....Baker, Egeland, Fricke, O. Carlsen
Finance ....Mortenson, Richardson
Music ....Van Hovel
Prayer ....Dugan
Press Corps ....Smith, Fricke, W. Carlson, Reapsome, Stobbe, Sorensen, Moore
Program ....Taylor, Frizen
Review ....King, Mortenson, Norton, Tenney, Climenhaga, Kantzer, Glasser

Program Personnel

Dr. Carl Amerding .... President, Central American Mission
Dr. Jacques Blocher .... Co-director, Nogent Bible Institue, France
Rev. James Bolarin .... Editor, *African Challenge,* Kenya, E. Africa
Rev. Roy I. Brill .... Deputation Secretary, African Inland Mission
Rev. R. P. Chavan .... Moderator, General Assembly Christian and Missionary Alliance of India
Dr. Arthur M. Climenhaga .... Executive Director, National Association of Evangelicals
Dr. Robert P. Evans .... European Director, Greater Europe Mission
Dr. Theodore H. Epp .... Director, Back to the Bible Broadcast
Dr. Horace L. Fenton, Jr. ..... General Director, Latin America Mission
Mr. Eric Fife .... Missionary Director, Inter-Varsity Christian Fellowship
Mr. Edwin L. Frizen, Jr....... Executive Secretary, Interdenominational Foreign Mission Association
Rev. Vergil Gerber .... Missionary, Conservative Baptist Home Mission Society
Dr. P. Kenneth Gieser......... President, Christian Medical Society
Dr. Arthur F. Glasser .... Home Director, Overseas Missionary Fellowship
Dr. Vernon Grounds .... President, Conservative Baptist Theological Seminary
Rev. Akira Hatori .... Director Radio Evangelism, Pacific Broadcasting Association, Japan
Dr. Don W. Hillis .... Associate Director, The Evangelical Alliance Mission

Rev. Melvin L. Hodges	Secretary for Latin America and West Indies General Council of the Assemblies of God
Rev. Juan Isais	Area Coordinator, Evaneglism-In-Depth, Mexico
Mr. Gadiel Isidro	Far Eastern Gospel Crusade, Philippine Islands
Mr. James Johnson	Executive Secretary, Evangelical Literature Overseas
Rev. Timothy Kamau	Radio Pastor, Africa Inland Church, Kenya, East Africa
Dr. Kenneth S. Kantzer	Dean, Trinity Evangelical Divinity School
Dr. Louis L. King	Foreign Secretary, Christian and Missionary Alliance
Rev. Gilbert W. Kirby	International Secretary, World Evangelical Fellowship
Dr. Raymond Knighton	Executive Director, Medical Assistance Programs, Inc.
Dr. Delbert Kuehl	Executive Assistant Director, The Evangelical Alliance Mission
Rev. Alfred Larson	Congo Field Leader, Unevangelized Fields Mission
Rev. Phu Hoang Le	former General Secretary, The Evangelical Church of Viet Nam
Rev. Ruben Lores	Director of Evangelism, Latin America Mission; International Coordinator, Evangelism-in-Depth
Dr. Vernon Mortenson	General Director, The Evangelical Alliance Mission
Dr. H. Wilbert Norton	Professor of Missions, Wheaton College Graduate School
Rev. Jack F. Shepherd	Director, Jaffray School of Missions
Dr. Clyde W. Taylor	Executive Secretary, Evangelical Foreign Missions Association

Rev. Philip Teng . . . . Chairman, Chinese Missionary Society, Hong Kong
Rev. A. G. Thiessen . . . . Deputation Secretary, Sudan Interior Mission
Rev. Doan Van Mieng . . . . President, Evangelical Church, Viet Nam
Dr. Fernando Vangioni . . . . Evangelist, Billy Graham Evangelistic Association, Argentina
Dr. John F. Walvoord . . . . President, Dallas Theological Seminary

Study Paper Consultants

Rev. Philip E. Armstrong . . . . . . Executive Secretary, Far Eastern Gospel Crusade
Rev. Erik Barnett . . . . Missionary (Africa), Africa Inland Mission
Rev. Linwood Barney . . . . Professor, Jaffray School of Missions
Rev. James Bolarin . . . . Editor, *African Challenge*
Dr. Raymond Buker . . . . Professor of Missions, Conservative Baptist Theological Seminary
Dr. Harold Cook . . . . Chairman, Department of Missions, Moody Bible Institute
Rev. Ralph Cox . . . . Missionary (Japan), The Evangelical Alliance Mission; Chairman, Department of Missions, Southeastern Bible College
Rev. Ralph Christensen . . . . Missionary (South Africa), The Evangelical Alliance Mission
Rev. Norman Cummings . . . . . . Home Director, Overseas Crusades, Inc.
Rev. W. Elwyn Davies . . . . Director for Canada, Bible Christian Union
Dr. Wesley Duewel . . . . Vice President, The Oriental Missionary Society
Dr. Horace L. Fenton, Jr. . . . . . . General Director, Latin America Mission

Rev. Junichi Funaki . . . . President, Japan Bible Seminary
Rev. Stuart P. Garver . . . . Executive Director, Christ's Mission
Dr. Arthur F. Glasser . . . . Home Director, Overseas Missionary Fellowship
Dr. David Gotaas . . . . Missionary (Venezuela), The Evangelical Alliance Mission, Instructor, Moody Bible Institute
Rev. Ian Hay . . . . Home Director, Sudan Interior Mission
Dr. Carl F. H. Henry . . . . Editor, *Christianity Today*
Rev. Art Johnston . . . . Missionary (France), The Evangelical Alliance Mission
Dr. Rufus Jones . . . . General Director, Conservative Baptist Home Mission Society
Rev. J. Herbert Kane . . . . Director of Missions, Lancaster School of the Bible
Rev. Francis Keida . . . . Research Secretary, *Christian Heritage Magazine*
Dr. Louis L. King . . . . Foreign Secretary, Christian and Missionary Alliance
Dr. Delbert Kuehl . . . . Executive Assistant Director, The Evangelical Alliance Mission
Dr. Harold B. Kuhn . . . . Chairman, Department of Philosophy of Religion, Asbury Theological Seminary
Rev. Sidney Langford . . . . General Secretary, Africa Inland Mission
Rev. Francisco Lievano . . . . Professor, Ebenezer Bible Institute (Venezuela), The Evangelical Alliance Mission
Dr. Harold Lindsell . . . . Associate Editor, *Christianity Today*
Rev. Ruben Lores . . . . Director, Division of Evangelism, Latin America Mission

Rev. William A. Mahlow ...... General Secretary, World Presbyterian Mission
Dr. Donald A. McGavran ..... Dean, School of World Mission, Fuller Theological Seminary
Rev. Douglas Percy .... Director of Missions, Toronto Bible College
Dr. George Peters .... Professor of World Missions, Dallas Theological Seminary
Dr. Earl Radmacher .... President, Western Conservative Baptist Seminary
Mr. Lorne Sanny .... President, The Navigators
Dr. Francis Steele .... Home Secretary, North Africa Mission
Dr. Clyde W. Taylor .... Executive Secretary, Evangelical Foreign Missions Association
Dr. Merrill C. Tenney .... Dean, Wheaton College Graduate School
Mr. Charles H. Troutman...... former General Director Inter-Varsity Christian Fellowship
Mr. I. Ben Wati .... Executive Secretary, Evangelical Fellowship of India
Dr. Lester Westlund .... Secretary of Foreign Missions, The Evangelical Free Church of America
Rev. Kermit Zopfi .... Director, German Bible Institute, Greater Europe Mission

CHAPTER 27

Congress Program

Sunday, April 10, 1966

10:00 A.M. Worship Service
Mission and the Resurrection Proclamation
Theodore Epp, *Back to the Bible Broadcast*
3:30 P.M. Public Rally
Timothy Kamau, Ruben Lores, Jacques Blocher, Akira Hatori, Doan Van Mieng, Vergil Gerber
7:30 P.M. Keynote Address
God's Gift to the Church: Louis L. King

Monday, April 11, 1966

8:30 A.M. Bible Exposition
Mission and the Church's Authority: Kenneth S. Kantzer
9:15 A.M. Study Paper
Mission and Syncretism: Jack F. Shepherd
10:30 A.M. Discussion Groups
2:15 P.M. Study Paper
Mission and Neo-Universalism: Arthur Climenhaga
3:30 P.M. Discussion Groups
7:30 P.M. Area Brief
Africa: James Bolarin
7:50 P.M. Ministry Briefs
Literature: James Johnson
8:15 P.M. Inspirational Address
Mission and Prayer: Don Hillis

Tuesday, April 12, 1966

8:30 A.M. Bible Exposition
Mission and the Church's Message: Arthur F. Glasser

9:15 A.M. Study Paper
Mission and Proselytism: Jacques Blocher
10:30 A.M. Discussion Groups
2:15 P.M. Study Paper
Mission and Neo-Romanism: Vernon Grounds
3:30 P.M. Discussion Groups
7:30 P.M. Area Briefs
Europe: Robert P. Evans
7:50 P.M. Ministry Brief
Radio: A. G. Thiessen
8:15 P.M. Inspirational Address
Mission and Mandate: Timothy Kamau

Wednesday, April 13, 1966

8:30 A.M. Bible Exposition
Mission and the Church's Endowment: Philip Teng
9:15 A.M. Study Paper
Mission and Church Growth: Melvin Hodges
10:30 A.M. Discussion Groups
2:15 P.M. Study Paper
Mission and Foreign Missions: R. P. Chavan
3:30 P.M. Discussion Groups
7:30 P.M. Area Brief
Latin America: Juan M. Isais
7:50 P.M. Ministry Brief
Education: Delbert Kuehl
8:15 P.M. Inspirational Address
Mission and Manpower: Ruben Lores

Thursday, April 14, 1966

8:30 A.M. Bible Exposition
Mission and the Church's Nature: John F. Walwoord
9:15 A.M. Study Paper
Mission and Evangelical Unity: Vernon Mortenson
10:30 A.M. Discussion Groups
2:15 P.M. Study Paper
Mission and Evaluating Methods: H. Wilbert Norton
3:30 P.M. Discussion Groups

7:30 P.M. Area Brief
S/SE Asia: Phu Hoang Le
7:50 P.M. Ministry Brief
Medicine: Kenneth Gieser
8:15 P.M. Inspirational Address
Mission and Discipleship: Roy F. Brill

Friday, April 15, 1966

8:30 A.M. Bible Exposition
Mission and the Church's Consummation: Eric Fife
9:15 A.M. Study Paper
Mission and Social Concern: Horace L. Fenton, Jr.
10:30 A.M. Discussion Groups
2:15 P.M. Study Paper
Mission and a Hostile World: Alfred Larson
3:30 P.M. Discussion Groups
7:30 P.M. Area Brief
Far East/Pacific: Gadiel Isidro
7:50 P.M. Ministry Brief
Mass Evangelism: Fernando Vangioni
8:15 P.M. Inspirational Address
Mission and Harvest: Clyde W. Taylor

Saturday, April 16, 1966

8:30 A.M. Business Session
Adoption of the Wheaton Declaration
11:00 A.M. Communion Service
Mission and Commitment: G. W. Kirby
The Lord's Supper
Adjournment

CHAPTER 28

Organizations Registered
For The
Congress On The Church's Worldwide Mission

Evangelical Foreign Missions Association (EFMA)
Interdenominational Foreign Mission Association (IFMA)

Africa Evangelical Fellowship
Africa Evangelical Office
Africa Inland Mission
American Advent Mission Society
American Messianic Fellowship
Andes Evangelical Mission
Appalachian Bible Institute (West Virginia)
Arctic Missions, Inc.
Asia For Christ Missionary Strategy Agency
Assemblies of God, Foreign Missions Dept.
Association of Baptists for World Evangelism
Back To The Bible Broadcast
Baptist General Conference, Board of Foreign Missions
Baptist General Conference, Board of Home Missions
Barrington College (Rhode Island)
Belgian Gospel Mission, Inc.
Berean Mission, Inc.
Berkshire Christian College (Massachusetts)
Bethel Theological Seminary (Minnesota)
Bible Christian Union
Bible Club Movement
Bible and Medical Missionary Fellowship
Bible Meditation League
Billy Graham Evangelistic Association

Biola College (California)
Brethren Church, Missionary Board Of
Brethren Church Foreign Missionary Society
Brethren in Christ World Missions
Bryan University (Tennessee)
Buffalo Bible Institute (New York)
Calvary Bible College (Missouri)
Calvin Theological Seminary & College (Michigan)
Campus Crusade International
Canadian Bible College (Canada)
Central American Mission
Central Bible Institute & Seminary (Missouri)
Ceylon and India General Mission
Child Evangelism Fellowship Int'l.
Children's Bible Fellowship
Chamber Of Evangelical Lit. For Brazil
Christian Medical Society
Christian & Missionary Alliance
Christian Missionary Fellowship
Christian Missions in Many Lands, Ltd.
Christian Reformed Board of Foreign Missions
Christian Service Brigade
Christian Training Institute (Canada)
Christian Nationals' Evangelism Commission
Church of God World Missions
Columbia Bible College (South Carolina)
Congo Inland Mission
Conservative Baptist Foreign Mission
Conservative Baptist Home Mission Society
Conservative Baptist Theological Seminary (Colorado)
Covenant Theological Seminary (Missouri)
Dallas Bible College (Texas)
Dallas Theological Seminary (Texas)
David C. Cook Foundation
Difusiones Inter Americanas
Distribuidory Editora De Literatura Evangelical
Eastern Baptist College & Seminary (Pennsylvania)
Eastern European Mission

Eastern Mennonite Board of Missions & Charities
Eastern Mennonite College (Virginia)
Egypt General Mission
Erickson Foundation
Evangel College (Missouri)
Evangelical Covenant Church Of America
Evangelical Fellowship Of India
Evangelical Free Church of America
Evangelical Friends Alliance
Evangelical Lit. Fellowship of E. Africa
Evangelical Lit. Fellowship of India
Evangelical Literature Overseas
Evangelical Mennonite Church
Evangelical Teacher Training Assoc.
Evangelical Union Of South America
Evangelistic Faith Missions, Inc.
Evangelized China Inc.
Far East Broadcasting Company, Inc.
Far Eastern Gospel Crusade
Federation Literature Committee
Fellowship of Evang. Bapt. in Canada
Fellowship Of Independent Missions
Fort Wayne Bible College (Indiana)
Free Methodist Church of North America
Free Will Baptist Bible College (Tennessee)
Free Will Baptists Board of Foreign Missions
Friends, California Yearly Meeting
Friends, Ohio Yearly Meeting
Friends, Oregon Yearly Meeting
Fuller Theological Seminary (California)
Fundamental Baptist Mission Of Trinidad
General Conference Mennonite Church
Geneva College (Pennsylvania)
Gordon College (Massachusetts)
Gordon Divinity School (Massachusetts)
Gospel Films, Inc.
Gospel Light Publications
Gospel Missionary Union

Gospel Mission of South America
Gospel Recordings, Inc.
Grace Bible Institute, Inc. (Nebraska)
Grace Mission, Inc.
Grace Theological Seminary (Indiana)
Grand Rapids School of Bible and Music (Michigan)
Greater Europe Mission
Haiti Evangelical Mission
Home of Onesiphorus
Houghton College (New York)
Huntington College (Indiana)
Independent Fundamental Churches of America
Inter-Church Ministries
International Christian Broadcasters
Int'l Church of the Foursquare Gospel
Int'l Fellowship of Evang. Students
International Gospel League
International Missions, Inc.
International Students, Inc.
Inter-Varsity Christian Fellowship
Japan Evangelical Mission
King's College (New York)
King's Garden
Lancaster School of the Bible (Pennsylvania)
Latin America Mission
Liebenzell Mission of USA, Inc.
Literature Crusades, Inc.
Lilly Endowment
London College of Bible & Missions (Canada)
Lutheran Brethren Foreign Mission
Mahon Mission
Maranatha Gospel Fellowship
Medical Assistance Programs, Inc.
Mennonite Board of Missions & Charities
Mennonite Brethren Bible College (Manitoba)
Mennonite Brethren Board of Missions
Mexican Indian Mission
Mexican Militant Mission, Inc.

Minnesota Sunday School Assoc.
Mission Biblique (France)
Mission to Europe's Millions
Missionary Aviation Fellowship
Missionary Church Association
Missionary Equipment Service
Missionary Internship, Inc.
Moody Bible Institute (Chicago)
Moody Literature Mission
Multnomah School of the Bible (Oregon)
National Assoc. of Evangelicals
National Negro Evangelical Association
New Tribes Mission
North Africa Mission
North America Indian Mission, Inc.
Nyack Missionary College (New York)
Omaha Baptist Bible College (Nebraska)
Open Bible Standard Missions
Oriental Boat Mission
Oriental Missionary Society
Orinoco River Mission
Orthodox Presbyterian Church
Overseas Crusades, Inc.
Overseas Missionary Fellowship
Pentecostal Assemblies of Canada
Peruvian Fellowship—Canada
Philadelphia College of Bible (Pennsylvania)
Pioneer Girls
Prairie Bible Institute (Canada)
Ramabai Mukti Mission
Reformed Presbyterian Church of N.A.
Regions Beyond Missionary Union
Rockmont College (Colorado)
St. Paul Bible College (Minnesota)
Scripture Press Foundation
Scripture Union (London)
Short Terms Abroad
Slavic Gospel Association

Soldiers of Christ
South America Indian Mission, Inc.
Southeastern Bible College (Alabama)
South-Eastern Bible College, Inc. (Florida)
Spanish Language School
Spring Arbor College (Michigan)
Sudan Interior Mission
Sudan United Mission
Sudan United Mission (Sydney, Australia)
The Christian Union
The Evangelical Alliance Mission
The Institute of Church Growth
The Missionary Dentist, Inc.
The Navigators
The World Radio Missionary Fellowship
Toronto Bible College (Canada)
Trans World Radio
Trinity College (Illinois)
Trinity Evangelical Divinity School & College (Illinois)
Tyndale Foundation
Unevangelized Fields Mission
Unevangelized Fields Mission (Australia)
United Brethren in Christ (Parent Board)
United Brethren in Christ (Women's Miss'y Asso.)
United Indian Mission, Inc.
United Missionary Society
United World Mission
Victory in Christ Literature Crusade
Wesleyan Methodist Church of America
West Indies Mission
Western Bible Institute (Colorado)
Wheaton College (Illinois)
Winona Lake School of Theology (Indiana)
Woman's Union Missionary Society
World Evangelical Fellowship
World Evangelical Fellowship (London)
World Gospel Mission
World Literature Crusade (Calif.)

World Mission Prayer League, Inc.
World Opportunities, Inc.
World Presbyterian Missions, Inc.
World Vision, Inc.
Worldwide European Fellowship
Worldwide Evangelization Crusade
Wycliffe Bible Translators, Inc.
Youth for Christ International

DATE DUE
HIGHSMITH # 45220